DOCUMENTS AN

THESE UNITED STATES
The Questions of Our Past

COMBINED CONCISE EDITION

Irwin Unger

PRENTICE HALL, *Upper Saddle River, New Jersey 07458*

© 1999 by PRENTICE-HALL, INC.
Simon & Schuster / A Viacom Company
Upper Saddle River, New Jersey 07458

10 9 8 7 6 5 4 3 2 1

ISBN 0-13-081609-4
Printed in the United States of America

CONTENTS

1

****

******** A HISTORICAL DOCUMENT ********

The "Indies" Described

While still aboard the *Niña*, Columbus composed a brief letter to his sovereigns describing his first voyage to America. This document was transmitted to Ferdinand and Isabella from Lisbon, where Columbus first made port after his return, and reached them at Barcelona sometime in March 1493. Called by different names, the letter is the first account in a European language of the New World, if we accept the Norse sagas of 500 years earlier. The document was quickly printed in Latin and other languages and widely circulated in Europe.

Columbus's account gave Europeans their first glimpse of the New World. Unfortunately it played on their greed in a way that would have tragic consequences for the native peoples of the Americas. Note the simultaneous appeal to his sovereigns' piety and greed.

"SIR. Since I know you will take great pleasure at the great victory with which Our Lord has crowned my voyage, I write this to you, from which you will learn how in . . . [thirty-three] days I reached the Indies with the fleet which the most illustrious King and Queen, our lords, gave to me. And there I found very many islands filled with people without number, and of them all I have taken possession of for their Highnesses, by proclamation and with the royal standard displayed, and nobody objected.

"When I reached Juana [Cuba], I followed the coast westward, and I found it to be so long that I thought it must be the mainland, the province of Catayo [a part of China]. And since there were neither towns nor cities on the coast, but only small villages, with the people of which I could not have speech because they all fled forthwith, I went forward on the same course, thinking that I should not fail to find great cities and towns. . . . [Later] I sent two men upcountry to learn if there were a king or great cities. They traveled for three days and found an infinite number of small villages and people without number, but nothing of importance; hence they returned. . . .

" . . . I saw toward the east another island . . . to which I at once gave the name *La Spanola* [Hispaniola, or Haiti]. And I went there and followed its northern part . . . to the eastward for 178 great leagues. . . . As Juana, so all the others are very fertile to an excessive degree, and this one especially. In it there are many harbors on the coast of the sea, incomparable to others I know in Christendom, and numerous rivers, good and large, which is marvelous. Its lands are lofty and in it are very many sierras and very high mountains. . . . All are most beautiful, of a thousand shapes, . . . and filled with trees of a thousand kinds and tall, and they seem to touch the sky; and I am told they never lose their foliage, which I can believe, for I saw them as green and beautiful as they are in Spain in May, and some of them were flowering, some with fruit. . . . And there were singing the nightingale and other little birds

1

of a thousand kinds in the month of November. . . . Upcountry there are many mines of metals, and the population is innumerable. *La Spanola* is marvelous, . . . and the lands are so beautiful and fat for planting and sowing, and for livestock of every sort, and for building towns and cities. . . .

"The people of this island and of all other islands which I have found and seen . . . all go naked, men and women, as their mothers bore them, except that some women cover one place only with a leaf of a plant or with a net of cotton which they make for that. They have no iron or steel or weapons, nor are they capable of using them, although they are well-built people of handsome stature, because they are wonderfully timorous. They have no other arms than arms of canes . . . to the ends of which they fix a sharp little stick. . . . [O]ftentimes . . . I have sent ashore two or three men to some town to have speech, . . . and as soon as they saw them coming, they fled. . . . It is true that after they saw them coming, they have been reassured and have lost this fear, they are so artless and so free with all they possess, that no one would believe it without having seen it. Of anything they have, if you ask them for it, they never say no; rather they invite the person to share it; . . . and whether the thing be of value or of small price, at once they are content with whatever little thing of whatever kind may be given to them. I forbade that they should be given things so worthless as pieces of broken crockery and broken glass, and ends of straps, although when they were able to get them, they thought they had the best jewel in the world; thus it was ascertained that a sailor for a strap received gold to the weight of two and a half *castellanos* [worth today about $500], and others much more for other things which were worth much less. . . . I gave them a thousand good and pleasing things which I had brought, in order that they might be fond of us, and furthermore might be made Christians and be inclined to the love and service of their Highnesses and of the whole Castilian nation, and try to help us and to give us of the things which they have in abundance and which are necessary to us. And they know neither sect nor idolatry, with the exception that all believe that the source of all power and goodness is in the sky, and they believe very firmly that I, with these ships and people, come from the sky, and in this belief they everywhere received me, after they had overcome their fear. . . .

"In these islands I have so far found no human monstrosities, as many expected; on the contrary, among all these people good looks are esteemed; nor are they Negroes, as in Guinea, but with flowing hair. . . . Thus I have neither found monsters nor had report of any, except in an island . . . which is inhabited by a people who are regarded in all the islands as very ferocious and who eat human flesh [the Carib Indians, that is]; they have many canoes with which they range all the islands of India and pillage and take as much as they can. . . . In another island, which they assure me is larger than *Espanola*, the people have no hair. In this there is countless gold, and from it and the other islands I bring with me Indios [that is, Indians] as evidence."

"In conclusion, to speak only of that which has been accomplished on this voyage, which was so hurried, their Highnesses can see that I shall give them as much gold as they want if their Highnesses will render me a little help, besides spice and cotton, as much as their Highnesses shall command; and gum mastic, as much as they shall order shipped; . . . and aloe wood, as much as they shall order shipped; and slaves, as many as they shall order, who will be idolators. And I believe that I have found rhubarb and cinnamon, and I shall find a thousand other things of value. . . .

"So, since our Redeemer has given this victory to our most illustrious King and Queen, and to their famous realms in so great a matter, for this all Christendom ought to feel joyful and make great celebrations and give solemn thanks to the Holy

Trinity with many solemn prayers for the great exaltation which it will have in the turning of so many people to our holy faith, and afterwards for material benefits, since not only Spain but all Christendom and hence have refreshment and profit. . . ."
"At your service.

THE ADMIRAL"

★★★★★★★★ A HISTORICAL PORTRAIT ★★★★★★★★

Isabella of Castile

Isabella, queen of Castile, was called "the Catholic" by her subjects to honor her piety and deep devotion to her faith. Though married to Ferdinand, king of Aragon, she was not merely a royal consort, for in her own realm, Castile, she was sovereign. Like that other reigning early modern queen, Elizabeth I of England, Isabella was not "womanly" in the traditional passive sense. She was one of the most powerful and vigorous rulers of early modern times and she helped transform Spain into a strong, modern nation.

Isabella was already married to Ferdinand, the young heir apparent of neighboring Aragon, when she came to the throne of Castile in 1474. When Ferdinand became king of Aragon several years later, their alliance united the two realms that occupied the largest portion of the Iberian peninsula and ultimately formed the core of the modern Spanish state.

But Spain was anything but united religiously, culturally, or politically when the two young monarchs took up their joint reign. For centuries the Iberian peninsula had been a meeting ground—and a battlefield—of diverse peoples. Conquered in the eighth century by "the Moors" (Muslims), it had been reclaimed by the Christians bit by bit through fierce struggle. The process was incomplete, however, and until the end of the fifteenth century the Moors continued to rule Grenada in the southeast. In addition, the peninsula was home to thousands of Jews, who formed a class of artisans, merchants, and professionals who contributed much-needed skills to Spanish society.

Few Spanish Christians believed religious or cultural tolerance to be a virtue. Non-Christians were infidels whose beliefs were wicked and dangerous. Though over the centuries there had been periods of relative harmony among the different Iberian communities, there had also been periods of fierce religious strife and intolerance. Such conflict had helped mold the passionate, valorous, and often ferocious temperament of the Spanish aristocracy. Isabella's accession to the throne of Castile ushered in the last stage of the Christian reconquest of the Iberian peninsula. By 1481 the Catholic monarchs were engaged in a final drive to conquer Grenada and thereby eliminate the last Muslim outpost in Western Europe.

Earlier Christian successes against the infidels had not led to internal order. Until Ferdinand and Isabella, Spain was a land wracked by turmoil and lawlessness, most of it inspired by the proud, warlike Spanish nobility. These men preyed on city folk and peasants alike, and their undisciplined retainers ravaged the towns and the countryside, stealing, murdering, and raping. The previous rulers of Castile had been too weak to stop these unruly grandees, whose defiance effectively reduced the central government to an empty shell. Spain at the time of Isabella's accession exhibited the worst aspects of the feudalism that had characterized the Middle Ages and kept Europe too feeble to exploit the growing geographic knowledge of distant lands.

Isabella determined to smash the unruly aristocrats, reassert the authority of the crown, and put an end to lawlessness in the realm. Her methods were not gentle. In the province of Galicia her agent, Don Fernand de Acuna, razed forty-seven castles of the unruly nobility and hanged some of the worst offenders. Hordes of brigands and assassins fled the province.

The monarchs' chief instrument for imposing order was the Hermandad, or brotherhood, a league of city people disgusted with the lawless aristocrats. Under the crown's sponsorship, the Hermandad contributed men and money for an internal police force to suppress brigandage and violence in the towns and along the highways. Its militia exacted terrible penalties of the culprits they caught. "The executioners," in the words of one later historian, "cut off feet and hands, shoulders and heads, neither sparing nor veiling the rigor of justice."

In their drive to consolidate Spain under royal authority, Isabella and Ferdinand waged implacable war against all those elements within the Iberian peninsula who marred the kingdom's religious unity. These included many converts from Judaism and Islam who had changed their faith to Christianity out of expediency. In 1478 the royal monarchs established, under papal authority, a tribunal called the Inquisition to root out secret backsliders among the "New Christians" and punish them, by burning at the stake if necessary. But this was not all: The practicing Jews and Muslims remained, and these groups, too, had to be dealt with. They were.

In that momentous year of 1492, the Jews of Spain were ordered expelled from the kingdom. At the very same time, after a decade of war, the Moorish kingdom of Grenada fell to the Christian knights and soldiers. Faced with the alternative of exile, most of Grenada's Muslim inhabitants accepted baptism into the Catholic faith.

Columbus was a major beneficiary of Isabella's determination and strength of will. Spain was ready for new projects. The success of its joint rulers in suppressing the aristocracy and establishing their authority gave the crown the resources needed to support such speculative ventures as voyaging west to reach India and the Far East. With its internal enemies defeated as well, there were new energies for further conquest. If the plan of the Genoese mariner succeeded, the newly united Spain would steal the lead on Portugal's attempt to bypass the Italian middlemen in the fabulous spice trade with the Orient.

Columbus also enjoyed a special rapport with the queen. He and Isabella were as alike, physically, as brother and sister: Both were blue-eyed and auburn-haired, rarities in southern Europe. More important, they had similar personalities. Isabella, like the Genoese mariner, was a visionary who responded to Columbus's bold schemes. Columbus would later write of his patroness: "In all men there was disbelief, but to the Queen, my lady, God gave the spirit of understanding and great courage and made her heiress of all. . . ."

But the queen was no instant convert to the "Enterprise of the Indies." Columbus visited the Spanish court several times over a span of seven years before Isabella agreed to sponsor and finance his expedition. Finally, early in 1492 the monarchs authorized the expedition, pledged financial support, and furnished "the Admiral" with the necessary documents to set his enterprise in motion.

They joyously greeted Columbus in Barcelona when he returned from his first voyage in 1493, confirmed all the titles and privileges they had promised, and provided him with the ships and men he needed to return to "the Indies" as soon as possible. During the following years, while the discoverer collected enemies in Spain and in the new colonies, the queen remained his champion. But by the time he returned from his fourth voyage in 1504, she was old, sickly, and bowed with cares. A devoted mother, she had seen three of her children die while still young. Another child, Joanna, sole surviving heir to the Spanish throne, was insane, and the queen trembled at the prospect of the kingdom under her rule.

During the last months of her life Isabella, always pious, turned more and more to her devotions. On November 26, 1504, she died. Her will made no provision for Columbus, and when he passed away scarcely eighteen months later, he was a near pauper.

Invigorated by the treasure of the New World, Spain would become the most powerful nation in Europe. But having driven from the realm some of its most creative people and confirmed a tradition of intolerance, it ultimately failed to benefit from its good fortune. In the following centuries Spain, once past the first flush of prosperity, became an economic backwater and surrendered leadership in science and the arts to other nations. In the end Isabella had bequeathed to her beloved nation an ambiguous legacy.

2

****

******** A HISTORICAL DOCUMENT ********

How Africans Came to America

The *Hannibal*, commanded by Captain Thomas Phillips, sailed to the west African coast in 1693–1694 to collect a cargo of slaves for the West Indies market. In the Caribbean many of these unfortunate people would be "seasoned" for later transport to the mainland colonies. Phillips was a merchant under contract to supply slaves to the Royal African Company, the firm which for many years possessed a monopoly on the slave trade to the English colonies.

Phillips was an unusual man. He kept a diary and also, despite his occupation, was capable of feeling some compassion for his victims. The portion of his account reproduced here tells of what followed the local king's sale of a slave parcel to the European slave traders.

"The negroes are so willful and loth to leave their own country, that they have often leap'd out of the canoes, boat and ship into the sea, and kept under water till they were drowned, to avoid being taken up and saved by our boats, which pursued them, they having a more dreadful apprehension of Barbados than we can have of hell. . . . [W]e have likewise seen divers [a number] of them eaten by the sharks, of which a prodigious number kept about the ships in this place. . . . We had about twelve negroes did willfully drown themselves, and others starved to death, for 'tis their belief that when they die they return home to their own country and friends again. . . .

". . . When our slaves are aboard we shackle the men two and two while we lie in port, and in sight of their country, for 'tis then that they attempt to make their escape, and mutiny, to prevent which we always keep sentinels upon the hatchways, and have a chest full of small arms, ready loaded and prim'd constantly lying at hand upon the quarter deck. . . . The men are all fed upon the main deck and forecastle, in case of any disturbance; the women eat upon the quarterdeck with us. . . . When we come to sea we let them all out of irons, they never attempting to rebel, considering that should they kill or master us, they could not tell how to manage the ship. . . . I never heard that they mutiny'd in any ships of consequence, . . . but in small [vessels] where they had but few men . . . then they surpriz'd and butchered them, cut the cables, and let the vessel drive ashore. . . . We often at sea in the evenings would let the slaves come up into the sun to air themselves, and made them jump and dance for an hour or two to our bag-pipes, harp and fiddle, by which exercize to preserve them in health; but notwithstanding all our endeavour, 'twas my hard fortune to have great sickness and mortality among them. . . .

"We spent in our passage from St. Thomas to Barbados two months eleven days. . . . [A]mong my poor men and negroes, that of the first we buried 14, and of the last 320, which was a great detriment to our voyage, the royal African company

6

losing ten pounds by every slave that died, and the owners of the ship ten pounds ten shillings. . . .

"I deliver'd alive at Barbados to the company's factors [agents] 372, which being sold, came to about nineteen pounds per head one with another. . . ."

******** A HISTORICAL PORTRAIT ********

John Winthrop

At fifteen Master John Winthrop, son of Squire Adam Winthrop of Groton Manor in Suffolk, went off to Cambridge University to acquire the polish and classical learning expected of a seventeenth-century gentleman. He returned two years later and married Mary Forth, as had been arranged between his father and hers. Ten months later while only seventeen, he became father of a son.

Life was usually short in seventeenth-century Europe, so it was necessary to cram a lot into a brief period. Yet the young man's course marked him as precocious even for his time. But it was not surprising that John would act quickly to take on the responsibilities of adulthood, for he had become a Puritan, and like others of the faith, was imbued with a new seriousness of purpose and a sense that he must follow the Lord's commandments.

The Puritan view of the Christian life placed an enormous strain on believers. They must avoid sin while living with the world's temptations. Yet they could not count on earning salvation merely by virtuous behavior. Salvation was God's gift alone and predestined from the beginning of time. The young Winthrop enjoyed hunting; he relished good food. Like most Puritans, he was not a dour killjoy. But he also feared excess and closely examined his conscience and conduct to see if his recreations and pleasures had "ensnared" his "heart so farre in worldly delights" that he had "cooled the graces of the spirit by them."

Despite his prudence, Winthrop's life had its share of tragedy. Mary died in 1615 after bearing him six children. He married his second wife six months later, and within the year she, too, died. But he had his portion of joys as well; in 1618 he married for a third time. He would later describe Margaret Tyndal as "a very gracious woman," and the relationship would be a long and happy one. Meanwhile, John became an attorney and in the late 1620s spent much time in London on cases heard before the royal courts.

During these years England, under Charles I, was a deeply troubled land. The king believed that he ruled by divine right and need not heed Parliament. He also despised the Puritans within the official Church of England and he and Archbishop Laud harassed and persecuted them. From his perch in London, Winthrop could see still another deplorable aspect of the existing regime: its extravagance and corruption.

For a time the Puritans hoped that their many friends in Parliament would help them, but in March 1629 the king disbanded that body and began to govern directly. To many Puritans the time now seemed ripe to "separate" from England and seek refuge in America.

Winthrop had misgivings about the move, and when approached by a group of other prominent Puritan leaders, men associated with the newly chartered Massachusetts Bay Company, he dithered. Should the virtuous depart, leaving behind their fellow Puritans to face the wrath of Laud and the king alone? Would the new colony be able to achieve economic independence and attain some prosperity? Most of Winthrop's doubts were resolved by mid-1629, and that fall, while still in England, he was elected governor of the new enterprise.

The four small vessels that braved the rough north Atlantic in April and May 1630 carried 400 people, each of whom cost £50 to transport. Many paid their own way; others had their passage and outfitting paid for by richer Puritans like Winthrop or one of the other "gentlemen." Another 600 men, women, and children arrived in Massachusetts soon after.

As in all the early settlements, even one so well planned and financed as the Puritan colony, the first months were hard. During this difficult time Governor Winthrop was a rock of strength, though he had to cope with the personal tragedy of his son Henry's drowning shortly after arrival. He moved the settlers from their initial landing point near Salem to the east shore of Massachusetts Bay and eventually brought them to the site of what would be named Boston. Food was in short supply, and before the community became self-sustaining, he dispatched vessels to Cape Cod to collect corn for the winter and contacted the settlers' friends in England to raise money to buy provisions. Despite the sickness, hunger, hard work, discomfort, and danger, he did not lose heart. That September he wrote Margaret, still in England: "I like so well to be heer, as I doe not repent my comminge. . . ." He had, he added, "never slept better, never had more content of minde."

Two hundred settlers died that first winter and an equal number returned to England in the spring. Yet the colony survived and eventually prospered. Margaret and the rest of Winthrop's family arrived in the fall of 1631, to be greeted en masse by the whole colony and presented with gifts of "fat hogs, kids, venison, poultry, geese, partridges, etc., so as the like joy and manifestations of love had never been seen in New England."

During the next eighteen years Winthrop served his community well as governor, deputy governor, and assistant. At times he was accused of excessive leniency, though he was adamant in his prosecution of Anne Hutchinson and her followers. From our modern perspective, this was not admirable behavior, but few contemporaries anywhere believed that dangerous heretics and sowers of sedition like Hutchinson should be allowed to spread their poison. Winthrop was not a democrat, but rather held the view that a good magistrate must act as he thought best without regard for the opinions of his constituents. That he was popular nonetheless is proved by the fact that he was reelected to office time and time again.

In 1647 Margaret died. In his journal John called her a "woman of singular virtue, prudence, modesty, and piety. . . ." He soon married a fourth time, but he was sixty and ailing, and in March 1649 he too went to his reward. Though he was not a perfect man, his strength of character, resolve, and good common sense stood the Puritan colony in good stead. His descendants would make distinguished contributions to Massachu-setts, and the community he helped to found and sustain would bear the imprint of his own conscientious personality. Ultimately, in the shape of the "New England conscience," a part of John Winthrop of Groton Manor would be incorporated into the essential character of America itself.

3

★★★★★★★★

★★★★★★★★ A HISTORICAL DOCUMENT ★★★★★★★★

Sinners and an Angry God

Jonathan Edwards became his grandfather's assistant as minister at the Northampton Congregational Church in 1726. There he continued the Reverend Stoddard's vivid preaching and helped to launch the Great Awakening.

Edwards was a throwback to the early days of Calvinism when preachers proclaimed the infinite majesty of the Lord and the limitless sinfulness of humankind. Only by surrendering themselves to God's mercy and preparing to accept grace could men and women be saved, and even then few would attain the kingdom of heaven. Edwards's passion and vivid imagery, always impressive, were given a new intensity by his contact with the English preacher George Whitefield during his visit to America in the 1740s. Edwards's famous *Sinners in the Hands of an Angry God* (1741) is the classic expression of the "fire-and-brimstone" sermon, designed to put the fear of God into his congregation and make them seek conversion. It helped confirm his reputation as the most powerful revivalist in the English colonies.

"The God that holds you over the pit of hell, much as one holds a spider, or some loathsome insect, over the fire, abhors you and is dreadfully provoked; His wrath towards you burns like fire; He looks upon you as worthy of nothing else, but to be cast into the fire; He is of purer eyes than to bear to have you in His sight; you are ten thousand times more abominable in His eyes, as the most hateful and venomous serpent is in ours. You have offended him infinitely more than ever a stubborn rebel did his prince. And yet, it is nothing but His hand that holds you from falling into the fire every moment. . . .

"O sinner! consider the fearful danger you are in: it is a great furnace of wrath, a wide and bottomless pit, full of the fire of wrath, that you are held over in the hand of that God, whose wrath is provoked and incensed as much against you, as against many of the damned in hell. You hang by a slender thread, with the flames of divine wrath flashing about, and ready every moment to singe it, and burn it asunder; and you have no . . . Mediator, and nothing to lay hold of to save yourself, nothing to keep off the flames of wrath, nothing of your own, nothing you have ever done, nothing that you can do, to induce God to spare you one moment. . . .

"Thus it will be with you that are in an unconverted state, if you continue in it; the infinite might and majesty, and terribleness, of the omnipotent God shall be magnified upon you. . . . You shall be tormented in the presence of the holy angels, and in the presence of the Lamb; and when you shall be in the state of suffering, the glorious inhabitants of heaven shall go forth and look on the awful spectacle, that they may see what the wrath and the fierceness of the Almighty is; and when they have seen it, they will fall down and adore that great power and majesty. . . ."

Benjamin Franklin

Benjamin Franklin was the first self-made American. When Ben was born in 1706, his father, Josiah, was a candlemaker and soap manufacturer with premises on Milk Street in Boston. Like most of his forebears, Ben was destined for a leather apron, not a silk waistcoat; at the age of twelve he was apprenticed to his older brother, James, who ran a print shop in the New England capital. Though he became an intellectual celebrity, a major political leader, and a favorite of royalty, Franklin never forgot his origins in the sober, hard-working American lower middle class.

Ben and his brother did not get along, yet the lad profited by his work in the print shop. James was not only a job printer, he was also publisher of one of America's earliest newspapers, *The New England Courant*. This was a single-sheet weekly, like the handful of other colonial newspapers, but it afforded abundant scope for young Ben's talents and energies. In the intervals between setting type, sweeping the floor, and running errands, he had time to make up for the deficiencies in his formal education. Ben read widely the ancient classics in translation, as well as in the best of contemporary English prose. He also learned to write with skill, and at sixteen composed a series of humorous articles for the *Courant* under a pseudonym. In later years he taught himself mathematics, Greek, Latin, and several modern languages, but he never lost the straightforward, unpretentious quality of the self-taught individual.

In 1723, following months of squabbling with James, Ben left Boston to seek his fortune as a printer elsewhere. He went first to New York, but unable to find work, he moved on to Philadelphia.

The young man of seventeen arrived in a town of 10,000, a community smaller than Boston, but one that was growing faster and was more open to the talented go-getter. During the remainder of his long life Franklin would spend extended periods abroad, in London and then in Paris, but practical, tolerant Philadelphia left an indelible impression on him and provided the base for all his later success. Here he established his own newspaper, *The Pennsylvania Gazette*, and made his fortune as editor, pamphlet and almanac publisher, bookseller, and paper maker. Here he achieved international fame as "Poor Richard," a fictional old man whose lips spouted wise maxims and proverbs recorded in *Poor Richard's Almanack*. Here he married Deborah Read Rogers, a young woman whose aid in the printshop-bookstore was an essential part of his financial success. Finally, the City of Brotherly Love provided the setting for Franklin's extraordinary and wide-ranging intellectual activities.

Franklin was a philosopher, a scientist, and an inventor. In London, while on a visit to buy a press and type for his paper, he picked up the fashionable deism of the day. He later wrote several pamphlets and articles defining the idea of a scientist-God who made "the glorious sun, with its attending worlds . . . and prescribed the wondrous laws, by which they move." But he gave him, characteristically, a practical twist. Franklin's God was not remote and aloof. He was a benevolent being who delighted in virtue and frowned on vice.

All knowledge interested Franklin. He was fascinated by the expanding world of contemporary science. He could not crack the mathematical complexities of Sir Isaac Newton's revolutionary work on gravity and planetary motion, but he was adept at empirical science. His famous kite experiments of 1752 proved that lightning was a form of the mysterious "electrical fluid" and made Franklin a celebrity. Colleges and universities hastened to confer honorary degrees on the Philadelphian. Thereafter he was universally addressed as "Doctor Franklin."

Franklin's intellectual labors were characteristically American. Even his most theoretical scientific work had a practical side. One important outcome of the kite experiment was the lightning rod to protect buildings in electrical storms. Besides this useful device, Dr. Franklin invented a fuel-efficient stove and bifocal eyeglasses.

Franklin also carved out a distinguished career as a public servant. He served as a member of the Pennsylvania Assembly, as a delegate to the 1754 Albany Congress, as Pennsylvania's "agent" in London, and as joint deputy postmaster general in North America. As the strains between the American colonies and the British Empire grew during the 1760s and 1770s, he emerged as a leading "patriot" who supported increased autonomy for America and opposed Britain's drive to tighten imperial controls. Most of his work for his countrymen he performed abroad. Between 1766 and 1775 he served in effect as ambassador and chief lobbyist of the American colonies in London. Franklin returned to America in 1775 in time for the dramatic final crisis that led to independence and served on the committee of Congress that drafted the Declaration of Independence. In late 1776 he went to France as one of the three commissioners of the new United States to negotiate an alliance that would offset powerful Britain in the fierce struggle now under way.

His work in France proved invaluable. He was more than the official United States envoy. Franklin fulfilled a fantasy about the "natural man" then in vogue among Europe's educated classes, and the French saw him as the very essence of the new American man, simple in dress and manner, practical yet learned, tolerant and industrious, and free of the Old World's corruptions. In all but possibly the last they were correct. Though there was a conscious element of guile and self-advertisement in Franklin, he was a blunt, pragmatic, unpretentious man. But he was also a man of strong appetites. His marriage to Deborah, with its long separations, did not meet his romantic needs. In France the American ambassador was especially popular among the ladies, and Abigail Adams, on a visit to the Franklin residence at Passy near Paris, was shocked by the free manners and the frankness of speech she encountered there. Fortunately for Franklin and the United States, his gallantry only made him more popular with the French people.

Franklin, of course, had more important things to do in France than please the ladies. While there he negotiated the Franco-American Alliance of 1778 and the accompanying commercial treaty. In 1783 he, John Jay, and John Adams negotiated the peace treaty with Britain that ended the war and confirmed American independence.

In July 1785 Franklin left France for America, having been away from his native land for still another decade. He arrived in Philadelphia to be greeted by pealing bells and roaring cannon. Soon after, he was elected president of the Pennsylvania Executive Council under the state's novel new constitution.

The last important role of his career was as Pennsylvania delegate to the Constitutional Convention in Philadelphia. He had not been among those who deplored the country's state during the immediate postindependence period, but he approved the convention's results and wrote in favor of his state's ratification of the Constitution. His last public act, at the age of eighty-four, was to sign, as head of the Pennsylvania Society for Promoting the Abolition of Slavery, a petition to end human bondage in the United States. To the end Franklin remained enlisted in the party of humanity and enlightenment.

11

4

★★★★★★★

★★★★★★★ A HISTORICAL DOCUMENT *★★★★★★★*

The Sons of Liberty

Sons of Liberty organizations first sprang up in many American towns in 1765 to oppose the Stamp Act. Often led by prosperous merchants and lawyers, these groups were responsible for much of the violence against Stamp Tax agents and citizens who complied with the detested act. In Boston the Sons of Liberty were responsible for burning the records of the vice-admiralty court and destroying the library and elegant home of Lieutenant Governor Thomas Hutchinson.

The Sons continued to be active through each confrontation with the English government over the next five years, but then, during the quieter years of the early 1770s, they became relatively dormant. The 1773 Tea Act revived the Patriot cause and reawakened the Sons of Liberty as a militant expression of that cause. The following resolution was adopted by the New York Sons of Liberty in late November 1773 to protest Parliament's apparent attempt to thrust East India Company tea on the colonists through favored agents, thus bypassing other merchants and creating a potential monopoly for British interests. The argument used, however, resembles the earlier protests against "taxation without representation."

". . . To prevent a calamity which, of all others, is the most to be dreaded—slavery, and its terrible concomitants—we subscribers, being influenced from a regard to liberty and disposed to use all lawful endeavors in our power to defeat the pernicious project, and to transmit to our posterity those blessings of freedom which our ancestors have handed down to us; and to contribute to the support of the common liberties of America which are in danger to be subverted, *do,* for these important purposes, agree to associate together . . . and faithfully to observe and perform the following *resolutions, viz.*

1st. *Resolved,* That whoever shall aid, or abet, or in any manner assist in the introduction of tea . . . into this colony, while it is subject . . . to payment of a duty, for the purpose of raising a revenue in America, he shall be deemed an enemy to the liberties of America.

"2d. *Resolved.* That whoever shall be aiding, or assisting, in the landing, or carting of such tea, from any ship or vessel, or shall hire any house, store-house, or cellar . . . to deposit the tea . . . he shall be deemed an enemy to the liberties of America.

"3d. *Resolved.* That whoever shall sell or buy . . . tea, or shall aid . . . in transporting such tea . . . from this city, until the . . . revenue act shall be totally and clearly repealed, he shall be deemed an enemy to the liberties of America.

"4th. *Resolved.* That whether the duties on tea, imposed by this act, be paid in Great Britain, or in America, our liberties are equally affected.

"5th. *Resolved.* That whoever shall transgress any of these resolutions, we shall not deal with or employ, or have any connection with him."

12

Sam Adams

Samuel Adams, a failure in business and law, was a resounding success in politics and propaganda. A man who could not manage his own family's financial affairs, he instigated the Boston Tea Party, the spark that ignited the American Revolution.

Samuel was a maverick member of the same Adams family that gave the nation two presidents, several distinguished historians, and a flock of business leaders. Born in Boston in September 1722, he was named after his father, "Deacon" Adams, a substantial brewer and merchant and a pillar of the Congregational church. His mother, Mary, was also a pious woman, a disciple of Jonathan Edwards, the fire-and-brimstone Calvinist preacher from Northampton. All his life the younger Samuel, though considered a political firebrand, would remain intensely loyal to his ancestral church and participate devoutly in its rites and affairs.

We have little information about Sam Adams's youth except the anecdotes he told in later years. Because his father was so busy, his mother raised the children and did so in a strict Puritan fashion. Mary Adams did not permit the products of the family brewery to be served in her prosperous home. Instead of lullabies, Samuel recounted, hymn tunes rocked him to sleep. The Bible was his first reading primer and deeply influenced his perceptions. Samuel played in the garden behind the house, but he was forbidden to eat the fruit that grew there. His plight made vivid to him the dilemma of Adam and Eve in the Garden of Eden.

Samuel was a lonely lad with few siblings or friends and, despite his mother's orders not to wander off, sought playmates among the sons of waterfront workers. At six, however, he entered Boston Latin School where he drilled daily in the "dead languages" like other middle-class youths preparing for college. In 1736, at the age of fourteen, he entered Harvard and acquired a smattering of geography, geometry, physics, logic, "natural philosophy," as well as Latin and Greek.

College was a time of drastic change in Adams's life. In his junior year he lived off campus, a privilege accorded only to "delicate" students who could not eat college food or to the high-toned student who could afford better accommodations. Sam, apparently, qualified in the second category. But then his father lost his fortune in the Land Bank fiasco, forcing Sam not only to return to the college dining room but also to wait on tables to help pay his expenses.

The Land Bank crash damaged more than Sam Adams's social standing at Harvard. Founded in 1741 to issue paper money against real estate security, the Land Bank was designed to offset the chronic colonial money shortage and ease the burden of debtors in thrall to creditors at home and in Great Britain. Deacon Adams, though himself a merchant, was one of the Land Bank's founders and when, in 1741, the British government, goaded by Governor Jonathan Belcher, declared the Land Bank and its paper money illegal, Sam's father suffered severe financial losses. This debacle, it is said, taught Sam two critical lessons: First, he must not identify with the privileged classes and, second, British rule in America was both arbitrary and selfish.

Sam graduated from Harvard without a strong sense of vocation. For a time he tried reading law but did not like it. He studied for an advanced degree at Harvard and wrote a master's thesis on the subject "Whether It Be Lawful to Resist the Supreme Magistrate if the Commonwealth Cannot Be Otherwise Preserved." The essay combined his reading of John Locke with his experiences during the Land Bank struggle. Its conclusion was "Yes."

By default Adams entered business, starting as a clerk with merchant Thomas Cushing, a family friend. Cushing quickly found that Sam was more interested in politics than the affairs of his counting house, and he asked him to leave. At this point the Deacon gave his son a thousand pounds to set up his own business. Sam lent half of it to a friend, who promptly absconded. In despair at his son's financial irresponsibility, the Deacon took him into his brewery where he could keep an eye on the feckless young man.

Sam spent as little time at the brewery as possible. He had no interest in making money, and somehow he could not pay attention to beer when there were so many exciting political issues in the air. In 1747 he and several friends founded a political discussion group, the Caucus Club, which soon issued a newspaper, the *Independent Advertiser*. This journal regularly attacked the governor and the aristocratic "prerogative party" with an "itch for riding the *Beasts of the People*," and demanded a return to an earlier day of Puritan simplicity. Adams was now well on his way to becoming a leader of the "country party" that would plague the royal governor and his pro-British associates until independence.

Meanwhile, Adams's financial circumstances continued to deteriorate. His father died in 1748, leaving Sam one-third of his property. But Adams quickly squandered this estate. In 1756 he became Boston's tax collector, but instead of profiting from this post he became personally responsible for £8,000 in back taxes. During these years Adams married twice. His first wife died in 1757, leaving him with two small children. He married again in 1764 to Elizabeth Welles, a woman who raised his children, supported his political positions, and managed his household remarkably well on his small income.

Seventeen sixty-four was also the year that Adams began the political course that led to fame. By this time the war with France was over and Britain was determined to put the empire and its finances in order. In April 1764 Parliament passed the Sugar Act, which extended the duties on sugar and molasses imported from the non-British West Indies and imposed higher duties on a wide range of colonial imports. Accompanying this measure was a law that strengthened the British custom's service in America and drastically reduced the rights of accused violators of imperial trade laws.

Adams and his colleagues of the Caucus Club immediately denounced the new measures as tyrannical. In a statement authored by Adams, the Boston Town meeting instructed the Massachusetts legislature to work for repeal of the Sugar Act and join with other colonies in this effort. The statement also condemned the policy of allowing appointed officials to have seats in the Massachusetts General Court, the colonial legislature. This attack was aimed primarily at Thomas Hutchinson, the lieutenant governor and chief justice of Massachusetts, a man who himself opposed the new British measures, but, as a member of the Court Party, believed they must be obeyed.

The following March Parliament made an even graver mistake when it passed the Stamp Act, in effect placing a tax on legal documents, dice, playing cards, newspapers, almanacs, and many other American items. The outcry against this novel imposition came first in Virginia, where Patrick Henry denounced King George III and first raised the issue of taxation without representation. The "Patriot" party in Massachusetts responded more violently. During the summer of 1765, mobs of artisans, merchants, apprentices, and seamen, loosely organized as the Sons of Liberty, attacked the home of Andrew Oliver, one of the new stamp tax collectors and a relative of Hutchinson. Twelve days later another mob burned the home of Hutchinson himself and destroyed most of his papers.

Adams's role in this violence, if any, cannot be established. As yet he was merely a private citizen attacking the emerging Tory interest from within the Sons of Liberty, the Caucus Club, and other informal groups. But soon after, Adams was elected by Boston voters to the General Court and was in a position to take a more visible part in opposing the Tory loyalists. In fact, he soon became the unofficial leader in the legislature of the enemies of the new imperial policies.

Over the next eight years, until 1774, Adams served in the General Court as leader of the radical party, a group of men who resisted expanded British power and demanded ever greater American autonomy. He and his colleagues, including James Otis, Josiah Quincy, Joseph Warren, and his cousin, John Adams, helped to drive from power governor Francis Bernard, and when Hutchinson replaced Bernard in 1769, he helped make the new governor's life miserable as well. Meanwhile, Adams became the sparkplug of opposition to the Townshend duties, the measure that replaced the Stamp Act as a means to raise revenue in America when the opposition finally forced Parliament to rescind the earlier law. Adams authored the Circular Letter in February 1768, soliciting united action among the thirteen colonies to resist British encroachment on American liberties. He was also a vital force behind the second Nonimportation Association designed to pressure the British government into rescinding the detested Townshend duties, just as the first boycott had forced repeal of the Stamp Act.

Adams denied supporting violence, but his barrage of published attacks against the redcoats sent to Boston in 1768 incited the public to riot. According to Adams the British regulars were "bloody-backed rascals" who spread crime, vice, and impiety throughout the city. They violated the sabbath, caroused shamelessly, beat small boys, and raped matrons and young girls indiscriminately. Exposed to this flood of invective, crowds of angry young men, referred to as Adams's "Mohawks," were soon shadowing the soldiers wherever they went. On March 5, 1770, the antagonisms between them erupted as the famous Boston Massacre.

In April 1770 Parliament repealed the Townshend duties, removing a major incitement to anti-British feelings. That October a Boston jury acquitted the British soldiers of wrongdoing during the March 5 violence. During the next two years, the Patriot cause, supported by no new grievance, ebbed. But Adams would not let go—not while his detested enemy, Thomas Hutchinson, now governor, was assaulting the reputations of the Patriot leaders and denouncing their cause. During the next few years Adams engaged in a war of words against the Tories, which was designed to keep the struggle alive. In 1772 he induced the Boston Town Meeting to appoint a Committee of Correspondence to lay out the rights of the American colonists and established a network of communication with Patriot leaders all over British North America.

In May 1773 Parliament shocked the Patriot cause once more to life by passing the Tea Act. This new law retained the small tax originally placed on tea by the Townshend duties, but now permitted the East India Company to market its tea in America through its own agents and reducing its cost by rescinding an export tea tax. Americans would get cheaper tea, but American merchants—whether "fair traders" who had bought English tea legally or "free traders" who had smuggled tea in from Dutch colonies—would be undercut.

Adams and his firebrand friends had no intention of allowing this latest assault on American rights to go unanswered. The tea must not be landed and placed in warehouses, for once ashore it would certainly be distributed. And once the British had made good the process, they would feel free to impose taxes on all necessities purchased in Britain and even on the "land purchased and cultivated by our hard laboring ancestors." These revenues would then pay the salaries of corrupt officials "whose vileness ought to banish them from the Society of Men."

Adams might have accepted the scheme of Governor Hutchinson to refuse to allow the ships to actually enter the harbor. That would permit them to return to Britain without paying the cargo duties and so avoid a crisis. Adams would have none of this, however. Instead, he induced the ship captains to dock, though not unload, their tea. Now there was no way under the law that they could avoid paying the duties, but at the same time the Patriots would insist that the tea not be sold. Adams had created a deliberate crisis in order to revive the Patriot movement.

He and his friends now resolved it in a way designed to provoke maximum confrontation. As dusk fell on December 16, 1773, several hundred Sons of Liberty, fortified with rum and made up as Indians, headed for the Boston waterfront followed by a crowd of spectators. Many of the "Narragansett Indians" were Adams's followers from the city's North End—merchants, artisans, seamen. The painted, be-feathered men clambered aboard the tea ships and in a matter of minutes dumped 342 chests of prime Bohea tea into the harbor waters.

Adams and his fellow radicals got just what they wanted. The London government reacted violently to this criminal defiance of law and imposed a series of coercive measures that seemed to confirm every Patriot charge of British oppression. British truculence in turn created sympathy for Boston and Massachusetts everywhere in America. Adams and the other firebrands were overjoyed. The Boston Tea Party was "a perfect Jubilee," they announced. Step by step each side moved closer to armed confrontation.

During the next few years Adams was in the midst of the drive for independence. In September and October 1774 he served as Massachusetts delegate to the First Continental Congress that met at Philadelphia. Adams and his fellow Massachusetts delegates stayed in the background to avoid frightening the more conservative delegates and keeping them from taking a bold stand against Britain. Adams even supported the choice of the Anglican clergyman, Jacob Duché, to give the opening prayers, though in Puritan Massachusetts he had long baited the Church of England as an extension of Britain's power. In May 1775, after Concord and Lexington, Adams returned to Philadelphia for the Second Continental Congress. There he was one of the most ardent defenders of early separation from Britain and voted for, and signed, the Declaration of Independence, which created the United States of America.

During the Revolutionary War Adams served in the Confederation Congress and then in 1781 returned to Boston. During Shays's Rebellion he upheld the state authorities against the rebels. Though a radical opponent of Britain and her defenders at home, he was not an extreme social egalitarian. In 1768 he had denounced "utopian schemes of levelling and a community of goods. . . ." Yet he so hated England that, during the 1790s, with Britain and France at war, he would support the French Jacobins. In 1794–97 he served one term as Massachusetts governor. Though he had, rather reluctantly, endorsed the Constitution, Adams became a Jeffersonian, exchanging affectionate letters with the leader of the new victorious party. By now he was an old and feeble man, however, and no longer a figure to be reckoned with in the country's political life.

Sam Adams died October 2, 1803, at the age of eighty. He had requested a quiet burial, but his state and city refused to let him go gentle into that good night. The church bells of Boston tolled, the city's shops were closed, and soldiers fired off the harbor guns at sixty-second intervals. Adams was interred in the old graveyard where his Puritan predecessors, who had also smote the wicked, were buried. It was a fitting place.

5

****

******* A HISTORICAL PORTRAIT *******

Benedict Arnold

Arnold was a respected name in colonial New England. The first American Arnold had been associated with Roger Williams in the founding of Rhode Island. His son, the first Benedict Arnold, was a rich merchant of Newport. Thereafter, though the family's fortunes fluctuated, Arnolds would remain prominent citizens of southern New England through four generations. The Benedict Arnold born in 1741 would make the family name synonymous with "traitor."

The fourth Benedict Arnold grew up in Norwich in southern Connecti-cut. As a child he was a leader, recognized by his neighbors as "bold, enterprising, ambitious, active as lightning." Though apprenticed to a merchant, his spirit of adventure led him to join the American forces during the French and Indian War. He served briefly during the French attack on Fort William at Lake George, returning soon after to complete his apprenticeship.

Despite his unauthorized flight to join the army, Arnold pleased his employers, the Lathrops, and in 1762, when he had completed his apprenticeship, they gave him £500 to establish an apothecary shop in New Haven. Arnold did well there. He not only sold medicines but he also invested in the West Indies trade and soon had a flourishing business selling horses and mules to the sugar planters of Antigua, St. Croix, and other Caribbean islands. In 1767 he married Peggy Mansfield, daughter of one of New Haven's respected merchants, and entered into business partnership with his father-in-law.

Like many New England merchants, Arnold was a passionate opponent of British imperial measures after 1763. In 1764 he led a mob protesting the Sugar Act. In 1774 he denounced the Boston massacre as "the most cruel, wanton, and inhuman murders. . . ." When news of Lexington reached New Haven, Arnold left with sixty militiamen under his command to join George Washington's forces outside of Boston.

Arnold rose rapidly in the ranks of the Continental Army. He fought at Ticonderoga as a colonel and in December 1775 led a hopeless attack during a snowstorm against the British bastion of Quebec, garrisoned by a larger force than his own. The attack failed, and Arnold's co-commander, General Richard Montgomery, was killed. Arnold was forced to lift the siege, but despite this failure, Congress recognized his skill and gallantry by promoting him to brigadier general. The following year he further distinguished himself by helping to stop Guy Carleton's advance from Canada on New York City. In 1777 Arnold commanded American troops in the battles that led to the defeat of Burgoyne at Saratoga, the campaign often judged the turning point of the war.

At no time during these tumultuous months was there any outward sign that General Arnold was anything but a fiercely loyal Patriot. But his sense of grievance had begun to build. In February 1777 Congress passed him over for a promotion to major general. He eventually got the promotion, but the delay rankled. His real disaffection, however, dates from mid-1778, when he was appointed military commander at Philadelphia, then newly evacuated by the British.

The general's first wife had died three years before, and Arnold soon became enamored of Peggy Shippen, the beautiful eighteen-year-old daughter of Edward Shippen, a prominent Philadelphia lawyer and admiralty judge allied before the war with the colony's proprietors, the Penn family. Despite this connection and his role as an officer of the crown, Judge Shippen, a timid man, had tried to stay neutral in the evolving struggle between the Patriots and the British government. When the first Continental Congress met in Philadelphia, Shippen invited the delegates to dinner. Then, when the British occupied the town in September 1777, Judge Shippen was happy to welcome the young English officers to his house to pay court to his daughter. Among those who vied for a smile from the lovely Peggy was Lieutenant John André, the young, dashing aide-de-camp of the British general Charles Grey.

The British evacuated Philadelphia in June 1778. Arnold, as American military commander, moved into the mansion formerly owned by the Penns and was soon emulating General Howe's grand style with housekeeper, coachman, groom, seven other servants, and a fine coach-and-four. Such an establishment could not be supported on the salary of a Continental officer, and General Arnold entered into several morally dubious deals with merchants in New York and other British-occupied towns to trade in illegal goods. These shady schemes got him into trouble with the Pennsylvania authorities and with Congress. To clear his name Arnold demanded a court-martial. Though declared innocent of most charges, he earned a public reprimand from Washington. During this time he also began to associate with Philadelphians who favored a negotiated peace without independence.

Inevitably the middle-aged general was drawn to the young and vivacious Peggy Shippen, who belonged to the circle of near-Tories. Ambitious for social distinction and wealth, Peggy was attracted to Arnold in turn. In April 1779 they were married in a simple ceremony appropriate to the now strained pocketbook of Edward Shippen, and went to live in Arnold's newly purchased mansion, Mount Pleasant, on the banks of the Schuylkill.

It was while in Philadelphia that Arnold began to correspond with British General Sir Henry Clinton, commander in chief of his majesty's forces in America. Arnold's motives for betraying his country were clearly mixed. First, came money. The general found good living irresistible, and with a young, extravagant wife to please, he was desperate for cash. He was also angry at the mistreatment he felt he had received at the hands of Congress and the Pennsylvania authorities. He may also have had less ignoble motives than lucre and resentment. As a good New England Protestant, Arnold despised the alliance with Catholic France and believed it tainted the American cause irretrievably. Better to abandon independence and return to the British fold than to accept association with the despised French.

From mid-1779 through 1780 Arnold sold information to André, now Clinton's aide, concerning American and French naval and troop movements, the disposition of supplies, and the identities of French spies in the British camp. Peggy conducted her own spying operation and at one point was paid £350 for her services. The couple's value to the British leaped when, in the summer of 1780, Washington appointed Arnold commander of the vital American post at West Point on the Hudson. Here was a real prize indeed, and Arnold demanded £20,000 for its surrender to the British. Clinton sent André to negotiate. On the way back from the meeting, André was intercepted by American militia while in civilian clothes. When

Arnold learned of the capture, he fled to a nearby British ship. André was tried as a spy and executed in October 1780.

During the remainder of the war Arnold served as brigadier general of Loyalist forces in the British army. In late 1780 he conducted a series of ruthless Tory raids in Virginia. Governor Thomas Jefferson offered a £5,000 reward for his capture. The following year Arnold led Tory attacks against the Americans in Connecticut. Soon after, he and Peggy sailed for England, where they remained permanently.

Like many Loyalist emigrés they found life away from their native land a grim trial. In their last years the Arnolds associated with the circle of Loyalist exiles in London. They found some comfort in these relationships, but it never consoled them for the self-inflicted wounds of betraying their native country. Arnold never received more than £5,000 or £6,000 for his treason, though he frequently petitioned the British government for a more generous reward. The best he could get was a land grant in Canada in 1797. He never visited his Canadian lands and never profited by them. Peggy's life in England was not happy. She kept in touch by letter with her family in Philadelphia, but missed her native city desperately. In late 1789 she visited Philadelphia, hoping to find a spirit of forgiveness. She was disappointed. Many of her old friends cut her and she went back to England after a few months, never to return. Toward the end of her life Peggy became a semi-invalid.

Arnold tried to get a military command from the British government during the Napoleonic Wars, but failed, though his grown sons were more fortunate. He turned to business once again, and for a time was active in the West Indies trade. His ventures did not restore his fortunes, however, and when he died in 1801, Peggy was left to pay off his many debts. Some would say he had paid the price for treason.

★★★★★★★★ A HISTORICAL DOCUMENT ★★★★★★★★

Slavery Struck Down

Though it was not a deep-running social upheaval, the American Revolution wiped away vestiges of the past's privileged order. Yet none of the social changes it produced was more significant than the blow against slavery north of the Mason-Dixon line. In most of those northern states that took steps to end slavery during the Revolution and immediately thereafter, the process was accomplished by act of the legislature. In Massachusetts, however, slavery ended as the result of a judge's decision as to the meaning of a provision of the state constitution of 1781. The case before the Massachusetts court involved an assault by a white man on a black man. The white man was indicted, but pleaded not guilty on the grounds that the man he had struck was his slave. This plea induced the judge, Chief Justice William Cushing, to consider the question of whether slavery legally existed in the commonwealth. His decision, expressed briefly below, reflects the liberating spirit of the Revolutionary era.

"CUSHING, C. J. As to the doctrine of slavery and the right of Christians to hold Africans in perpetual servitude, and sell and treat them as we do our horses and cattle, [it is true that it] has been heretofore countenanced by the Province Laws . . . but nowhere is it expressly enacted or established. It has been a usage—a usage which took its origins from the practice of some of the European nations, and the regulations of British government respecting the then Colonies, for the benefit of trade and wealth. But whatever sentiments have formerly prevailed in this particular or slid in upon us by the example of others, a different idea has taken place with the people of America, more favorable to the natural rights of mankind, and to that natural, innate desire of Liberty, with which heaven (without regard to color, complexion, or shape of noses . . .) has inspired all the human race. And upon the ground our Constitution of Government, by which the people of this Commonwealth have solemnly bound themselves, sets out with declaring that all men are born free and equal—and that every subject is entitled to liberty and to have it guarded by the laws, as well as life and property—and in short is totally repugnant to the idea of being born slaves. This being the case, I think the idea of slavery is inconsistent with our own conduct and Constitution; and there can be no such thing as perpetual servitude of a rational creature, unless his liberty is forfeited by some criminal conduct or given up by personal consent or contract. . . . *Verdict Guilty*."

6

****

******* A HISTORICAL DOCUMENT *******

Annapolis Convention

Many steps intervened between first perceptions that the Articles of Confederation were inadequate and the actual meeting of the Constitutional Convention at Philadelphia during the summer of 1787. One of the more important was the Annapolis Convention, called originally by Virginia as a commercial meeting to discuss the chaotic trade relations among the states. Nine states accepted the invitation, but only five actually sent delegates. The poor turnout made it impossible for the twelve delegates present in the Maryland capital to proceed with their business. But the nationalists were not to be deterred from their purposes. Under the leadership of New York's Alexander Hamilton, they drafted a "call" for a new convention to meet in Philadelphia in May. This meeting would discuss not only trade disunity, but all the weaknesses of the government under the Articles. The following is a shortened version of that call.

"To the Honorable, the legislatures of Virginia, Delaware, Pennsylvania, New Jersey, and New York—

"The Commissioners from the said States, respectively assembled in Annapolis, humbly beg leave to report . . .

"That the express terms of the powers of your Commissioners supposing a deputation from all the States, and having for object the Trade and Commerce of the United States, your Commissioners did not conceive it advisable to proceed on the business of their mission, under the Circumstances of so partial and defective a representation.

"Deeply impressed, however, with the magnitude and importance of the object confided in them on this occasion, your Commissioners cannot forbear to indulge an expression of their earnest and unanimous wish that speedy measures be taken, to effect a general meeting of the States, in a future Convention, for the same, and other purposes, as the situation of public affairs may be found to require. . . .

"That there are important defects in the system of the Federal Government is acknowledged by the Acts of all those States which have concurred in the present Meeting; that the defects, upon a closer examination, may be found greater and more numerous, than even these acts imply, is at least so far probable, from the embarrassments which characterise the present state of our national affairs, foreign and domestic, as may reasonably be supposed to merit a deliberate and candid discussion, in some mode, which will unite the Sentiments and Councils of all the States. In the choice of the mode, your Commissioners are of the opinion that a Convention of Deputies from the different States, for the special and sole purpose of entering into this investigation, and digesting a plan for supplying such defects as may be discovered to exist, will be entitled to a preference from considerations which will occur without being particularised.

"Your Commissioners decline an enumeration of those national circumstances on which their opinion respecting the propriety of a future Convention, with more enlarged powers, is founded; as it would be a useless intrusion of facts and observations, most of which have been frequently the subject of public discussion, and none of which can have escaped the penetration of those to whom they would in this instance be addressed. They are, however, of a nature so serious, as, in the view of your Commissioners, to render the situation of the United States delicate and critical, calling for an exertion of the united virtue and wisdom of all the members of the Confederacy.

"Under this impression, your Commissioners . . . beg leave to suggest their unanimous conviction that it . . . may advance the interests of the union if the States. . . would themselves concur, and use their endeavours to procure the concurrence of the other States, in the appointment of Commissioners to meet at Philadelphia on the second Monday of May next, to take into consideration the situation of the United States, to devise such further provisions as shall appear to them necessary to render the constitution of the Federal Government adequate to the exigencies of the Union, and to report such an Act for that purpose to the United States in Congress assembled, as when agreed to by them, and afterwards confirmed by the Legislatures of every State, will effectively provide for the same."

******** A HISTORICAL PORTRAIT ********

Daniel Shays

The people of Massachusetts found the peace after Yorktown a dubious blessing. In the coastal regions of the state the end of hostilities brought nothing but difficulties. The Barbary pirates cut off trade with the Mediterranean. The English vengefully excluded American vessels from the West Indies. Hardship for the merchants also meant hardship for the sailors, the sailmakers, the ship carpenters, and all the other "mechanics" who worked in the port towns and earned their living from overseas commerce.

The difficulties soon spread to the farmers of the interior. The people of Massachusetts had gone on a buying spree when British goods became available soon after Yorktown. Unable to ship goods to the English West Indies colonies in exchange, they had to pay for these British goods in specie—gold and silver. The import deluge quickly drained the community of all hard money and compelled hard-pressed import merchants to demand quick repayment of all outstanding debts. Soon they were dunning their customers among the retail shopkeepers of the interior market towns. The retail merchants in turn had no alternative but to pressure *their* customers—the local farmers and mechanics—to immediately pay all outstanding debts, and in coin, not farm produce as in the past. By this chain reaction, before many months the cash shortage of the coastal port towns had been transmitted to the entire state.

The cash dearth proved a bonanza to local lawyers, for when their farm customers refused to pay, the besieged storekeepers turned to the courts. Between August 1784 and August 1786 the Hampshire County Court of Common Pleas prosecuted almost 3,000 debt cases, a 260 percent increase over 1770–72. Matters were made worse by the state's tax system. Land bore two-thirds of the total Massachu-

23

setts tax burden, while the personal property of the business and professional classes escaped taxation. The result of this combination was that many farmers in the interior and western counties faced not only suits for debts but also the forced sale of their property for nonpayment of state taxes.

Into this picture of severe rural distress intruded the figure of Daniel Shays of Pelham in Hampshire County. Shays was seen as Robin Hood by his supporters; his foes considered him a dangerous social leveler. He was really neither. A former captain in Washington's army, Shays had fought gallantly at Bunker Hill, Saratoga, and Stony Point. But Captain Shays had none of the "nobler" qualities expected of a hero. In 1780 he sold for cash a sword that the Marquis de Lafayette had presented to him as a mark of esteem. The act scandalized many of his fellow officers. Soon after this event Shays resigned his commission and returned to his native state.

Shays was not the chief mover of the events that have been given his name. The "rebellion" started as a wave of peaceful petitions to the state legislature for relief in the form of paper money and the closing of the courts where creditors had brought suit against the farmers. Patience soon wore thin, however, and during the late summer, fall, and winter of 1786 spontaneous bands of "regulators," attempting to stop the lawsuits and the forced sales, shut the courts in western Massachusetts. Captain Daniel Shays played little part in the earliest of these attacks. But when in late September the rebels tried to stop the sitting of the court in Springfield, he was abruptly catapulted into leadership. Wearing his old buff-and-blue Continental officer's uniform, Shays rode up and took charge of the protesters in front of the courthouse. He talked General Shepard, commander of the militia, into allowing the regulators to parade around the town square without interference to express their grievances. He was now a marked man.

During the remainder of 1786 Shays was in the thick of the growing disorders. In late November, following the violent capture of two rebel leaders by the loyal militia, Shays signed a manifesto proclaiming that "the seeds of war are now sown. . . ." He was soon busy planning an attack on the court scheduled to meet in Worcester in early December.

A thousand insurgents assembled in Worcester to stop the meeting of the court, prepared if necessary to die for their cause. The sacrifice proved unnecessary. A winter storm descended on central Massachusetts the evening before the court session, completely blocking the roads and preventing the judges from getting to the town. The insurgents, cold, wet, and miserable, soon drifted off for home. Shays and a number of other disappointed leaders had to settle for another proclamation detailing the sufferings of the farmers and demanding the release of rebel prisoners and the suspension until spring of the courts in three western counties.

By this time the conservative citizens of the commonwealth were in a state of panic and demanding "condign punishment" of the rebels. The state legislature responded with a barrage of measures punishing rioting, suspending the writ of habeas corpus, and making "the spreading of false reports to the prejudice of government" an indictable crime. It also passed an Act of Indemnity pardoning all rebels who would take an oath of allegiance. Meanwhile, an alarmed Confederation Congress in New York, at the behest of the Massachusetts authorities, voted to raise a force of federal troops to put down the rebellion, the money to be supplied by a requisition on the states of $530,000.

As usual, nothing came of Congress's good intentions. The states refused to appropriate the money and the Massachusetts authorities were forced to suppress the rebellion by themselves. In January 1787 Governor James Bowdoin began to organize a small army of volunteers, financed by private contributions, to put down the rebels. Money and recruits poured in, and by the end of the month five companies of troops under General Benjamin Lincoln were on their way to the scene of the disorders. Before they arrived, Shays and his associates, in quest of arms and ammunition, attacked the federal arsenal at Springfield. The attack was met by the militia, who opened fire with artillery loaded with grapeshot. The third volley smashed into the charging rebels, killing three. Shays tried to rally the men, but most had never faced gunfire before. Crying "Murder!", they broke and ran for cover.

During the next few weeks Shays and his little army retreated before the approaching forces of General Lincoln. At Petersham, Lincoln and his men caught up with the Shaysites and surprised them at breakfast. Fortunately there were few casualties. The rebels once again panicked and ran from the field. Most escaped and over the next few months continued a sort of guerrilla war against the authorities. But the Petersham defeat broke the back of the rebellion.

Shays himself fled to Vermont with a price on his head. In 1788, with order restored in the commonwealth, the Massachusetts legislature pardoned the rebel leaders. Shays returned home and for a while lived quietly in Pelham. Then he joined the trek of many rural Yankees to western New York, where he spent his remaining years as a Revolutionary War pensioner.

Occasional visitors came to see the notorious rebel. They were generally disappointed. The firebrand was just a genial old man, a little too fond of the bottle. Shays died in Sparta, New York, in 1825 at the age of 84. By this time few remembered the man who had inspired terror among the rich and mighty of the commonwealth of Massachusetts and, by giving a final push to the nationalists' demand for a stronger federal union, helped alter the course of American history.

7

***

********* A HISTORICAL DOCUMENT *********

Report on Manufactures

A critical issue separating the two political parties during the 1790s was whether the country's future lay with agriculture or with industry and commerce. The apostle of the second course, one that required major changes in America's economy and social system, was the first secretary of the treasury, Alexander Hamilton. In his *Report on Manufactures* of 1791 Hamilton argued for government policies that would transform America from a land of farms into one of workshops, mills, and busy cities as well. This document, the last of four major reports, did not lead to immediate congressional action, but like the others it helped define the coherent political philosophy that we associate with the Federalist party. By its challenge to those who wished to keep America as it was, it also helped to clarify the position of the Jeffersonian Anti-Federalists.

"There . . . are . . . respectable patrons of opinions unfriendly to the encouragement of manufactures. The following are . . . the arguments by which these opinions are defended.

"In every country (say those who entertain them) Agriculture is the most beneficial and *productive* object of human industry. This position . . . applies with peculiar emphasis to the United States on account of their immense tracts of fertile territory, uninhabited and unimproved. Nothing can afford so advantageous an employment for capital and labor, as the conversion of this extensive wilderness into cultivated farms. . . .

"To endeavor, by the extraordinary patronage of Government, to accelerate the growth of manufactures, is, in fact, to endeavor, by force and art, to transfer the natural current of industry from a more, to a less beneficial channel. Whatever has such tendency must necessarily be unwise. . . . To leave industry to itself, therefore, is . . . the soundest as well as the simplest policy.

"This policy is not only recommended to the United States by considerations which affect all nations . . . it is [also] dictated to them . . . by the smallness of their population compared with their territory. . . . [This fact] conspires to produce . . . a scarcity of hands for manufacturing occupations, and dearness of labor generally. . . .

"If contrary to the natural course of things, an unseasonable and premature spring can be given to certain fabrics, by heavy duties, prohibitions, bounties, or by other forced expedients, this will only be to sacrifice the interests of the community to those of particular classes. Besides the misdirection of labor, a virtual monopoly will be given to the persons employed on such fabrics; and an enhancement of price, the inevitable consequence of every monopoly, must be defrayed at the expense of the other part of society. . . .

"[In reply to these arguments] . . . it ought readily to be conceded that the cultivation of the earth . . . has *intrinsically a strong claim to pre-eminence over every other kind of industry*. . . . But, that it has a title to anything like an exclusive predilection in any country, ought to be admitted with great caution. . . .

". . . [M]anufacturing establishments not only occasion a positive augmentation of the Produce and Revenue of the Society, but . . . they contribute essentially to rendering them greater than they could possibly be, without such establishments. These circumstances are—

1. The division of labor.

2. An extension of the use of Machinery.

3. Additional employment to classes of the community not ordinarily engaged in the business.

4. The promoting of emigration from foreign Countries.

5. The furnishing of greater scope for the diversity of talents and dispositions which discriminate from each other.

6. The affording a more ample and various field for enterprise.

7. The creating in some instances a new, and securing in all, a more certain and steady demand for the surplus produce of the soil.

"Each of these circumstances has a considerable influence upon the total mass of industrious effort in a community. Together, they add to it a degree of energy and effect, which are not easily conceived. . . ."

★★★★★★★★ A HISTORICAL PORTRAIT ★★★★★★★★

Timothy Pickering

Timothy Pickering came by his reputation for self-righteousness honestly. His father, a prosperous farmer and businessman of Salem, Massachusetts, and deacon of the Third Congregational Church, was the town scold, constantly embroiled in public battles with those whose views on political and religious issues he considered wicked. The elder Pickering's appearance betrayed his personality. John Adams noted of the man that "he has an hypocritical demure on his face . . . ; his mouth makes a semicircle when he puts on that devout face."

Timothy attended Harvard, graduating in 1763 at the age of eighteen with almost nothing good to say about his four years in Cambridge. Back in Salem, he studied law and became an attorney, but he was never interested in legal practice. By this time the American colonies were embroiled in the struggle with Britain for autonomy, and Pickering, like his father before him, found public controversy more compelling than the humdrum pursuit of a legal career.

Salem, though more conservative than Boston, was a Patriot town, and Pickering joined the ranks of those opposed to the British attempt to tighten control over their American empire. During the War for Independence he served as adjutant general and quartermaster general in the army. In these posts he became a close associate of Washington and many of the leading politicians of the new republic. During the months following Yorktown Pickering was one of those army officers who despaired at the feebleness of Congress, especially its inability to meet its back-pay obligations to the Continental soldiers. During the Critical Period he moved his family to Philadelphia and established himself as a commission merchant. But the postwar deluge of British imports soon drained the country of cash and badly hurt the firm of Pickering and Hodgdon.

Unable to make the private fortune he craved, in 1790 Pickering accepted appointment as federal agent to treat with the Iroquois Indians. He proved to be remarkably generous and fair and was rewarded for his success by appointment as postmaster general in Washington's cabinet.

Pickering at first stayed clear of the factional disputes that divided Washington's cabinet and shaped the first political parties. Not until he became secretary of state in 1795 did he become an ardent Federalist, and his conversion derived from his attitudes toward France rather than his views on domestic issues. Retained in Adam's cabinet, the secretary became a member of the "war party," who held that nothing would "satisfy the ambitious and rapacious" French Directory except "universal dominion." England, he told the British minister, was "the last bulwark against the usurper of civilization." Following the revelations of French contempt for the United States in the XYZ Affair, Pickering urged an actual military alliance with Britain. His fear of France led him to support the Alien and Sedition Acts, which were designed to purge the nation of all "Gallomen" who might subvert the government. President Adams, though shocked by the XYZ revelations, rejected war and eventually resumed talks with the French. The president's conciliatory attitude placed him on a collision course with his warlike secretary of state, and in May 1800 he dismissed Pickering.

After a brief professional detour while he tried pioneer farming and land development in western Pennsylvania, Pickering and his family returned to Salem. Here he resumed his political career as a High Federalist, and in 1803 the Massachusetts legislature elected him to the United States Senate. Pickering arrived in Washington when that raw capital was in the hands of the Jeffersonians. He might have assumed leadership of the Federalist opposition, but many of his party colleagues considered him an extremist and consigned him to the obscure party backbench. Out of touch with the give-and-take of everyday politics, Pickering indulged his imagination and constructed a conspiracy theory that depicted his Republican opponents as subverters of the nation's institutions. Jefferson, he convinced himself, was plotting to make himself president for life. The Republicans would not let the Constitution get in their way, he believed. Their sponsorship of the Louisiana Purchase, an act not authorized by the Constitution, made that clear. Pickering's penchant for controversy and extremist statements made him a favorite target of the Jeffersonians, who cited his intemperate remarks as a way of stigmatizing the entire Federalist party.

During the crisis with Britain that culminated in the War of 1812, Pickering predictably opposed the Republican administration's foreign policy. In 1813, after he had been rejected for a second Senate term, he returned to Washington as Representative from the Essex County district of eastern Massachusetts. As early as 1803 Pickering had conceived the idea of an independent confederacy of New England and other northeastern states opposed to the policies of the Jeffersonians. Now, in the midst of war, he once again entertained the scheme of New England secession from the Union and heartily endorsed the Hartford Convention called in late 1814 to consider regional grievances against the Madison government. When the convention adjourned without proposing secession, Pickering was bitterly disappointed.

During most of his political career Pickering's views had coincided with those of his eastern Massachusetts constituents, though he often expressed them in exaggerated ways. After the war, however, a gap opened between him and the Essex County voters. Eastern Massachusetts by 1815 had begun to turn away from the sea and foreign trade and to take up manufacturing. Pickering's constituents supported the tariff bill of 1816, and when he opposed it, they were angry enough to repudiate him at the polls.

At the age of 72, Pickering left Washington to spend his remaining twelve years in Salem battling with everyone in sight. Fittingly for this son of the old deacon, he would embroil himself in religious controversy—but not as a defender of the old order. Pickering was a rationalist in religion and took the side of the Unitarians when they challenged the old Congregational establishment. The final irony of his career was his support of Andrew Jackson in 1824 over John Quincy Adams. But perhaps it was not so surprising after all. Resentment had always been a prime motivating force in his life, and he could never forget that the younger Adams's father had dismissed him from office a quarter century before. Pickering died in January 1829, still defending his actions and denouncing his enemies.

8

****

******* A HISTORICAL DOCUMENT *********

Jefferson in Office

Once elected, Thomas Jefferson, like most other victorious presidential candidates, sought to make peace with his opponents. His inaugural address of March 1801 was intended as an overture to the more moderate Federalists. The new president hoped to cool the heated feelings aroused by the election campaign. His goal was to make governing the nation a less difficult task. But the address also expressed some of Jefferson's most characteristic ideas: the rights of minorities, frugal and limited government, assured civil and religious liberties, the dangers of militarism, and the primacy of agriculture. Unfortunately he was not always as good as his words, but the inaugural address is an eloquent statement of traditional liberal principles.

"During the contest of opinion through which we have passed the animation of discussions and of exertions has sometimes worn an aspect which might impose on strangers unused to think freely and to speak and to write what they think; but this being now decided by the voice of the nation, . . . all will, of course, arrange themselves under the will of the law, and unite in common efforts for the common good. All, too, will bear in mind this sacred principle, that though the will of the majority is in all cases to prevail, that will to be rightful must be reasonable; that the minority possess their equal rights, which equal law must protect, and to violate would be oppression. Let us, then, fellow citizens, unite with one heart and one mind. Let us restore to social intercourse that harmony and affection without which liberty and even life itself are but dreary things. . . .

". . . [E]very difference of opinion is not a difference of principle. We have called by different names brethren of the same principle. We are all Republicans, we are all Federalists. If there be any among us who would wish to dissolve this Union or to change its republican form, let them stand undisturbed as monuments of the safety with which error of opinion may be tolerated where reason is left free to combat it. I know, indeed, that some honest men fear that a Republican government cannot be strong, that this Government is not strong enough; but would the honest patriot . . . abandon a government which has so far kept us free and firm on the theoretic and visionary fear that this Government, the world's best hope, may by possibility want energy to preserve itself? I believe this, on the contrary, the strongest Government on earth. I believe it is the only one where every man, at the call of the law, would fly to the standard of the law, and would meet invasions of the public order as his own personal concern. Sometimes it is said that man cannot be trusted with the government of himself. Can he then, be trusted with the government of others? Or have we found angels in the forms of kings to govern him? Let history answer this question.

"Let us, then, with courage and confidence pursue our own Republican and Federal principles, our attachment to union and representative government. Kindly separated by nature and a wide ocean from the extermininating havoc of one quarter of the globe; too high-minded to endure the degradation of the others; possessing a chosen country, with room for our descendants to the hundredth and thousandth generation; entertaining a due sense of our equal right to the use of our own faculties, to the acquisitions of our own industry, to honor and confidence from our own fellow-citizens, resulting not from birth, but from our own actions and their sense of them; enlightened by a benign religion, professed, indeed, and practiced in various forms, yet all of them inculcating honesty, truth, temperance, gratitude, and the love of man; acknowledging and adoring an overriding Providence, which by all its dispensations proves that it delights in the happiness of man here and his greater happiness hereafter—with all these blessings, what more is necessary to make us a happy and prosperous people? Still one more thing, fellow-citizen—a wise and frugal Government, which shall restrain men from injuring one another, shall leave them otherwise free to regulate their own pursuits of industry and improvement, and shall not take from the mouth of labor the bread it has earned. This is the sum of good government, and this is necessary to close the circle of our felicities.

"About to enter, fellow-citizens, on the exercize of duties which comprehend every thing dear and valuable to you, it is proper you should understand what I deem the essential principles of our Government, and consequently those which ought to shape its Administration. I will compress them within the narrowest compass they will bear. . . . Equal and exact justice to all men of whatever state or persuasion, religious or political; peace, commerce, and honest friendship with all nations, entangling alliances with none; the support of the State governments in all their rights, as the most competent administrations for our domestic concerns and the surest bulwarks against antirepublican tendencies; the preservation of the General Government in its whole constitutional vigor, as the sheet anchor of our peace at home and safety abroad; a jealous care of the right of election by the people—a mild and safe corrective of abuses which are lopped by the sword of revolution where peaceable remedies are unprovided; absolute acquiescence in the decisions of the majority, the vital principles of republics, from which is no appeal but to force, the vital principle and immediate parent of despotism; a well-disciplined militia, our best reliance in peace and for the first moments of war, till regulars may relieve them; the supremacy of the civil over the military authority; economy in the public expense, that labor may be lightly burthened; the honest payments of our debts and sacred preservation of the public faith; encouragement of agriculture, and of commerce as its handmaid; the diffusion of information and arraignment of all abuses at the bar of the public reason; freedom of religion; freedom of the press, and freedom of person under the protection of the habeas corpus, and trial by juries impartially selected. . . .

"Relying, then, on the patronage of your good will, I advance with obedience to the work, ready to retire from it whenever you become sensible how much better choice it is in your power to make. And may that Infinite Power which rules the destinies of the universe lead our councils to what is best, and give them a favorable issue for your peace and prosperity."

★★★★★★★★ A Historical Portrait ★★★★★★★★

Albert Gallatin

One of the most prominent leaders of the party established by Thomas Jefferson was not even American-born. Not until 1780, when he was nineteen, did Albert Gallatin come to the United States, the country where he was to achieve such great political distinction.

Gallatin was born in Geneva, an independent city-republic in what is now Switzerland, of a distinguished French-speaking Protestant family. Given a classical education in the local schools, he reached his teens discontented with the limited economic opportunity and conservatism of his community. In school he had become acquainted with the writings of the Enlightenment philosopher Jean-Jacques Rousseau, himself a native of Geneva, and belonged to a circle of young men who yearned for a better political and social order than existed in Europe under the Old Regime. By now all of "enlightened" Europe knew of the brave cause of the Americans fighting against British tyranny, and in 1780 Gallatin and a friend left Geneva to cast in their lot with America.

Gallatin spent his first few years in the United States in quest of a vocation. By the time he arrived, the war was virtually over, so a military career was precluded. For a while he taught French at Harvard, but he was drawn to the West and western opportunities. For a number of years he tried to make money as a speculator in western lands. Though these schemes did not work out, he came to know western Pennsylvania and, in 1785, established his permanent home there.

Fayette County in the 1780s was frontier, with all the frontier openness to newcomers. Even a foreigner like Gallatin who spoke heavily accented English could make his mark. In 1788 his fellow citizens sent the young man to represent them at a convention in Harrisburg called to change the recently adopted federal Constitution. There Gallatin met other men like himself who feared the centralizing tendencies of the new frame of gov- ernment. This concern would remain an important part of Gallatin's political ideology and a major bond with the Jeffersonians.

Gallatin's career following this debut was meteoric. In 1790 he was elected to the Pennsylvania state legislature and served there for three terms. As a legislator he sponsored bills for a statewide system of public education, the abolition of slavery, and reform of the penal code. His program closely echoed the work that the great Jefferson had accomplished in Virginia as governor during the war. Yet at the same time, Gallatin was no enemy of banks or "fiscal responsibility." He helped rid Pennsylvania of its depreciated paper money, got the state to pay its public debt in specie, and sponsored a state-controlled bank. In many ways this program resembled Hamilton's almost simultaneous efforts at the federal level. But there was one crucial difference: Hamilton believed a permanent federal debt was a useful political and economic device; Gallatin, like all Republicans, believed public debt undesirable. The state must always follow the principle of pay-as-you-go for all its expenses.

In 1793 the legislature elected Gallatin to the United States Senate and he went to Philadelphia to take his seat. In the nation's temporary capital he met and married Hannah Nicholson, member of a New York family with close ties to the emerging Republican or Anti-Federalist party. Soon after, Gallatin was disqualified for his Senate seat on the grounds that he had not met the constitutional requirement of citizenship for nine years. He returned to his farm on the Monongahela with his new bride and a total fortune of £600 in cash.

He arrived in Fayette County just in time to become embroiled in the uprising against the federal authorities over the 1793 excise tax that we call the Whiskey Rebellion. Though a Republican and man of the West, Gallatin played a moderating role and succeeded in preventing a civil war. By the time the federalized militia appeared, the rebellion was over and nothing remained to be done but arrest a few holdouts and drag them to Philadelphia to be tried.

In 1794 Gallatin was elected to the federal House of Representatives. Here, during the three terms he served, he became a major Republican leader, second only to Madison, and a prime target for Federalists, who derided his accent and foreign birth and accused him of being a ringleader of the Whiskey Rebels. He quickly became known as an expert in finance who could argue with the Federalists on their own ground and show where their much-vaunted financial measures had been costly and unnecessary to the economic health of the nation. He also succeeded in establishing the House Ways and Means Committee as Congress's permanent watchdog over treasury affairs.

Because he was one of the few Republicans who understood the intricacies of national finance, it was inevitable that Gallatin would become Jefferson's secretary of the treasury. He would serve in that office for almost thirteen years, until well into Madison's second term.

As secretary, Gallatin's first priority was debt reduction. His second, related to the first, was reduction of taxes. This in turn required cutting the budget drastically, especially the outlays for the army and the navy. Finally, he believed that Congress must be more careful in overseeing the finances of the country than it had been under the Federalists. All told, it was a good Jeffersonian program of frugality, simplicity, and limits on the operations and ambitions of government.

Yet Gallatin was also a man of vision. He did not oppose the Louisiana Purchase, though paying Napoleon's price required going many millions of dollars further into debt. Unlike his chief, Gallatin was not an inveterate enemy of the Bank of the United States. When the president demanded that the treasury transfer a large part of its deposits to various state banks, Gallatin resisted. Also at odds with the president was his support of "internal improvements" legislation to tie the country together with a network of roads and canals. In 1808 he issued a report laying out a grand design, estimated to cost $10 million, that would rectify all the deficiencies of nature's own plan for connecting the various parts of the Union. Congress, dominated by more conventional Jeffersonians, refused to fund this proposal. Not until the War of 1812 had demonstrated the dangers of a fragmented nation did party leaders reconsider their position.

Gallatin was skeptical of the War Hawks' zeal for war in 1811 and 1812, especially after the votes of many of these same men helped defeat a bill to recharter the Bank of the United States. Without the bank to help, the treasury would have trouble raising money for the government during the war. Fortunately for the secretary, he would not have to face all the difficulties of financing the war, for in May 1813 he left the treasury and went to Europe as American peace envoy. Eventually he helped negotiate the Treaty of Ghent, bringing peace between Britain and America.

Gallatin was never again active in American domestic politics. From 1816 to 1823 he served as American envoy to France. When he returned to the United

States, he was disappointed at the low level of politics in his adopted homeland. He soon went off to England as American envoy, but returned again after a single year.

In 1830 Gallatin moved his family to New York, where he accepted the offer of tycoon John Jacob Astor to become president of a bank. The move to the country's commercial metropolis enabled Gallatin to help his two sons establish themselves financially and allowed him to be close to his married daughter, Frances, and his seven grandchildren. Gallatin continued to be active in public affairs, however. In 1830 he was approached by a group of New York business and civic leaders to lend his name and influence to establishing a modern university in the city. Gallatin joined the enterprise as a strong advocate of a new, more commercially and scientifically oriented institution of higher education. His help proved vital to the formation of what would later become New York University.

During his last years the alert old gentleman took an active interest in the city's intellectual life. He served as president of the New York Historical Society and helped found the discipline of "ethnology," the forerunner of modern anthropology. He also continued to pronounce on financial and political questions. When sectional issues came to the fore during the 1840s, he endorsed excluding slavery from the newly acquired regions in the West. In May 1849 Gallatin's wife of fifty-five years died. Six months later, at the age of eighty-eight, Gallatin himself died quietly at his daughter's summer house on Long Island.

Though a creator of one of the two great parties that have dominated American political life, Albert Gallatin was a voice for moderation and reason, a man who could see the best in the other side.

9

★★★★★★★★ A HISTORICAL PORTRAIT ★★★★★★★★

Samuel F. B. Morse

The career of Samuel Finley Breese Morse refutes the conventional view that artists are quixotic dreamers. One of America's foremost pre–Civil War painters, Morse was also the inventor of a practical system of transmitting messages by electricity and the creator of the telegraph industry, precursor of the vast telecommunications enterprise of today.

Born in Massachusetts in 1791, Morse came of distinguished New England forebears who included famous preachers, scholars, judges, and a colonel in the Continental Army. His father, Jedidiah, was a prominent Congregational minister, Federalist leader, and one of America's first geographers. Samuel (called Finley by his family after one of his middle names) grew up near Boston, in a household where people prized learning and knowledge.

Though his family was well equipped to educate him at home, he was sent away to school at Phillips Academy in Andover when he was just eight. The young Finley disliked boarding school and did not do well, but he found consolation in drawing. His father preferred books to pictures, but he did not at first discourage the lad and in fact proudly sent a specimen of his work to Finley's grandfather with the comment: "[H]e is self taught—has had no instructions."

In 1805, at the age of 14, Morse entered Yale. The college was scarcely an intellectual feast in the early nineteenth century. It had only three professors and its curriculum was almost exclusively devoted to the classical languages. Yet at Yale, Morse first learned about electricity. Equally important, to earn pocket money, he began to paint miniature portraits on ivory, a genre much admired in that day. The acclaim of his peers convinced him that his future lay in art, and on graduation he told his father that he wished to study with Washington Allston, an American painter then passing through Boston. The Reverend Morse put his foot down. His oldest child, he said, would become a bookstore clerk in Boston while considering a proper career.

Though bitterly disappointed, Morse obeyed his father. But while working at Mallory's bookstore he continued to paint. The work he did in his spare time so impressed influential people that his father relented and agreed to send him to England in the company of Allston to perfect his talents and learn from the masters of Europe.

Morse spent the next four years in London, studying with Allston and painting a number of important canvasses. He returned to Boston in 1815 and opened his own studio, full of hope that he could make a living from his painting and at the same time launch an artistic renaissance in America. He was disappointed. People admired his pictures and liked the young man personally, but they did not give him commissions. No one wanted the landscapes and historical paintings that Morse preferred to paint. He did manage to make a little money doing portraits, but this required him to move from place to place to accommodate patrons. In the next eight years Morse wandered from Concord, New Hampshire, to Charleston, South Carolina, finally settling in New York in 1823.

During this period his talent matured, but it did not lead to the fame and recognition he craved. These were not good years for Morse. His wife, Lucretia, died in 1825, leaving him with four young children. His father and mother died soon after. In 1829 he returned for a while to Europe, where he believed that art and artists were better appreciated. When he came home in 1832, he was appointed professor of painting and sculpture at New York University, but the position was purely honorific, without salary. During these disappointing years his frustrations led him into nativist, anti-Catholic politics, a position he later came to regret.

During the 1830s Morse also drifted away from painting. On a return voyage from Europe he had first conceived the idea that electricity could be used to transmit messages over a wire. By 1832 he had set down in his notebook the plan for a device that would send signals by the opening and closing of a circuit, a receiving apparatus that would record the signals as dots and spaces on a paper strip moved by clockwork, and a code to translate the dots and spaces into the letters of the alphabet. Over the next few years Morse perfected his device, relying heavily on the scientific knowledge of Joseph Henry, a science professor at Princeton, and the financial backing of Alfred Vail, a rich young man whom he had taught at the university.

Morse filed his "electric telegraph" patent in 1837, but for the next seven years he could not secure enough financial support to demonstrate his invention's practical value. During this period, rather than go into debt, Morse actually went hungry at times. Finally, in 1843, Congress appropriated $30,000 to build an experimental telegraph line between Washington and Baltimore. On May 24, 1844, surrounded by friends and associates in the Supreme Court chamber of the Capitol, Morse tapped out the biblical phrase: "What hath God wrought!" In Baltimore Vail received the message and responded. The effect of this demonstration was strongly reinforced when the telegraph was used immediately after to transmit news of the Democratic national convention meeting in Baltimore. Vail sent news from the scene of the convention; Morse tacked up the messages on a board in the Capitol rotunda. It was the beginning of the new "information age" that is still evolving in our day.

Despite these successes, neither Morse nor the telegraph experienced clear sailing thereafter. Morse would have been happy to accept a government award and return to his art. But Congress refused his request for $100,000, and he was forced to seek commercial support for his invention. He was not a businessman, but fortunately he had Vail and a former postmaster general, Amos Kendall, to handle his business affairs. Morse and his partners beat off numerous lawsuits by other claimants to the invention and competed energetically with other companies offering telegraph services to newspapers and private users. Together the Morse associates and their competitors helped to wire the nation into a network of instantaneous communication. In 1858 Morse and his friends formed the Magnetic Telegraph Company in a deal that finally made the inventor a rich man after twenty years of struggle.

Morse lived until 1872, long enough to see a functioning Atlantic cable tie Europe to America. His last years were marked by contentment. He lived with his second wife and second family at an estate on the Hudson, while enjoying a townhouse in New York City. Colleges showered him with honorary degrees and governments awarded him medals and decorations. In 1871 the telegraph operators of America commissioned a bronze statue of the man who had created their industry, to be mounted in New York's Central Park. Morse did suffer one major disappointment in this period of his life, otherwise marked by comfort and acclaim. In 1864,

36

when he tried to resume painting, he discovered that his talent had ebbed and he gave up the attempt.

Morse's death was marked by memorial services all over the nation. It was the inventor whom the country honored; little was noted of the artist. Posterity has been kinder to the artistic side of his career, however. He is now regarded as one of the nation's greatest painters. Morse now seems, in the words of his chief biographer, the "American Leonardo"—like the great da Vinci, a genius in art as well as technology.

★★★★★★★★ A HISTORICAL DOCUMENT ★★★★★★★★

The Lowell Girls

Not all the workers at the Lowell Mills were content with their lot. As early as 1834 angry factory girls at Lowell "turned out" to protest wage cuts and other acts of the corporation "agents" that they considered arbitrary and unjust. Yet life at Lowell was a mixture of good and bad, and many of the farm girls found it a welcome relief for a few years from the boredom and narrowness of life in the declining New England countryside.

Harriet Hanson Robinson, whose account of her Lowell experience in the mid-1830s is excerpted below, was not entirely typical of the Lowell "operatives." She was born in Boston and moved to Lowell with her mother shortly after her father's death. There Mrs. Robinson ran a boardinghouse for girls who worked in the Tremount mill. Harriet herself, along with her three siblings, entered the mill at the age of ten and remained there until her mid-teens. She later married a newspaper editor and became an active women's suffrage leader. Below, from the perspective of over half a century, she tells what it was like to be a "doffer" in the mill.

"I had been to school constantly until I was about ten years of age, when my mother, feeling obliged to have help in her work besides what I could give, and also needing the money which I could earn, allowed me, at my urgent request (for I wanted to earn *money* like the other little girls), to go to work in the mills. I worked first in the spinning-room as a 'doffer.' The doffers were the very youngest girls, whose work was to doff, or take off, the full bobbins, and replace them with the empty ones.

"I can see myself now, racing down the alley, between the spinning frames, carrying in front of me a bobbin-box bigger than I was. These mites had to be very swift in their movements, so as not to keep the spinning-frames stopped long, and they worked only about fifteen minutes in every hour. The rest of the time was their own, and when the overseer was kind they were allowed to read, knit, or even to go outside the mill-yard to play.

"Some of us learned to embroider in crewels, and I still have a lamb worked on cloth, a relic of those early days, when I was first taught to improve my time in the good old New England fashion. When not doffing, we were often allowed to go home, for a time, and thus were able to help our mothers in their housework. We were paid two dollars a week; and proud I was when my turn came to stand up on the bobbin-box, and write my name in the paymaster's book, and how indignant I was when he asked me if I would 'write.' 'Of course I can,' said I and he smiled as he looked down on me.

"The working hours of all the girls extended from five o'clock in the morning until seven in the evening, with one-half hour for breakfast and for dinner. Even the doffers were forced to be on duty nearly fourteen hours a day, and this was the greatest hardship in the lives of these children. For it was not until 1842 that the hours of labor for children under twelve years of age were limited to ten per day; but the 'ten-hour law' itself was not passed until long after some of these little doffers were old enough to appear before the legislative committee on the subject, and plead, by their presence, for a reduction of the hours of labor.

"I do not recall any particular hardship connected with this life, except getting up so early in the morning, and to this habit I never was, and never shall be, reconciled, for it has taken nearly a lifetime for me to make up the sleep lost at that early age. But in every other respect it was a pleasant life. We were not hurried any more than was for our good, and no more work was required of us than we were able easily to do."

10

★★★★★★★★★★

★★★★★★★★ A HISTORICAL DOCUMENT ★★★★★★★★

Jacksonian Democracy

Mrs. Margaret Bayard Smith, wife of a Washington banker, editor, and Jeffersonian politician, witnessed the transition from the Virginia dynasty to the age of Jackson. A keen observer of politics as it was played out in the nation's capital early in the nineteenth century, she recorded her impressions in letters to friends and family, later collected as *The First Forty Years of Washington Society*. The following excerpt from that work describes Inauguration Day, 1829, when the "people's" hero, Andy Jackson, became president of the United States, ushering in a new, more democratic age. It was an age that clearly did not fully please Mrs. Smith, who was unused to the unruly exuberance of the masses come to celebrate their day in the sun.

"A national salute was fired early in the morning, and ushered in the 4th of March. By ten o'clock the Avenue was crowded with carriages of every description, from the splendid Barronet and coach, down to waggons and carts, filled with women and children, some in finery and some in rags, for it was the people's President, and all would see him. . . . Some one came and informed us [that] the crowd before the President's house, was so far lessen'd, that they thought that we might enter. This time we effected our purpose. But what a scene did we witness! *The Majesty of the People* had disappeared and a rabble, a mob, of boys, negros, women, children, scrambling, fighting, romping. What a pity, what a pity! No arrangements had been made; no police officers placed on duty, and the whole house had been inundated by the rabble mob. We came too late. The President, after having been *literally* nearly pressed to death and almost suffocated, and torn to pieces by the people in their eagerness to shake hands with Old Hickory, had retreated through the back way or south front and had escaped to his lodgings at Gadsby's. Cut glass and china to the amount of several thousand dollars had been broken in the struggle to get the refreshments. . . . [P]unch and other articles had been carried out in tubs and buckets, but had it been in hogs-heads it would have been insufficient. . . . [They supplied] ice-creams, and cake, and lemonade, for 20,000 people, for it is said that [that] number were there tho' I think the estimate exaggerated. Ladies fainted, men were seen with bloody noses and such a scene of confusion took place as is impossible to describe,—those who got in could not get out by the door again, but had to scramble out of windows. At one time, the President, who had retreated and retreated until he was pressed against the wall, could only be secured by a number of gentlemen forming around him and making a kind of barrier of their own bodies, and the pressure was so great that Col Bomford who was one said that at one time he was afraid they should have been pushed down, or on the President. It was then the windows were thrown open, and the torrent found an outlet, which otherwise might have proved fatal.

"This concourse had not been anticipated and therefor not provided against. Ladies and gentlemen only had been expected at this Levee, not the people en masse. But it was the People's day, and the People's President and the People would rule. God grant that one day or other, the People do not put down all rule and rulers. . . ."

******** A HISTORICAL PORTRAIT ********

Peggy Eaton

Peggy Eaton was a beautiful woman who loved not wisely but too well. Her sex denied her an official role in politics, but for a time during the Jackson administration, her vivacity and charm made her a force in the political life of her nation.

Born Margaret O'Neale in 1796, Peggy learned early the skills that would make her a political presence. Her father, William, was Scotch-Irish, and his brick house on I Street in Washington was one of the first in the new federal district. William O'Neale offered board and lodging for members of Congress and the executive branch who came to the raw, new capital for only a few months each year, leaving their wives and families at home. The congressmen and government officials, deprived of their own children, spoiled the pretty little girl shamelessly. She in turn learned early how to please men, even those busy ones deeply immersed in high affairs of state.

Her father's boarding house cum tavern, which he called the Franklin House, was the source of still another sort of education for Peggy. Women were totally excluded from politics in this era, and the few who tried to influence the course of political events indirectly were scorned. As one contemporary publication described it, "a female politician is only less disgusting than a female infidel." Yet it was difficult for Peggy to avoid absorbing political ideas or learning political strategy with so many argumentative and brilliant politicians dining each day at the family table or puffing their pipes around the Franklin House tavern fire.

Though her father was only a "tavernkeeper," Peggy went to the best school for young ladies that the capital afforded. There she was exposed to the standard curriculum of the day for girls: reading and writing, penmanship, French, drawing and painting, and twenty-five different kinds of needlework. Her favorite subjects, however, were music and dancing. In 1812 Peggy's dancing skill impressed President Madison's wife, Dolley, when she served as judge for the ball that Mr. Generes, the capital's most prestigious dancing master, gave each year for his pupils. Mrs. Madison awarded Peggy the prize as Carnival Queen, a triumph that reinforced her romantic streak and magnified her yearnings for fame and fortune.

That same year, when she was still not yet sixteen, Peggy tried to elope with a handsome army officer stationed in Washington. She was caught by her father wriggling down a rope from her second-floor bedroom window and sent off to a finishing school in New York where she would be far from the dashing captain. But William O'Neale, like most other men, found it difficult to deny Peggy her wishes and he soon allowed her to return home.

For the next year or two Peggy, now the object of much tongue-wagging among Washington's respectable matrons, served as hostess in her father's tavern. In June 1816 she met John B. Timberlake, a purser in the U.S. Navy. Impressed by his blond good looks she accepted his proposal of marriage. At twenty, Peggy became a wife.

The marriage was not happy. Timberlake was a rolling stone who refused to settle down. He also drank too much. He and Peggy had three children, but the marriage never really jelled. Timberlake was away on duty much of the time, and Peggy and the children generally stayed at the O'Neale boarding house where she, though now a young matron herself, continued to charm the politician boarders.

One of these was the young senator from Tennessee, Major John Eaton, a good friend of Andy Jackson, the hero of New Orleans. In 1823 Jackson himself was elected to the Senate and came to reside at the O'Neale house with his young, though politically senior, colleague. Both men were enchanted with Peggy Timberlake. Jackson wrote home to his wife, Rachel, of the "amiable" O'Neale family and particularly of Mrs. Timberlake, who "plays the Piano Delightfully & every Sunday evening entertains her pious mother with Sacred music to which we are invited."

Andrew Jackson would always retain the image of Peggy playing "Sacred music" for the pious Mrs. O'Neale. John Eaton apparently found her person more attractive than her accomplishments, and rumors were soon circulating that his attentions to Mrs. Timberlake were more than old-fashioned gallantry. One congressman who served in Washington during this period wrote that Peggy Timberlake "was considered as a lady who would be willing to dispense her favors wherever she took a fancy." Peggy became so notorious that Eliza Monroe, the president's proper wife, excluded her from White House receptions.

In 1828, while on duty with the Mediterranean squadron, John Timberlake died and was buried in Spain. Major Eaton quickly resolved to marry the young widow, but before acting he consulted his friend Jackson, now president-elect. Jackson was a generous and loyal man who, moreover, remembered how the gossips had tried to besmirch the reputation of his own beloved Rachel, claiming that she had lived in sin with him before they were legally married. He told Eaton to go ahead. "[I]f you love the woman, and she will have you, marry her by all means." In January 1829 Eaton and Peggy were married by the chaplain of the Senate at Franklin House. Hours before, Congressman Churchill C. Cambreleng of New York wrote his friend, Governor Martin Van Buren, in Albany: "Poor Eaton is to be married tonight to Mrs. T...! There is a vulgar saying of some vulgar man ... on such unions— about using a certain household [item] and then putting it on one's head."

The marriage might have become a minor footnote to the social history of Jacksonian Washington if the president had not asked Senator Eaton to join his cabinet as secretary of war. Eaton at first refused the bid, probably because he feared to embarrass his friend, but Jackson insisted and Eaton "very reluctantly" agreed.

Eaton's doubts proved sound. At the inaugural ball the wives of the politicians ignored Peggy, though their husbands flocked around the witty and vivacious young matron and the president himself singled her out for "marked attention." Worse was to follow. Enemies of Eaton were soon circulating rumors that he and Peggy had taken trips and registered in hotels together while she was still Mrs. Timberlake and that she had conceived a child a year after her husband had departed for overseas duty. The gossips were to be found in the president's own household. Rachel Jackson had died shortly before Jackson's first term began, and the president's young niece, Emily Donelson, served as his official hostess. Mrs. Donelson quickly made it clear that she would not "receive" or call on Mrs. Eaton.

Nor were the other cabinet wives any more cordial. Leading the anti-Peggy pack was Floride Calhoun, the wife of Vice President John C. Calhoun and a very proper southern lady. With their wives so adamant, it proved difficult for other administration officials to accept Peggy Eaton socially. They avoided invitations to affairs that included the Eatons. They excluded the secretary of war and his wife from their balls and dinners. One exception was Martin Van Buren, now secretary of state. A widower whose own father had been a tavernkeeper, Van Buren saw no reason to snub Peggy Eaton. Indeed, the canny New Yorker recognized that Peggy's ostracism was causing the president pain, and he went out of his way to be chivalrous to his cabinet colleague's wife.

But Van Buren's generosity was not enough for Jackson. On September 10, 1829, he called his official family together to lay to rest the stories concerning the Eatons' premarital relations. With Eaton himself absent, the president denounced gossip in general and defended both his Tennessee friend and his friend's wife. John Eaton was innocent. As for Mrs. Eaton, she was "as chaste as a virgin."

Jackson's effort to lay down an official line on Peggy to his subordinates did not work. The president's colleagues and advisers split in two, one group willing to abide by his desire that Peggy be treated with respect, the other strongly opposed. The division disrupted his household. In mid-1830 Jackson exiled Emily and his nephew, Andrew Jackson Donelson, from the White House for refusing to socialize with the Eatons. It also had political consequences. Jackson was a fierce partisan. Those who did not agree with him were his sworn enemies and he would not cease until he had destroyed them.

The president's commitment to the Eatons helped split the Jackson party, contributing to the emerging Whig–Democratic rivalry that would soon enliven the political scene. It affected the political fortunes of Van Buren and Calhoun, both of whom nursed presidential ambitions and, even this early, sought the endorsement of the popular hero.

Jackson had other reasons to dislike Vice President Calhoun besides his disdain for Peggy Eaton. Back in 1818, when Calhoun was secretary of war under Monroe, he had harshly criticized General Jackson's "unauthorized" incursion into Florida, the bold stroke that had led to the hanging of Arbuthnot and Ambrister. In 1832 Jackson would clash again with the South Carolinian over the right of a state to nullify an act of Congress. But clearly the vice president's attitude toward Mrs. Eaton contributed to the antagonism. Meanwhile, Van Buren had become the general's favorite. In 1840, after Jackson stepped down, Van Buren would win the Democratic nomination; Calhoun had by this time become the champion of the South's special interests.

Peggy at first had stubbornly sought vindication, though even some of John Eaton's friends felt the president was risking too much for her cause. But finally even she lost heart and began to withdraw from possibly embarrassing social occasions. Having lost the battle for the rights she believed she deserved, she had no objection when her husband agreed to resign his post in 1831 in a general cabinet reorganization. Peggy hoped to remain in Washington where she had lived all her life and where, the prudes aside, she had made friends. But Eaton preferred to return to Tennessee and soon after they took up residence in the Eaton family house near Nashville.

But the major found private life dull. In 1832 he decided to run for the Senate. Though beaten, he continued to seek office, and in 1834 Jackson appointed him governor of Florida Territory. There, in Tallahassee, Peggy's health, not good since leaving Washington, improved. Yet she was not happy. The shabby little territorial capital seemed dull after Washington. Fortunately, in 1836 Eaton was sent as ambassador to Spain, and Peggy had a new, and far more cosmopolitan, social world to conquer.

Peggy liked Madrid. She, her husband, and her two surviving children by Timberlake—Margaret and Virginia—lived in the beautiful former home of the Duke St.

Lorenzo. She adored the Spanish people. The common folk were joyous yet respectful. The men of the upper class were courtly—much like President Jackson—and their wives, daughters, and sisters showed none of the priggishness of American women. Especially gratifying was the friendly attitude of Maria Cristina, the queen, a woman who, like Peggy, had had her share of flirtations and amorous escapades. Peggy would describe the four years in Spain as the happiest in her life, a time full of balls, bullfights, fiestas, and other lively distractions.

The idyll was disrupted in 1840 when Jackson's successor as president, none other than Martin Van Buren, recalled Eaton so that he could replace him with the famous New York author Washington Irving. The Eatons returned to America and settled once again in Washington where the major, perhaps disgruntled by Van Buren's recall, became a Whig. The change of party did not lead to preferment. Bored with inactivity, Eaton drank too much. In 1856 he died, leaving Peggy, now a 60-year-old grandmother, a rich woman.

Peggy Eaton did not settle down to respectable old age. In 1859, the elderly widow startled Washington, and revived all the lurid old stories, by marrying Antonio Buchignani, a dancing instructor of nineteen, one-third her age! Despite the scandal, the marriage was happy for a time. The couple were even accepted by Washington's respectables. Then "Tonio" began to show his true colors, stealing silver from his wealthy wife and playing on the affections of Emily, Peggy's sixteen-year-old granddaughter.

In 1866, after seven years of marriage, Tonio ran off to Europe with Emily and most of Peggy's fortune. The errant couple set up as husband and wife in Leghorn, Italy, had a child, and quickly squandered their ill-gotten wealth. They returned to America in September 1868, and Peggy had Tonio arrested as a swindler and seducer.

Peggy divorced Buchignani soon after and resumed use of her former name. She lived in New York for a time and then returned to her beloved Washington. In 1874 a Washington newspaper reporter interviewed her for a feature story for his paper. She was, he wrote, "a hale, vigorous, well-preserved lady," in whose "form and face" could be detected "many of the lines and lineaments of that queenly beauty which once held captive so many men." This story launched a flock of others, and for a time Peggy once again became a celebrity. Mathew Brady, the famous photographer, asked to take her portrait. The picture is the only photograph we have of her and, notwithstanding the newspaper reporter's chivalrous remarks just a few years before, it shows an old lady dressed in black with only the faintest traces of the charm and beauty she once possessed.

On a gray day in November 1879, Margaret O'Neale Timberlake Eaton Buchignani died. The president's wife, Lucy Hayes, sent a large wreath of white roses to the funeral, and the Washington chief of police was the head pallbearer. Once again Peggy made the headlines. One paper called her a "One-Time Society Queen." The *New York Times* reviewed her life and marveled at its strange twists. Another daily, the *New York Tribune*, was ungallant. She had "created a noise quite out of proportion to her importance," Horace Greeley's old paper concluded. The judgment is unfair. Peggy Eaton was only a minor mover and shaker in politics, it is true. As a woman in her day she could not be more. But for a time in the 1820s, she demonstrated the power of elemental human drives to mold a nation's public life even in a repressed era.

11

★★★★★★★★★★

★★★★★★★★ A HISTORICAL DOCUMENT ★★★★★★★★

Manifest Destiny

Every nation with expansionist designs has found a rationale for its urges. The United States was no exception. Its justification was called Manifest Destiny, and it was the creation largely of a New York lawyer-journalist named John Louis O'Sullivan, who probably first used the phrase in 1845.

In the July-August 1845 issue of his paper, *The United States Magazine and Democratic Review*, O'Sullivan argued in favor of Texas annexation against those who attacked it as either a "slave power" scheme or an act of pure greed against a weaker neighbor. The excerpt of this editorial included here carries the argument beyond Texas to justify all of American continental expansion. Note O'Sullivan's emphasis on demography and his prediction of America's population a century ahead. He was not too far off the mark.

". . . Texas has been absorbed into the Union in the inevitable fulfillment of the general law which is rolling our population westward; the connexion of which with that ratio of growth in population which is destined within a hundred years to swell our numbers to the enormous population of *two hundred and fifty millions* (if not more), is too evident to leave us in doubt of the manifest design of Providence in regard to the occupation of this continent. It was disintegrated from Mexico in the natural course of events, by a process perfectly legitimate on its own part, blameless on ours; and in which all the censures due to wrong, perfidy, and folly, rest on Mexico alone. And possessed as it was by a population which was in truth but a colonial detachment from our own, . . . their incorporation into the Union was not only inevitable, but the most natural, right and proper thing in the world—and it is only astonishing that there should be any among ourselves to say it nay. . . .

"California will, probably, next fall away from the loose affiliation which, in such a country like Mexico, holds a remote province in a slight equivocal kind of dependence on the metropolis. Imbecile and distracted, Mexico can never exert any real governmental authority over such a country. The impotence of the one and the distance of the other, must make the relation one of virtual independence, unless, by stunting the province of all natural growth, and forbidding that immigration which alone can develop its capabilities and fulfill the purposes of its creation, tyranny may retain a military dominion which is no government in the legitimate sense of the term. In the case of California this is now impossible. The Anglo-Saxon foot is already on its borders. Already the advance guard of the irresistible army of the Anglo-Saxon emigration has begun to pour down upon it, armed with the plough and the rifle, and making its trail with schools and colleges, courts and representative halls, mills and meeting-houses. A population will soon be in actual occupation of California, over which it will be idle for Mexico to dream of dominion. They will necessarily

44

become independent. All this without agency of our government, without responsibility of our people—in the natural flow of events, the spontaneous working of principles, and the adaptation of the tendencies and wants of the human race to the elemental circumstances in the midst of which they find themselves placed. . . .

"Whether they will then attach themselves to our Union or not, is not to be predicted with any certainty. Unless the projected railroad across the continent to the Pacific be carried into effect, perhaps they may not; though even in that case, the day is not far distant when the Empires of the Atlantic and the Pacific would again flow together into one. . . . But that great work . . . cannot remain long unbuilt. Its necessity for this very purpose of binding and holding together in its iron clasp our fast settling Pacific region with that of the Mississippi valley . . . gives assurance that the day cannot be distant which shall witness the conveyance of the representatives from Oregon and California to Washington within less time than a few years ago was devoted to a similar journey by those from Ohio. . . .

"Away, then, with all idle French talk of *balances of power* on the American Continent. There is no growth in Spanish America! Whatever progress of population there may be in the British Canadas, is only for their own early severance of their present colonial relation to the little island three thousand miles across the Atlantic; soon to be followed by Annexation, and destined to swell the still accumulating momentum of our progress. And whatsoever may hold the balance, though they should cast into the opposite scale all the bayonets and cannon, not only of France and England, but of Europe entire, how would it kick the beam against the simple solid weight of two hundred and fifty or three hundred millions . . . destined to gather beneath the flutter of the stripes and stars, in the fast hastening year of the Lord 1945?"

******** A HISTORICAL PORTRAIT ********

John Charles Frémont

Whether John Charles Frémont was a pathfinder, a pathmaker, or merely a pathfollower is open to question, but there is no doubt that he is one of the most romantic figures in America's history.

Frémont's mother was Anne Beverly Whiting, a descendant of one of the Founding Fathers and member of a distinguished but impoverished family. His father was John Charles Frémont, a French royalist who had fled from Napoleonic France on a ship bound to Santo Domingo and ended up in Richmond, Virginia, in 1808.

It was in Richmond that the dashing French émigré met Anne, the childless and unhappily married wife of Major John Pryor, a tyrannical and wealthy man forty-five years her senior, and began a romantic relationship. After a showdown with the angry husband, the couple eloped and, without benefit of legal ceremony, settled in Savannah where Anne took in boarders and John Charles taught dancing and French. On January 21, 1813, their first child, John Charles Frémont, Jr., was born.

The family moved to Nashville soon after and then to Norfolk. There Anne and John, Sr., were married after Major Pryor's death. John, Sr., died of pneumonia in 1818 when his eldest son was only five. Gossip about the family continued to haunt Mrs. Frémont, so she moved to the more cosmopolitan, less puritanical city of

Charleston, where she supported her three children on a small inheritance, supplemented by paying guests at her house.

Young John was brilliant, handsome, and charming, and although his social credentials were not impeccable by class-conscious southern standards, he made many friends among Charleston's best families. He also attracted powerful patrons, a talent he would retain all his life. The first of these was John W. Mitchell, a lawyer who gave him a clerkship in his office and sent him to be educated at a fancy preparatory school. At sixteen he was able to enter Charleston College where he excelled in mathematics and natural science. Mitchell continued to help him financially as did the rector of St. Philip's, Charleston's most socially prominent Episcopal church. Unfortunately, John fell in love, neglected his studies, and cut classes. After several warnings he was expelled, just three months short of his graduation, for "habitual irregularity and incorrigible negligence."

Frémont was now forced to earn money to help support himself, his mother, and his siblings. Luckily his intellectual reputation won him a teaching position at a private secondary school in Charleston. Through his teaching he continued to meet and charm distinguished Charlestonians who were happy to help the talented and personable young man. One of these newest patrons was Joel Roberts Poinsett, Jacksonian politician, member of the St. Philip's congregation, first U.S. minister to Mexico, and the man who introduced the red tropical flower, the poinsettia, to the United States. Poinsett got John a job as mathematics teacher to navy midshipmen on the U.S.S. *Natchez*, then about to undertake a training cruise down the coast of South America. Two years later, when the *Natchez* returned, Frémont passed the examination for professor of mathematics in the navy. While he was debating whether to accept this position, Poinsett secured his appointment to the United States Topographic Corps as assistant engineer to survey the route of a projected railroad to run from Louisville to Charleston. When Poinsett became secretary of war in 1837, he commissioned his protegé second lieutenant in the army and appointed him assistant to Joseph Nicolett, a famous French scientist, on two government-sponsored surveys of the territory between the upper Missouri and Mississippi rivers. The two expeditions took lieutenant Frémont all through present-day Minnesota and the Dakotas. Here Frémont saw for the first time the vast sea of buffalo that then covered the Great Plains. When he returned to Washington in 1839, he and Nicolett collaborated on a series of maps and scientific reports.

In Washington, the ever-obliging Poinsett introduced the twenty-six-year-old Frémont to Democratic Senator Thomas Hart Benton, a leader of the expansionists in Congress and a strong supporter of government-sponsored exploration of the West. The young officer was soon dining regularly at the Benton home and paying court to his host's beautiful and intelligent teenage daughter, Jessie. However much they liked Frémont, the Bentons were opposed to the match. Jessie was too young and the handsome lieutenant's prospects were not very good. When their lecturing failed to deter the young couple, Senator Benton prevailed on Poinsett to send John Charles off on another expedition.

With Nicolett ill, Frémont was put in charge of the trip, a survey of the Des Moines River and Iowa Territory, a region rapidly being settled by farmers. Frémont spent the spring and summer of 1841 exploring and mapping Iowa Territory and by August was back in Washington ready to resume his courtship. Unable to overcome the Bentons' objections, the couple were secretly married in October. In November they informed the senator, who finally accepted the situation when his daughter clutched her husband's arm tightly and quoted the words of Ruth in the

Bible: "Whither thou goest, I will go." Frémont had won himself not only a rich and beautiful wife but another powerful patron.

Through Benton's influence Frémont was chosen to head a succession of major western expeditions. In 1842, with Christopher (Kit) Carson as his guide, he explored the Plains as far as South Pass in Wyoming. This trip produced a scientific map of the Oregon Trail and a report that confirmed the fertility of the adjacent lands and furnished practical advice to would-be emigrants. The following year Benton induced Congress to sponsor the second American expedition to the mouth of the Columbia. This trip was almost canceled when Frémont decided to take with him a portable howitzer cannon. The War Department feared that this would tag the expedition as a military venture against Mexico and dispatched an order asking Frémont, then collecting supplies in St. Louis, to return to Washington. Jessie Frémont, ascribing it to jealousy of her beloved husband, intercepted the order, and wrote her husband urging him to speed up his departure. Fortunately, when the defiance was discovered, the senator deflected blame from his daughter. But his son-in-law was branded within the professional army as an officer who would not obey orders.

The expedition took Frémont to California, a place with which his name would always be connected. But first he visited the Great Salt Lake and wrote a glowing report of its surroundings that would attract the attention of Mormon leader Brigham Young four years later when he was looking for a refuge for his persecuted people. When he reached the Dalles in Oregon in October 1843, prudence suggested that Frémont turn back before winter struck. Instead, he turned south to explore the forbidding Great Basin. In February, after struggling through deep snows, the Frémont party crossed the Sierras into California and arrived in the warm Sacramento Valley. Soon after, they reached Fort Sutter, not far from the present California capital. Here they were treated hospitably by Captain John Augustus Sutter, the Swiss entrepreneur who had arrived in California six years before and established a combination ranch–farm–fort on 50,000 acres granted by the Mexican government. Sutter filled in the American officer on the volatile politics of the province and the restlessness of the many American settlers under Mexican rule.

From Fort Sutter Frémont continued to move southeast, exploring parts of Nevada and Utah before finally returning to Washington at the end of the year. During the winter of 1844–1845 he and Jessie together drafted the report on this second trip to the far West, emphasizing the fertility and beauty of the region and the practicality of the Oregon Trail. Congress received this report with enthusiasm and ordered the printing of 100,000 copies at government expense.

In March 1845 the fiery expansionist James K. Polk took the oath of office as president. Manifest Destiny was in the air. Soon after, Benton and Frémont induced Congress to authorize another western reconnaissance. Like the others, the ostensible purpose of this trip was scientific, but Frémont later admitted in his *Memoirs* that "in arranging this expedition the eventualities of war were taken into consideration." Secretary of the Navy George Bancroft, he explained, expected him to convert his party of sixty-two into a military force if he found that war had begun by the time he reached California.

Blazing a new trail through Nevada, Frémont reached Sutter's Fort on December 9, 1845. From there he and his men proceeded to Monterey on the pretext of collecting additional supplies and contacted Thomas Larkin, the American consul, who told the young officer about the confused state of affairs in the province and described the American settlers' movement for secession from Mexico. Under orders from the suspicious Mexican authorities to leave, Frémont set off for Oregon. Though

Frémont did not yet know it, by this time Mexico and the United States were at war.

In early May, while camped at Klamath Lake, Frémont and his men received dispatches sent originally to Larkin from Washington directing the consul to seek peaceably to detach California from Mexico with the ultimate goal of annexation to the United States. Though he did not know that Mexican and American armies were already fighting along the Rio Grande, Frémont turned south and prepared to enter into the struggle for California's fate.

By this time the American settlers in the province were chafing under the repressive hand of the Mexican authorities; many feared massacre by the Indians. Frémont's arrival in Sonoma helped to precipitate a revolt. Inspired by the presence of the soldiers, on June 14 a tiny party of American settlers attacked the Mexican military post in the seedy town and raised the banner of the "Republic of California," inscribed with a grizzly bear. When the Mexican officials sent troops, Frémont dropped all pretense that his was purely an exploring expedition and intercepted them. Still without official knowledge of events in the East, he had personally declared war on Mexico.

When official news of hostilities finally reached the West Coast, Commodore Robert Stockton appointed Frémont major of the California Battalion, a force composed of his own small military unit, plus volunteers among the American settlers. After the American capture of Los Angeles, Stockton made him military governor of the province. This put Frémont on a collision course with General Stephen W. Kearny, who claimed to have official sanction to set up a government in the captured province. With Stockton's support, Frémont ignored Kearny's claims. When Kearny's orders were confirmed, Frémont was arrested, court-martialed, and found guilty of mutiny and conduct prejudicial to military discipline. President Polk eventually remitted his sentence of dismissal from the army, but let the guilty verdict stand. Hurt and indignant, Frémont resigned from the military.

Shortly after, Senator Benton and some wealthy St. Louis friends financed a fourth Frémont expedition to survey routes for a Pacific railroad. Frémont arrived in California in time for the great gold discovery at Sutter's Fort. Providentially, before he had left California in disgrace two years before, he had bought for $3,000 the large Las Mariposas tract in the Sierra foothills as a future home. In 1849 Mexican laborers discovered rich veins of gold ore on this property. Overnight Frémont became a millionaire. He soon abandoned his survey work, acquired real estate in San Francisco, developed his foothill property, and for a brief time lived an affluent life in Monterey with Jessie and their three children.

When California became a state in 1850 Frémont was elected ad interim United States senator, but failed to win the regular election in 1851. By this time the Frémonts, their land claims in dispute and their financial prospects in doubt, left California for the East. Frémont made another exploratory trip west, this one again to survey a Pacific railroad route. The expedition was not especially fruitful.

By this time the nation was in the throes of the sectional struggle over slavery extension. Though southern bred, Frémont was a free soiler, and in 1856, as a glamorous popular hero, won the presidential nomination of the newly formed Republican party. He lost to James Buchanan by an electoral vote of 174 to 114 and half a million fewer popular votes than his Democratic rival. When the Civil War broke out Lincoln appointed him major general and commander of the Western Department headquartered at St. Louis. Frémont's problems in his new post were almost insurmountable. Missouri was strongly secessionist and full of angry men determined to defy the Union authorities. Surrounded by enemies, the general had few arms and insufficient supplies and manpower to impose loyal government on the state. But he made matters still worse by declaring martial law and issuing his own, premature emancipation proclamation for the state's slaves. Lincoln might have retained him if he had proven an effective military leader. He was not, and his defeats in three minor battles prompted Lincoln to remove him from command. As usual, if Frémont had made enemies, he had also made friends. The radical antislavery Republicans protested his removal, and Lincoln reappointed him head of the Mountain Department with headquarters at Wheeling.

Having proven ineffective against Confederate general Stonewall Jackson, he once more lost his command. Senator Benton had died in 1858, but Frémont still did not lack for powerful friends and patrons. In 1864 a radical faction within the Republican party pushed him as an alternate to Lincoln in the presidential election. Though he was skeptical of Lincoln, he withdrew for the sake of party unity.

Frémont's life went downhill from this point on. During the war dishonest business associates cheated him of his Mariposa estate. Then, after the war, he invested his remaining capital in an unprofitable Pacific railroad enterprise. When this scheme failed, he lost his mansion in Manhattan and his estate in Westchester, and he and Jessie were forced to give up their extensive travels in Europe. Jessie sought to keep the poorhouse at bay by writing newspaper articles, children's stories, and travel accounts. Frémont himself wrote his *Memoirs*, a 650-page tome published in 1886. It was not a financial success, and his labors on it exhausted him. In 1887 he and Jessie went once more to California, this time for health reasons. Two years later John returned East to look after his remaining business affairs leaving Jessie behind in Los Angeles. In July 1890, while staying with one of his sons, he died of peritonitis at the age of 77. Jessie was not at his bedside.

Although his life ended in failure, Frémont had helped conquer a western empire for his country. His name, conferred on over twenty geographic sites scattered across the western third of the nation, marks his achievements.

12

****

******** A HISTORICAL DOCUMENT ********

Women's Rights

Lucy Stone was a founder of the pre–Civil War women's rights movement. Determined to get an education at a time when women were considered incapable of exercising the higher mental faculties, she was fortunate when Oberlin College in Ohio opened its doors to women and blacks. In 1847, soon after earning her degree, she joined the abolitionist movement and for several years worked for the American Antislavery Society. For Lucy Stone, as for other women, abolitionism served as a bridge to the women's rights movement. In 1850 she helped to organize the first national women's rights convention at Worcester, Massachusetts, and eventually became a leader of the women's suffrage movement as well. During her lifetime she was notorious for keeping her maiden name after marriage to Henry B. Blackwell. Other feminists who imitated her came to be called "Lucy Stoners."

The selection below is part of a speech Lucy Stone delivered extemporaneously at a women's rights convention in Cincinnati in 1855. It is a remarkable capsule summary of women's grievances and aspirations during the antebellum era as perceived by the feminists of the day.

"The last speaker alluded to this movement as being that of a few disappointed women. From the first years to which my memory stretches, I have been a disappointed woman. When, with my brothers, I reached forth after the sources of knowledge, I was reproved with 'It isn't fit for you; it doesn't belong to women.' Then there was but one college in the world where women were admitted, and that was in Brazil. I would have found my way there, but by the time I was prepared to go, one was opened in the young State of Ohio—the first in the United States where women and Negroes could enjoy opportunities with white men. I was disappointed when I came to seek a profession worthy an immortal human being—every employment was closed to me, except those of the teacher, the seamstress, and the housekeeper. In education, in marriage, in religion, in everything, disappointment is the lot of women. It shall be the business of my life to deepen this disappointment in every woman's heart until she bows down to it no longer. I wish that women, instead of being walking show-cases, instead of begging of their fathers and brothers the latest and gayest new bonnet, would ask of them their rights.

"The question of Women's Rights is a practical one. The notion has prevailed that it was only an ephemeral idea, it was but women claiming the right to smoke cigars in the streets, and to frequent barrooms. Others have supposed it is a question of comparative intellect; others still, of sphere. Too much has already been said and written about woman's sphere. Trace all the doctrines to their source and they will be found to have no basis except in the usages and prejudices of the age. This is seen in the fact that what is tolerated in women in one country is not tolerated in another. . . .

"I have confidence in the Father to believe that when He gives us the capacity to do anything He does not make a blunder. Leave women, then, to find their sphere. And do not tell us . . . that our province is to cook dinners, darn stockings, and sew on buttons. We are told woman has all the rights she wants; and even women, I am ashamed to say, tell us so. They mistake the politeness of men for rights—seats while men stand in this hall tonight, and their adulations; but these are mere courtesies. We want rights. The flour-merchant, the house-builder, and the postman charge us no less on account of our sex; but when we endeavor to earn money to pay all these, then, indeed, we find the difference. Man, if he has energy, may hew out for himself a path where no mortal has ever trod, held back by nothing but what is in himself; the world is all before him, there to choose; and we are glad for you, brothers, men, that it is so. But the same society that drives forth the young man, keeps woman at home—a dependent—working little cats on worsted, and little dogs on punctured paper; but if she goes heartily and bravely to give herself to some worthy purpose, she is out of her sphere and she loses caste. Women working in tailor-shops are paid one-third as much as men. Someone in Philadelphia has stated that women make fine shirts for twelve and a half cents apiece; that no woman can make more than nine a week, and the sum thus earned, after deducting rent, fuel, etc., leaves her just three and a half cents a day for bread. Is it any wonder that women are driven to prostitution? Female teachers in New York are paid fifty dollars a year, and for every such situation there are five hundred applicants. I know not what you believe of God, but I believe He gave yearnings and longings to be filled, and that He did not mean all our time should be devoted to feeding and clothing the body. The present condition of woman causes a horrible perversion of the marriage relation. It is said of a lady, 'Has she married well?' 'Oh, yes, her husband is rich.' Woman must marry for a home, and you men are the sufferers by this; for a woman who loathes you may marry you because you have the means to get money which she cannot have. But when woman can enter the lists with you and make money for herself, she will marry you only for deep and earnest affection. . . ."

******** A HISTORICAL PORTRAIT ********

Frederick Douglass

The expression "a credit to his race" used to be applied to a certain kind of well-educated black man who conformed to white expectations. Such people had acquired an education, taken on the white man's speech, and dressed in a white-middle-class way. Above all, they accepted the racial status quo and did not seek to change it. Frederick Douglass was "a credit to his race" by all but the last criterion. He did not accept the way blacks were treated in the United States. Indeed, he was one of the boldest, most resolute enemies of the cruel racial regime that, whether in slavery or "freedom," white America imposed on his people.

Douglass was born in 1818 in Maryland, son of a slave mother and an unidentified white father. Like all North American blacks, he followed his mother's condition, and like her was the property of Aaron Anthony, a Maryland planter with thirty slaves and three farms.

Frederick's mother died while he was still a young child and he went to live on a distant plantation owned by Anthony. Here he observed floggings for the first time and learned that the violence done to blacks by their white masters sometimes made them cruel to one another. Fortunately his stay on the Anthony plantation was brief. In 1825 Frederick was sent to Baltimore to be the companion of the son of Hugh and Sophia Auld. Mrs. Auld was a kind woman and taught the boy to read and write. Her husband, however, was mean-spirited and disapproved of her act. Literacy, he shouted, would "spoil the best nigger in the world." Mrs. Auld never again taught the bright slave boy anything.

Yet Frederick never gave up his quest for learning. When he left the Aulds' household to work in a Baltimore shipyard, he continued to read. The white South was right to forbid slave literacy. At the age of thirteen Frederick bought a book of rhetoric that contained model speeches by the great orators declaiming the principles of freedom and even of slave emancipation. From this work he learned many of the skills and eloquent arguments he would later use with devastating effect against the "peculiar institution."

Following Hugh Auld's death, Frederick was shunted around from one heir to another and employed as a field hand far from the stimulating life of the city. His resentment of his new condition finally induced his latest master to return him to Baltimore, to be apprenticed to a trade and freed when he reached twenty-one.

But Douglass could not wait till then. In September 1838, dressed as a seaman, he hopped a train northward and arrived in New York soon after. In New York he was befriended by the black abolitionist Charles Ruggles, who gave him shelter. Ruggles also helped him resume contact with Anna Murray, a free-born black woman Douglass had met in Baltimore, and it was in Ruggles's house that Frederick and Anna were married.

Soon after, at Ruggles's urging, the young couple left for New Bedford, Massachusetts, a community where they believed Frederick was less likely to be betrayed as a fugitive slave than in New York. It was in New Bedford that Frederick abandoned his slave name and took "Douglass" as a further disguise.

A new life began for Douglass in New England. He soon came to the attention of the prominent abolitionist leader William Lloyd Garrison, and in August 1841 he was invited to speak at an antislavery convention. Douglass created a sensation. Even abolitionists seldom knew educated blacks and at times they, too, exhibited race prejudice and condescension. But no one could doubt that this imposing, eloquent black man was a superior being and a living reproach to slavery. The lesson must be spread. Douglass was immediately hired at $450 a year as speaker for the Massachusetts Antislavery Society.

During the next three years Douglass toured the North, denouncing slavery at dozens of abolitionist meetings. His effect on his audiences was powerful but, like many abolitionists, he was also heckled and even attacked physically. In 1845 Douglass published the first of three autobiographies recounting his life as a slave and harshly condemning slavery. Soon after, he took ship for England under the sponsorship of the American Antislavery Society to bring his message to the many friends of black emancipation in Europe.

Like many black Americans during slavery days—and after—Douglass found his contact with Europe liberating. Europeans had little of the color prejudice of white Americans. Douglass could go anywhere in Europe, speak to anyone, and never be treated as an inferior.

Despite this exhilarating experience, in 1847 Douglass concluded that he must return to his native land. Recognizing the danger that he would be recaptured as a fugitive when he set foot on American soil, his English friends purchased his freedom from his legal owner. Douglass arrived back in the United States in April 1847 at the age of thirty, a free man for the first time in his life.

Back home, Douglass decided to establish a newspaper to expound his views. His friends in the abolitionist movement tried to dissuade him, arguing that there were already too many abolitionist papers and that if he failed, it would reflect on the capabilities of his race. But Douglass was now unwilling to accept white direction; blacks, he believed, must have an independent voice in the movement. His persistence led to a break with Garrison, though not with the less doctrinaire white abolitionists. With their help Douglass began publishing the *North Star* out of Rochester, New York, in 1847.

He soon discovered how hard it was to run a newspaper, and there would be many times in the next dozen years when he would consider abandoning the enterprise. But the paper afforded a far better outlet for Douglass's views than the lecture platform. The *North Star*'s columns and editorial pages covered not only the antislavery movement but also temperance, discrimination against free blacks, and national politics. Douglass and his paper were particular friends of women's rights. He was one of the sixty-seven men who attended the historic Seneca Falls Convention in 1848, which effectively launched the women's rights movement, and throughout his career he remained a strong supporter of Susan B. Anthony and Elizabeth Cady Stanton, the women's rights leaders.

As the country approached the final sectional crisis, Douglas became increasingly critical of Garrison's antipolitics position. He supported the Liberty party and its successor, the Republican party. In 1860 he endorsed Lincoln, though he had no illusions that the roughhewn man from Illinois would attack slavery head-on. Douglass considered the war that followed Lincoln's election providential. Here was the opportunity to finally strike slavery a mortal blow. But this result could not be left to chance. Through the early months of the war Douglass hammered away in print and from the platform at the necessity of destroying slavery in order to put down the rebellion. He was jubilant when the president announced in September 1862 his intention to issue the Emancipation Proclamation.

On the night of December 31, 1863, Douglass and 3,000 other antislavery men and women gathered in Boston's Tremont Temple to await word from Washington that the Proclamation was finally in force. At 10 P.M. a man came running through the crowd shouting: "It is coming! It is on the wires!" The crowd burst into spontaneous cheers. Prayers were offered up and joyous speeches continued until dawn. After two and a half centuries the evil institution was dead in America.

Douglass would live for thirty more years. During the Reconstruction era he would demand "immediate, unconditional, and universal enfranchisement of the black man in every State in the Union." He was one of the black leaders who visited Andrew Johnson in the White House in February 1866 to ask the president's support for giving freedmen the vote. The outspoken Douglass offended Johnson, who later told one of his private secretaries that he was "just like any nigger, and he would sooner cut a white man's throat than not." The suffrage issue put strains on the alliance of blacks and women. Susan B. Anthony and Elizabeth Cady Stanton wanted Douglass to support the simultaneous enfranchisement of women and blacks, but Douglass refused on the grounds that such linkage would jeopardize votes for blacks. Now, he said, "was the Negro's hour."

In 1872 Douglass and his family moved to Washington, where, during the administrations of Hayes and Garfield, he held minor but well-paying patronage jobs with the federal government. Republican preferment, plus the added years, cooled Douglass's ardor for change and curbed his critical pen and tongue. So much had been accomplished since slavery days for black people; it was hard to carp at the many inequalities that remained. Fortunately, successive versions of his autobiography sold well and provided the income he needed to live comfortably in the capital.

In 1882 Anna, Douglass's wife of forty-four years, died. Theirs had not been a happy relationship; Frederick was too public a man and had too many admirers, many of them female. He was a doting father to his three children and helped them whenever he could, but none of them achieved independence or conventional success. In 1884 Douglass scandalized blacks and whites alike by marrying a white woman. Yet despite the uproar, in 1889, when Douglass was seventy-one, President Benjamin Harrison appointed him minister to the black republic of Haiti. But Douglass disliked the climate and soon resigned.

He lived until February 1895, and in his last years regained some of his zeal for the black cause. Among his last writings was a series of attacks on the new epidemic of lynching that was sweeping the South. Seven months after he died another black leader would rise to speak at the Atlanta Cotton States Exposition. Booker T. Washington would make a pact with white America that would freeze the racial status quo for fifty years. A later generation of black leaders would condemn the Atlanta Compromise, but in all likelihood, his latest biographer believes, Frederick Douglass, who had waited so long to see even a flawed freedom, would have approved.

13

****

******* A HISTORICAL DOCUMENT *******

The Slaves Speak Out

We have many surviving accounts of slavery from the inside, but virtually all of these were written by unusual people—literate black men and women who escaped from bondage and went north or to Canada. An exception is the collection of Slave Narratives made by the New Deal Works Progress Administration (WPA) during the 1930s. The WPA workers interviewed several hundred elderly southern blacks who had lived under the slave regime before 1863, and recorded their descriptions of personal experiences. The following selection is excerpted from the account of Mingo White of Burleson, Alabama, who at the time of the interview was between eighty-five and ninety years old.

"I was born in Chester, South Carolina, but I was mostly raised in Alabama. When I was about four or five years old, I was loaded in a wagon with a lot more people in it. Where I was bound I don't know. Whatever became of my mammy and pappy I don't know for a long time. I was told dere was a lot of slave speculators in Chester to buy some slaves for some folks in Alabama. I 'members dat I was took up on a stand and a lot of people came round and felt my arms and legs and chest, and ask me a lot of questions. Before we slaves was took to de tradin' post Old Marsa Crawford told us to tell everybody what asked us if we'd ever been sick dat us'd never been sick in our life. Us had to tell 'em all sorts of lies for our marsa or else take a beatin'.

"I was just a li'l thing, tooked away from my mammy and pappy, just when I needed 'em most. . . . My pappy and mammy was sold from each other, too, de same time I was sold. I used to wonder if I had any brothers or sisters, as I had always wanted some. . . .

"I weren't nothin' but a child endurin' slavery, but I had to work de same as any man. I went to de field and hoed cotton, pulled fodder and picked cotton with de rest of de hands. I kept up, too, to keep from gettin' any lashes dat night when us got home. In de winter I went to de woods with de menfolks to help to get wood or to get sap from de trees to make turpentine and tar. Iffen us didn't do dat we made charcoal to run de blacksmith shop with.

"De white folks was hard on us. Dey would whip us about de least li'l thing. It wouldn'ta been so bad iffen us had comforts, but to live like us did was 'nough to make anybody soon as be dead. De white folks told us dat us born to work for 'em and dat us was doin' fine at dat. . . .

"De white folks didn't learn us to do nothin' but work. Dey said dat us weren't supposed to know how to read and write. Dere was one feller name E. C. White what learned to read and write even durin' slavery. He had to carry de chillen's books to

55

school for 'em and go back after dem. His young marsa taught him to read and write unbeknownst to his father and de rest of de slaves.

"After de day's work was done dere weren't anything for de slaves to do but go to bed. Wednesday night they went to prayer meetin'. We had to be in de bed by nine o'clock. Every night de drivers come around to make sure dat we was in de bed. . . .

"On Saturday de hands worked till noon. Dey had de rest of de time to work dey gardens. Every family had a garden of deir own. On Saturday nights de slaves could frolic for a while. Dey would have parties sometimes and whiskey and home-brew for de servants. On Sundays we didn't do anything but lay round and sleep, 'cause we didn't like to go to church. On Christmas we didn't have to do no work, no more'n feed the stock and do de li'l work round de house. When we got through with dat we had de rest of de day to run round wherever we wanted to do. 'Course we had to get permission from de marsa. . . .

"[After the war] I married Kizi Drumgoole. Reverend W. C. Northcross perform de ceremony. Dere weren't nobody dere but de witness and me and Kizi. I had three sons, but all of 'em is dead 'ceptin' one and dat's Hugh. He got seven chillens."

★★★★★★★★ A HISTORICAL PORTRAIT ★★★★★★★★

William Gilmore Simms

It is ironic that William Gilmore Simms failed to gain from Charleston, South Carolina, his beloved birthplace, the appreciation and recognition that his achievements deserved. In the years between 1833 and the outbreak of the Civil War, Simms published more than thirty works of fiction. Most of these dealt with the South's heroic exploits during the colonial period or the nobility of the settlers on the frontier of the lower South. They helped create the mythology by which the Old South explained itself to the world. And yet, though honored elsewhere and by posterity, during his lifetime he never won the approval he wanted from his native city.

William Gilmore Simms was born in April 1806. Two years later his father, a Scotch-Irish immigrant, depressed by his wife's death and humiliated by his recent bankruptcy, left little William in the care of his maternal grandmother and went off to rebuild his life. Mrs. Gates, a "proper" Charlestonian, brought William up, sending him first to public schools and then, at the age of ten, to the College of Charleston.

His formal schooling, however, was not as important in molding his literary imagination as was his family history. Grandmother Gates captivated him with tales of his great-grandfather, who had battled the British invaders of Charleston during the Revolutionary War and fought alongside Francis Marion, the "Swamp Fox," to liberate the city. His father's exploits, transmitted through long letters from distant places, also stimulated his mind. After leaving Charleston, the elder Simms had become a friend of Andrew Jackson and had been with Old Hickory at the battles of Tallahatchie and New Orleans.

The port of Charleston was still another source of material for Simms's tales and novels. After school, William sat on the docks, enthralled by visiting sailors' accounts of escapades in faraway places. When he was somewhat older he took advantage of

Charleston's cultural and intellectual life, attending performances at the Broad Street Theater and joining the discussion at the Charleston Library Society.

While in his early teens his grandmother apprenticed him to a druggist, hoping it would eventually lead to a career in medicine. Simms found pharmacology boring, however, and compensated himself for the dull work by reading all night. He soon abandoned medical studies and went to serve an apprenticeship with an attorney who also loved literature. By this time, his father had become a plantation owner in Georgeville, Mississippi. He invited his son to visit, in hopes that he would come to live with him permanently. William traveled through the backroads and backwoods of the frontier, enjoying the time spent with his father and using his experiences as material for his Border Romances. But in the end he decided to return to Charleston, possibly because he had fallen in love with Anna Malcolm Giles, a local belle. His father advised him that he would be able to do more with his life if he stayed in Mississippi, that without connections and wealth he would never make a mark in Charleston. "I know it," he told his son, "only as a place of tombs." In later years his son bitterly regretted this choice, feeling it had done him "irretrievable injury." "All that I have," he wrote, "has been poured to waste in Charleston, which has never smiled on any of my labors, which has steadily ignored my claims, which has disparaged me to the last. . . ." The entire South, and particularly his home city, recognized only narrow avenues of success and were indifferent or hostile to those whose talents lay off the beaten track.

When he was nineteen and still studying law, Simms's first published poem appeared, a work commemorating the death of Charleston native Charles Cotesworth Pinckney, soldier, Federalist leader, and diplomat. In 1825 also, Simms brought out his first volume of poetry and worked as editor of the *Album*, a short-lived literary and political magazine. The next year, having completed his law studies, he married Anna, the daughter of a city clerk. It was thought to be a love match, for many felt that Simms might have improved his standing in the community by choosing a girl from a "better" family.

He could not practice law until he was twenty-one. While he waited for admission to the bar, he continued to write poetry, publishing two more volumes, which were reviewed admiringly by critics and readers. His literary progress convinced him that he might make a career out of writing rather than law. Although he passed the bar in 1827 and practiced law successfully for a while, Simms was truly seduced by *belles lettres*. In 1830 he invested what was left of his maternal inheritance in the *Charleston City Gazette*, a daily newspaper, which he conceived of as a forum for the free exchange of important ideas.

The position he took in the nullification controversy bankrupted his paper and temporarily ruined him. Simms loved his nation as well as his state, and he hoped that they could resolve their difficulties without resorting to extreme measures. Although he believed that the federal government was treading on the constitutional rights of South Carolina, he thought that the state's loyalty to the Union should triumph over its disagreements. "There are some . . . ," he declared, "who would destroy the body, to preserve a member—we are not of the class." He was viciously attacked by prominent politicians throughout the state. The mayor of Charleston suggested that he "confine himself to witticisms, poetry (good luck!) and literature for ladies (girls?). . . ." Eventually Simms lost most of his subscribers and all of his money. In 1832 he was forced to sell the *Gazette* at a loss.

The sale of his journal was not the only tragedy that befell Simms that year. Anna died, leaving him with a young daughter. By this time his father and grandmother had died as well. He had no desire to return to law, and with the Nullifiers in control of Charleston, he decided to go north. There he met the poet and journalist William Cullen Bryant, who introduced him to the New York literary scene. These writers, publishers, and editors were members of "Young America," a group that favored a cultural declaration of independence from Europe and the creation of a distinctive American literature.

In New York Simms published a long poem, "Atalantis," and a maritime adventure; wrote for the *American Quarterly Review*; and worked on his first novel, *Martin Faber*, a Gothic romance about a young frontiersman whose lust for status and money results in murder. Readers liked it, buying all but one of the printed copies. He soon followed with *Guy Rivers*, a "tale of Georgia . . . of a frontier and wild people, and the events [that] . . . may occur among a people & in a region of that character." Critics, who praised it, remarked on the uniqueness of the locale and urged the author to write more about those "untrodden paths" of fiction.

In 1835 Simms published *The Yemassee*, a fictional biography of a colonial governor of South Carolina and an account of the British conquest of the Yemassee Indians. The book also contains the first in a long series of upright, brave, imaginative, and ambitious southern heroes and virtuous, virginal (but physically alluring), intelligent southern women, the future mothers of a "Noble Race." In this book, which is the best known of all Simms's works and still in print, he praised slavery as a necessary and beneficial system and argued that slaves were content with their lot. In the same year he also brought out a romantic history of the Revolutionary era called *The Partisan*. The critical and commercial successes of these volumes finally convinced Simms that his destiny was to be a professional writer.

Although he had made friends and found success in New York, he longed to return to South Carolina. On a visit in 1836 he met and married Chevillette Roach, daughter of a rich plantation owner. His marriage enabled him to stay in his home for much of the year. For the next quarter-century Simms and his wife spent the months from October through May at Woodlands, an estate of 3,000 acres near Charleston. In the summer the Simmses went to Charleston or to New York and New England. While at Woodlands, Simms spent his mornings in the library writing, his afternoons managing the plantation, and his evening hours entertaining guests at dinner. A visitor described Simms's new life: "For a whole morning have I sat in that pleasant library . . . watching . . . the tall, erect figure at the desk, and quick steady passage for hours of the indomitable pen across page after page—a pen that rarely paused to erase, correct, or modify. . . . At dinner he talked a great deal, joked, jested, and punned, . . . or, if a graver theme arose, he would often declaim. . . ."

Now that he was a member of the planter class, Simms's sectional sympathies became more pronounced. He wrote a review for the *Southern Literary Messenger* attacking *Society in America* by Harriet Martineau, a British social observer. In Simms's view, Martineau had not only ignored the North's social problems while criticizing slavery, but she had also failed to note that the southern system was in fact ethically superior. The slaveholder actually bettered the lives of his slaves by improving their morals and intelligence. Someday, Simms promised, when blacks had been elevated to the proper level, they would be freed. Martineau had claimed that since the manufacturing North dominated the country's finances, the South was totally dependent on the North for its economic well-being. Not so, Simms declared. Northern industry could not operate without the South's cotton; therefore, slavery was the financial backbone of the whole nation. This article was acclaimed throughout the South.

A version of what came to be called the "King Cotton" argument, it was widely reprinted and became a leading apology for slavery.

Pleased by his success, Simms continued to defend slavery and publicize the South's unique image. He compiled a history and geography of South Carolina. He wrote biographies of representative southern figures. He edited the *Southern Quarterly Review* and established *Simms Magazine*. Between 1844 and 1846 he was a member of the South Carolina legislature, and in the 1850s he actively advocated secession. But he did not give up on fiction. In these years before the Civil War he wrote nine novels, each in its own way glorifying his section and its people.

The era of the Civil War was a tragic one for Simms. The year before the war started, two of his sons died of yellow fever. Then his oldest son and namesake was wounded in battle. In 1863 his wife died at the age of forty-seven, having given birth the year before to her thirteenth child. Simms himself became mentally and physically ill for many weeks. In 1865 General William Sherman's men torched Woodlands and destroyed his art gallery and 10,000-volume library. Two weeks later he was an eyewitness to the burning and pillaging of Columbia, South Carolina, which affected him violently. At the end of the war he wrote to a friend: "Of all that I had . . . I have nothing left. . . ."

Yet he persisted in writing and turned out many poems, articles, and stories, earning money to rebuild his house and support his children. He wrote "Sack and Destruction of the City of Columbia, S.C.," describing vividly his experiences on "Black Friday," the day the beautiful old town went up in flames. In addition, he composed three more book-length southern romances. A month before his death he delivered the opening speech at the Charleston County Floral Fair.

Simms died on Saturday, June 11, 1870. Charleston appreciated him more in death than in life. The bells of St. Michael's tolled in his honor, and all sectors of the Charleston community sent condolences to his family. The *Charleston Courier* printed an appreciative editorial on Monday, the day of his funeral, when throngs of mourners came in a driving rain to pay their respects. But his best tribute had been written a decade earlier in *Debow's Review* of New Orleans: Simms, this article declared, "reflects . . . the spirit and temper of Southern civilization; announces its opinions, illustrates its ideas, embodies its passions and prejudices, and portrays those delicate shades of thought, feelings, and conduct, that go to form the character and stamp the individuality of a people. . . ."

14

★★★★★★★★★★

★★★★★★★★ A HISTORICAL PORTRAIT ★★★★★★★★

Harriet Beecher Stowe

Harriet Beecher Stowe came from a family of high achievers. Her father was the Reverend Lyman Beecher, the most famous clergyman in America. Her younger brother was Henry Ward Beecher, a man who would be called "the archbishop of American Protestantism." Older sister Catherine was a well-known pioneer of women's education. Another brother, Edward, founded Illinois College; another sister, Isabella, was a leading woman suffragist. And there were other successful Beechers as well. Yet Harriet is undoubtedly the most renowned member of this prominent American clan. Today, we know her as author of *Uncle Tom's Cabin*, one of those rare books that influenced the course of history.

Harriet Beecher Stowe was born in Litchfield, Connecticut, in 1811, a time when many village men still wore three-cornered hats, knee breeches, and powdered wigs. Her father, Lyman, was a Congregational minister, not yet well known beyond his small community, but a man of great learning and strong opinions. Her mother, Roxana, was a warm, loving woman who died young in 1817. Roxana's children would remember her as a saint, but perhaps that was because her successor as their father's wife, Harriet Porter, was a reserved woman who seemed overwhelmed by her ready-made family of small children and adolescents.

Harriet was a cheerful little girl despite the loss of her beloved mother. Litchfield was only a village, and she enjoyed the unconfined life of the accessible countryside. She possessed few manufactured toys, but willowbark whistles, barnyard animals and pets, and the horses in the stable were all diversions and sources of delight. Yet Harriet was no country bumpkin. The Beecher parsonage was an island of high culture and the source of its residents' lifelong interest in literature and ideas. Lyman Beecher made it a point to immerse his children, even the youngest, in books and issues. And not only the dour literature and theology of Puritanism. Harriet read the *Arabian Nights*, the novels of Sir Walter Scott, and even the poetry of that dangerous heathen, Lord Byron. The Reverend Beecher, was no dour kill-joy and he delighted the children by playing lively old tunes like *Auld Lang Syne, Bonnie Doon*, and *Mary's Dream* on his fiddle.

At thirteen Harriet left Litchfield to attend the new Hartford Female Academy just founded by her older sister Catherine. The experience was maturing. With 6,000 people, Hartford was the largest city that Harriet had ever known, and it introduced her to more cosmopolitan sights and ways. Harriet was not an extraordinary student, but at the academy she acquired a good grounding in literature, languages, and even the sciences. After graduation she remained in the academy as a teacher of rhetoric and composition. But in her eight years in the Connecticut capital she did not attract a suitor. Harriet was not a beautiful young woman. Tiny, barely over five feet tall, her face was marred by the large prowlike nose of all the Beechers. It looked as if she were destined to become another spinster schoolteacher living with her father or older brother and making do with the leavings of his life.

Her fate changed abruptly when, in 1832, Lyman Beecher accepted the call to head Lane Seminary, a new school for training ministers, in the fast-growing Queen City of the West, Cincinnati. Harriet and most of the younger children, including several half-siblings, accompanied their father west and for the next eighteen years Harriet would make the thriving city of 30,000 her home.

Cincinnati would provide many of the crucial experiences she would later draw on for her novels and stories. There she would meet Calvin Stowe, professor of biblical literature at Lane, and marry him in 1836, two years after his first wife died of cholera. There she would be exposed for the first time to slavery and its human costs.

Just across the Ohio River from the slave state of Kentucky, Cincinnati was a way station for runaways from the "peculiar institution" of slavery. Cincinnatians themselves were divided on slavery. The city had an elite of transplanted Yankees who were susceptible to the new appeal of the "immediate abolitionists" who demanded that freeing the South's slaves be commenced right away. But the city's white working class often disliked blacks, and many of its merchants had close business connections with the South. Both groups despised the antislavery agitators, and in 1836 angry mobs attacked abolitionists and destroyed an antislavery press established by James Birney. Lane Seminary itself soon became a battlefield between moderates like Calvin Stowe and Lyman Beecher and a circle of immediate abolitionist students led by Theodore Weld, a firebrand inspired by the writings of William Lloyd Garrison. No radical herself, Harriet and other moderates were shocked by the widespread antiabolitionist vigilantism, and soon after the attack on Birney she published an anonymous article defending law and order and the right of abolitionists to express their views freely.

The years in Cincinnati were financially hard for the Stowes and their growing family. Calvin Stowe was an impecunious professor at an institution that had trouble recruiting students, especially after Weld and his followers left for the more congenial new seminary at Oberlin. All the Beechers, in fact, found the years after the Panic of 1837 financially difficult. The Lane trustees were frequently slow in paying Lyman's salary. Older sister Catherine too was sorely pressed. She had joined the family hegira to Cincinnati and, after selling her Hartford school, had founded, jointly with Harriet, the Western Female Institute. In 1838 it closed, dashing Catherine's hopes to repeat in the growing West her Hartford success as an educator. Harriet earned a few dollars by writing sentimental sketches for magazines and New Year's annuals. The money enabled her to employ household help but made little further dent in the family's genteel poverty. And there were worse times as well. In 1849 the dreaded Asiatic cholera struck the city, killing over 4,400 Cincinnatians. One of the victims was little Samuel (Charley) Stowe, Harriet's youngest child.

In 1850 Bowdoin College, Calvin's alma mater, offered him the Collins Professorship, and the family left for Brunswick, Maine, with few regrets. Their first experiences confirmed the wisdom of the change. The Bowdoin faculty wives took pity on the shabby and pregnant little Mrs. Stowe and her brood of ill-dressed but well-mannered children, and they helped them get settled in a spacious frame house where Henry Wadsworth Longfellow had lived as a student years before. Calvin Stowe would soon get a still better academic offer, and in 1852 the Stowes would leave for Andover, Massachusetts. But it was in Brunswick that Harriet Beecher Stowe would write a novel that would resound through the nation's history and catapult her to fame.

By 1851 the nation was in a furor over the recently adopted Fugitive Slave Law.

Part of the Compromise of 1850, the measure tightened the rules for recovering slaves who fled the South to free territory and ignited a fierce northern reaction to federal efforts to recapture accused fugitives and remand them to slavery. Soon after passage of the bill, antislavery mobs in Syracuse, New York, and Boston expressed northern indignation by storming the jails where fugitives were confined and threatening federal marshals attempting to return them to their southern masters.

Among the Beechers, Harriet and her younger brother, Henry Ward Beecher, now a prominent pastor at Brooklyn's Plymouth Church, were the most deeply offended by the brutal "man-catchers." Both decided to attack slavery and the harsh new law. Henry's method was to dramatize the plight of runaways by staging before his congregation an "auction" of a beautiful slave girl whose master had agreed to free her if she could raise enough money. The prosperous Brooklyn congregation rose to the challenge and more than met the shortfall. Henry's little dramas no doubt made converts among his congregation for the antislavery cause, but Harriet's assault electrified the nation.

For some time Harriet had been writing articles for a Washington, D.C., antislavery weekly, the *National Era*, published by an old Cincinnati friend, Dr. Gamaliel Bailey. In March 1851 she wrote Bailey to tell him of a new project she had in mind. It would be a series of sketches that would "give the lights and shadows of the 'patriarchal institution,' written either from observation . . . or in the knowledge of my friends." "I shall," she said, "show the *best side* of the thing, and something *faintly approaching the worst*." Bailey liked her description and offered her $300 for a series of three or four installments. On June 5, at the top of the first column of page one of the *National Era*, appeared the heading:

UNCLE TOM'S CABIN
or
LIFE AMONG THE LOWLY
By Mrs. H. B. Stowe

There followed three and a half columns of text, the first words of a story set in Kentucky and Louisiana and describing the evils of slavery through a series of brilliant scenes involving the brutal slave overseer Simon Legree; the saintly "old darky," Uncle Tom; the courageous slave mother Eliza; the well-intentioned but weak slave owner, Augustine St. Clair, and a large cast of vivid characters caught in the toils of the "patriarchal institution."

Once begun the words poured from her with little delay for revision. She later ascribed her fluency to God. It "all came to me in visions, one after another, and I put them down in words," she explained. At first the public response was muted, but as episode followed episode—far beyond the anticipated three or four—reader enthusiasm grew. Before many weeks thousands of northerners were borrowing copies of the obscure antislavery paper to read the weekly installments to their families. By the time the last episode appeared in early 1852 Harriet had procured a book contract for the entire series from a Boston publisher. In early March the first advertisements for the novel *Uncle Tom's Cabin* appeared in New York and Boston newspapers, and bookstores all over the North were soon announcing that they intended to stock the new book in quantity.

Their optimism was fulfilled beyond anyone's dream. The novel became an instant best-seller. The public snapped up 10,000 copies in the first week. In a year 300,000 had been sold. Sales were even greater in Europe and especially Britain. Royalties rolled in and the Stowe's immediate financial troubles were over. Yet they never became rich. Harriet got a 10 percent royalty on American sales, but all the foreign editions were pirated—sold without royalty to the author—a system that flourished in the absence of international copyright laws.

Few copies of *Uncle Tom's Cabin* were sold in the South. By 1852 most southerners had lost patience with any attack on the peculiar institution, and they turned angrily on the Yankee authoress. The *Southern Literary Messenger* called the book a "criminal prostitution of the high functions of the imagination." Other southern critics charged her with ignorance of slavery and blind prejudice against it. Harriet replied in 1853 with *A Key to Uncle Tom's Cabin*, a book that was in effect a long footnote, providing the documentation to *Uncle Tom's Cabin*. It changed few southern minds.

But *Uncle Tom's Cabin* did change minds elsewhere. Inevitably, wherever people deplored slavery, the novel made a deep impression. And it also made converts to antislavery among thousands of complacent people who had accepted slavery as a necessary evil. The book made Harriet famous. When she visited England in 1853 she was treated as a celebrity. Everywhere in the British Isles people gathered to see or grasp the hand of the famous writer who had so touched their hearts. She met Charles Dickens, Lord Palmerston, the Lord Mayor of London, the Duchess of Sutherland, and other grandees. She even met the young queen, Victoria, though the meeting was unofficial lest it offend the American government, then firmly dominated by proslavery northerners and the powerful southern bloc. The Stowes would make several trips to Britain and the European continent during the 1850s and would make many prominent European friends.

Uncle Tom's Cabin was the start of a long and successful literary career. Her second novel, *Dred, A Tale of the Great Dismal Swamp*, published in 1856, was another commercial success. Some of her later works—*The Minister's Wooing, The Pearl of Orr's Island*, and *Oldtown Folks*—were also critically acclaimed and widely read. For almost thirty years, Harriet Stowe would churn out almost a book a year. Not all of this flood was choice. Mrs. Stowe was a slapdash stylist, often sentimental and trite. As one later critic would note harshly, "the creative instinct was strong in her but the critical was wholly lacking." Yet she always remained popular with the reading public.

The Civil War affected the Stowes deeply. Fred Stowe, their second son, joined a Massachusetts regiment in 1861 and went off to fight the rebels. He was wounded in action at Gettysburg and mustered out on disability before the war ended. The Beechers were fierce defenders of the Union cause. Harriet sought to use her influence in Britain to deflect the British upper classes from their pro-Confederate views. She made the abolition of slavery her fondest dream. She, Henry, and indeed the whole Beecher clan cheered Lincoln's preliminary Emancipation Proclamation. But they worried that the president would not come through with the definitive proclamation as promised. In the fall of 1862, on a visit to Washington to see First Lieutenant Fred Stowe, Harriet spent an hour with Lincoln at the White House. She told him of her efforts to influence British opinion and he, apparently, assured her that he would indeed make the Emancipation Proclamation official. It was on this occasion that, according to Stowe family lore, Lincoln exclaimed: "So this is the little lady who wrote the book that made this big war!"

The postwar years were not kind to the Beechers. Fred never readjusted to civilian life and eventually became an alcoholic. In 1870 he disappeared while on a visit to San Francisco and was never heard from again. The Beecher finances remained shaky. Though she earned much from her pen, she also spent much. Harriet poured thousands of dollars into building a large house in Hartford that was never comfortable to live in. She also invested money in an ill-conceived postwar scheme to grow cotton in Florida. After that failed, she retained an expensive winter home, Mandarin, near Jacksonville. Calvin, in retirement from Andover Seminary, surprised everyone with a tome on the origin of the books of the Bible that sold well. But still Stowe expenses constantly threatened to exceed Stowe income, and Harriet was forced to grind out stories, articles, and novels for the market.

In 1869 Harriet wrote an article for *Atlantic Monthly*, followed by a full-scale book, defending an English friend, Lady Anne Isabella Byron, Lord George Byron's widow, against charges of cruelty toward her famous deceased husband. In absolving her friend of blame for the early breakup of the Byron marriage, Harriet accused the dead poet of having committed incest with his half-sister. The charge created a sensation. In this mid-Victorian era the mere mention of incest was itself a scandal, and Harriet was blasted as a pornographer and a sensation-monger. *Atlantic Monthly* lost thousands of subscribers and almost went under.

Harriet and *Atlantic* both survived, but then in 1875 Theodore Tilton, editor of the influential weekly the *Independent*, publicly accused Henry Ward Beecher, his pastor at Plymouth Church, of having seduced his wife, Elizabeth Tilton, another of Henry's parishioners. During the sensational trial for alienation of affections that followed, Harriet rushed to the defense of her favorite brother. Henry was acquitted, but forever after the suspicion of hypocrisy and adultery clung to him.

Harriet's last years were marred by family and personal ill-health. In 1883 Calvin, whose voluminous white beard made him resemble the Old Testament prophets he wrote about, developed a serious kidney ailment. He died three years later. Henry too died in 1886. Harriet lingered on, living in the house in Hartford while her spinster twin daughters, Eliza and Hatty, took care of her needs and ran the household efficiently. In 1889, at the age of 78, she suffered a stroke. She recovered physically, but her mind was impaired. In 1893, during a lucid moment, she wrote her old friend Oliver Wendell Holmes that while *his* "lamp burns as brightly as ever," *hers* was "but a feeble gleam." Her mental condition, she said, had become "nomadic." There were few good times after that, and she died on July 1, 1896, two weeks after her eighty-fifth birthday.

She was buried at Andover cemetary between Calvin and little Charley, who had died so long before in Cincinnati. Harriet Beecher Stowe had outlived many of her contemporaries, and the funeral party gathered by the grave was small. Yet she had not been forgotten. On her casket was a wreath sent by the black community of Boston. The card was signed: "The Children of Uncle Tom."

15

****

******** A HISTORICAL DOCUMENT ********

Lincoln on Slavery

Lincoln despised slavery, but he loved the Union even more. For months following Fort Sumter his primary concern, perforce, was to keep more states from joining the Confederacy and to bring back into the Union, by force if necessary, those that had left. Slavery could wait. Other Americans—the abolitionists and other strong antislavery people—reversed the priorities. On August 19, 1862, Horace Greeley, the editor of the prominent antislavery newspaper the *New York Tribune*, published an editorial, "The Prayer of 20,000,000 People," demanding that the president attack slavery head on, without worrying about the political consequences. Lincoln replied in the letter below three days later. It is the statement of a man with little doubt about where his first loyalty lay, and suggests to what extent the abolition of the "peculiar institution" was a by-product of the war.

"Executive Mansion. Washington
"August 22, 1862

"Hon. Horace Greeley.

Dear Sir: I have just read yours of the 19th, addressed to myself through the New York *Tribune.* If there be in it any statements or assumptions of fact which I may know to be erroneous, I do not, now and here, controvert them. If there be in it any inferences which I may believe to be falsely drawn, I do not, now and here, argue against them. If there be perceptible in it an impatient and dictatorial tone, I waive it in deference to an old friend whose heart I have always supposed to be right.

"As to the policy I 'seem to be pursuing,' as you say, I have not meant to leave any one in doubt.

"I would save the Union. I would save it the shortest way under the Constitution. The sooner the national authority can be restored, the nearer the Union will be 'the Union as it was.' If there be those who would not save the Union unless they could at the same time save slavery, I do not agree with them. My paramount object in this struggle is to save the Union, and it is not either to save or to destroy slavery. If I could save the Union without freeing any slave, I would do it; and if I could save it by freeing all the slaves; I would do it; and if I could save it by freeing some and leaving others alone, I would also do that. What I do about slavery and the coloured race, I do because I believe it helps to save the Union; and what I forbear, I forbear because I do not believe it would help save the Union. I shall do less whenever I shall believe what I am doing hurts the cause, and I shall do more whenever I shall believe doing more will help the cause. I shall try to correct errors when shown to be errors, and I shall adopt new views so fast as they shall appear to be true views.

"I have here stated my purpose according to my view of official duty, and I intend no modification of my oft-expressed personal wish that all men everywhere could be free.

Yours, A. Lincoln"

######## A HISTORICAL PORTRAIT ########

Mary Boykin Chestnut

Mary Boykin Chesnut's fame rests on her Civil War diary. She kept it locked up and out of her husband's sight, but won renown in later years for the journal she worked on in secret. When *Diary from Dixie* was finally published, it was favorably compared to the famous diaries of Cotton Mather and John Quincy Adams.

Mrs. Chesnut's life was that of a privileged southern belle. Her family was prominent in South Carolina. At the time of her birth in March 1823, her father, Stephen Decatur Miller, was a state senator who, five years later, became governor and then United States senator. Mary was a precocious, intelligent child who responded to the politically active environment around her. In a letter written before her ninth birthday she told her father she was looking forward to reading his Senate speech on the tariff.

In 1833 Miller resigned his Senate seat and moved with his family to his cotton plantation in Mississippi. When Mary was twelve, she was sent back to Charleston to acquire a "finishing school" education at Madame Talvande's French School for Young Ladies. In addition to the "accomplishments" expected of every well-bred antebellum southern woman, she learned history, rhetoric, natural sciences, literature, and German, and became particularly fluent in French. She was an excellent student and a popular classmate, as well as a boisterous social leader who occasionally had to pay the price for her pranks. Her training at Madame Talvande's resulted in a life-long attraction to intellectual pursuits and literary conversation, and a love of music, novels, the theater, and French culture.

Charleston, one of America's most gracious cities, became the scene of Mary's lifetime love affair. When she was a thirteen-year-old schoolgirl, she went for moonlight strolls on the Battery, the walk skirting the harbor, with James Chesnut, Jr., of Mulberry° Plantation, a twenty-one-year-old Princeton graduate. Mary was brought back to Mississippi to cool her romance, but her parents soon returned her to Madame Talvande's to finish her education. Following her father's death in 1838, she became formally engaged to Chesnut. Soon after, her fiancé went to Europe to study and travel. He wrote Mary from Paris that he would try to "become worthy of the girl I love and honor." He had "no hopes that stir my soul, no visions bright . . . which amuse my fancy that are not colored with thoughts of you. . . ."

On June 23, 1840, when Mary was seventeen and Chesnut twenty-five, they married and went to live at Mulberry Plantation, where her husband's parents, a couple in their mid-sixties, still lived. Although Mary assumed she would soon become mistress of Mulberry, her in-laws, both physically and mentally energetic, lived into their eighties and continued to direct the operations of house and lands. While his parents ran the plantation, James practiced law in neighboring Camden

66

and served in the state legislature as representative, senator, and president until 1858, when, like his father-in-law, he was elected to the United States Senate.

During these years, with her in-laws in charge of her home, her husband involved in politics, and unable to have children, Mary often felt restless and useless. She occupied her time by reading, taking care of her young nieces and nephews, and visiting Charleston, Columbia, and the northern spas at Saratoga and Newport. She also acted as her husband's hostess and secretary and maintained her interest in politics. In 1845 she persuaded James to take her to London on a literary pilgrimage to the homes of Dickens and Thackeray, hoping that the sea journey would help her health and the mental stimulation of travel would lift her spirits. But these activities did not really fill the time or energies of this bright, vivacious woman, and her years at Mulberry Plantation were troubled by depression and poor health.

Her husband's election to the United States Senate in 1858 provided Mary with the opportunity to live in Washington. She was extremely happy during these next two years. She made friends easily with both the politicians and their wives, and charmed everyone she met with her intelligence, sense of humor, and conversational skill. She was soon invited to all the capital's important social functions and became a close friend of Varina Davis, wife of Jefferson Davis, the distinguished senator from Mississippi.

Her Washington years came to an end, however, after Lincoln's election in 1860. James resigned from the Senate to help draft the South Carolina Ordinance of Secession and organize the Southern Confederacy. In 1861 Mary accompanied her husband to Montgomery, Alabama, seat of the new Confederate government, and ran a lively salon where the men politicked and planned the strategy of the new nation, and their wives, excluded from such weighty matters, gossiped and intrigued.

Mary began her diary at this time. She was in Charleston in April 1861 when Fort Sumter was attacked, and watched the proceedings from a rooftop. In her original account she wrote: "At half past four we heard the booming of the cannon—I started up—dress & rush to my sisters in misery—we go on the housetop & see the shells bursting. . . ." When the smoke had cleared hours later, the Union had surrendered the fort to the Confederates and it was revealed, to Mary's relief, that no lives had been lost. Mary joined the celebration of the victory.

The Chesnuts returned to Montgomery for the second session of the Provisional Confederate Congress and in June 1861 went to Richmond, the new Confederate capital. Dreading to return to isolated Mulberry where her tyrannical father-in-law still presided, Mary hoped her husband would be appointed minister to France when he lost his bid for reelection to the Confederate Senate. No such foreign appointment saved her, and she was forced to spend a half year in Camden, where she frequently complained in her diary of her husband's lack of interest in the war. "If I had been a man in this great revolution—I should have either been killed at once or made a name & done some good for my country. Lord Nelson's motto would be mine—Victory or Westminster Abbey."

She was rescued from the plantation in January 1862 when her husband accepted the chairmanship of the South Carolina Executive Council in Columbia. In the fall Chesnut became an aide to Jefferson Davis, a position that brought the couple back to Richmond. In the Confederate capital Mary involved herself in both serious and frivolous things. The Chesnut's quarters at the Arlington Hotel was the scene of dinners, parties, and amateur theatricals. They had frequent house guests, including family and friends from all over the South. The Chesnuts and the Davises were devoted friends and visited each other constantly. Mary and her circle often chatted about personal affairs as well as news of the war and sometimes enjoyed a touch of scandal. "We discussed," read a diary entry for June 1862, "clever women who help their husbands politically. . . . These lady politicians—if they are young and pretty—always get themselves a 'little bit' talked about."

Behind the lively and gracious social screen, however, were more somber thoughts. Mary's diary for these war years reveals her underlying despair at the numbers of brave young men killed or maimed, the beautiful plantations destroyed, and the growing hardship of life in Richmond as the Yankee noose tightened. As early as March 1862 she would note that her "world, the only world we cared for," was being "kicked to pieces. . . ." In January 1865, with James away on military business, she was frightened. "Yesterday, I broke down—" she admitted, "gave way to abject terror. The news of Sherman's advance—and no news of my husband."

After Appomattox the Chesnuts moved back to Camden, living temporarily in one of her father-in-law's plantation houses that had been spared destruction. Mulberry itself had been sacked by Union soldiers and its cotton burned, but it survived, and was eventually restored. Mary continued her diary until July 1865. During the first months of Reconstruction she was ill with a heart condition and depressed by both the South's defeat and her own isolation. But her natural vivacity reasserted itself and she took over the management of the household, kept financial records, helped oversee the affairs of the plantation and the farm, and ran a butter-and-egg business with her maid, Molly. In 1873 the Chesnuts moved into a new home, Sarsfield, built with bricks from the old kitchen buildings at Mulberry.

During the 1870s and early 1880s, Mary wrote fiction to make additional money. In 1881 she began to work on a book based on her wartime diaries. James became ill in 1884 and Mary took time off to nurse him. He died at the end of the year, and then a week later her mother died as well. James had so many debts that Mary lost most of the land to his creditors, keeping only Sarsfield and a small dairy business. She continued to work on *Diary from Dixie*, but died on November 22, 1886, of a heart attack before the book was published.

Mary Chesnut was a perceptive reporter who vividly documented southern society during the Civil War. She had a sharp eye for the foibles of human nature and a keen understanding of life's contradictions. Her presence in the Confederate capital during the important years of the Civil War and her ability to record her observations of events and personalities make her *Diary from Dixie* an invaluable historical document. It is also a lively personal portrait that reveals Mary Boykin Chesnut as an outstanding woman of her time and, in the words of Lyman Butterfield, editor of the Adams Papers, "a great lady."

16

★★★★★★★★★★

★★★★★★★★ A HISTORICAL DOCUMENT ★★★★★★★★

Black Reconstruction

Black southerners were not passive participants in the Reconstruction process. In the South they joined the militia companies and the Union Leagues, as well as the Republican party. They also spoke out against their enemies and appealed to their white northern friends for support. The following is an early instance of such an appeal. It is a statement adopted by a black convention held in Virginia in August 1865, soon after the end of the war. Note how many of the things the delegates asked their white allies for were actually granted.

"We, the undersigned members of a Convention of colored citizens of the State of Virginia, would respectfully represent that, although we have been held as slaves, and denied all recognition as a constituent of your nationality for almost the entire period of the duration of your Government, and that by *your permission* we have been denied either home or country, and deprived of the dearest rights of human nature: yet when you and our immediate oppressors met in deadly conflict on the field of battle—the one to destroy and the other to save your Government and nationality, we, with scarce an exception, in our inmost souls espoused your cause, and watched, and prayed, and waited, and labored for your success. . . .

"When the contest waxed long, and the result hung doubtfully, you appealed to us for help, and how well we answered is written in the rosters of the two hundred thousand colored troops now enrolled in your service; and as to our undying devotion to your cause, let the uniform acclamation of escaped prisoners, 'whenever we saw a black face we felt sure of a friend,' answer.

"Well, the war is over, the rebellion is 'put down,' and we are *declared* free! Four fifths of our enemies are paroled or amnestied, and the other fifth are being pardoned, and the President has . . . left us entirely at the mercy of these subjugated but unconverted rebels, in *everything* save the privilege of bringing us, our wives, and little ones, to the auction block. . . . We *know* these men—know them *well*—and we assure you that, with the majority of them, loyalty is only 'lip deep,' and that their professions of loyalty are used as a cover to the cherished design of getting restored to their former relations with the Federal Government, and then, by all sorts of 'unfriendly legislation,' to render the freedom you have given us more intolerable than the slavery they intended for us.

"We warn you in time that our only safety is in keeping them under Governors of the *military persuasion* until you have so amended the Federal Constitution that it will prohibit the States from making any distinction between citizens on account of race or color. In one word, the only salvation for us besides the power of the Government is in the *possession of the ballot*. Give us this and we will protect ourselves. . . .

"We are 'sheep in the midst of wolves,' and nothing but the military arm of the Government prevents us and all the *truly* loyal white men from being driven from the land of our birth. Do not then, we beseech you, give to one of these 'wayward sisters' the rights they abandoned and forfeited when they rebelled until you have secured *our* rights by the aforementioned amendment to the Constitution. . . .

"Trusting that you will not be deaf to the appeal herein made, nor unmindful of the warnings which the malignity of the rebels are constantly giving you, and that you will rise to the height of being just for the sake of justice, we remain yours for our flag, our country, and humanity."

******** A HISTORICAL PORTRAIT ********

Thaddeus Stevens

His enemies in the South accused him of murder, adultery, misanthropy, and treason. His friends in the North considered him a sterling defender of democracy and freedom. His admirers called him "the old Commoner" after the eloquent and witty William Pitt, leader of the British House of Commons. Detractors called him "old Clubfoot" because of his congenital deformity. This man who attracted scandal and controversy all his life was Thaddeus Stevens, leader during Reconstruction of the Radical Republicans in the House of Representatives.

Born in April 1792, Stevens was the second son of a sometime farmer, surveyor, wrestler, and shoemaker who disappeared permanently after the birth of his fourth son. His mother, Sarah, was a religious, strong-willed, and energetic woman who ran the farm and taught her sons to read from the Bible. It was she who showed Thaddeus how to fight failure and finally overcome it. She was a firm believer in the value of education, moving her four fatherless children to Peacham, Vermont, when an academy was founded there.

Thaddeus was a bright boy who justified his mother's faith in him. He was also rebellious, a trait that lasted his entire life. As a senior at the academy, he took part in a theatrical performance "by candlelight," an activity expressly forbidden by the stern puritan headmaster. After signing "articles of submission" stating that he regretted his misdeed, he was allowed to finish school. He graduated from Datmouth in 1814, and in his commencement speech he defended luxury and wealth, claiming they were necessary for progress. Paradoxically, Stevens later attacked the South as a bastion of entrenched privilege and inequality.

In 1815 he went to York, Pennsylvania, where he taught for a year at the local academy and continued his study of law, begun in Vermont. Although the county insisted on a two years' residency requirement for admission to the bar, Stevens thought he was ready after a year because of his previous training. The lawyers of York did not like him and were unwilling to grant him a dispensation, so he crossed the border to Maryland. Here he answered a few questions on Blackstone's *Commentaries*, and a few on evidence and pleading, gave the judge two bottles of Madeira, and received his certification.

Stevens liked Pennsylvania, but did not want to return to York, where he had been snubbed. Instead, he opened his law office in Gettysburg. After a hard first year with few clients, he defended a mentally defective farmhand who had murdered a constable, using insanity as his plea. This was not a recognized defense at the time, and Stevens lost his case. He won himself a reputation for genius and boldness, however, and business poured into his office. He quickly bought himself a horse, a house and property in town, and a farm for his mother in Vermont. By 1830 he had become the largest property owner in the county, had invested in an iron business, and had been elected president of the Borough Council.

During his Gettysburg years Stevens survived an attack of typhoid fever that left him completely bald and added to his feelings of physical inferiority. Although he had many chances to marry, he rejected them all, feeling that his baldness and lameness made him unattractive and that any woman who wanted him must have reasons other than love.

Stevens also became an enthusiastic Anti-Mason, in part because of his rejection at Dartmouth and in York by secret societies. In 1831, in a speech at Hagerstown, Maryland, he attacked the Masons as corrupt, accused them of encouraging crime, and charged them with attempting to stop "the regular action of government." Jacob Lefever, a leading Mason and the owner of a Gettysburg newspaper, who had long been printing anonymous letters blaming Stevens for his supposed part in two recent murders, printed the Hagerstown speech in its entirety with a comment suggesting that Stevens had "blood" on his "skirts." Stevens sued him for criminal libel and damages. Lefever was sentenced to three months in jail and ordered to pay $1,500 in damages.

Despite the Masons' attacks, the Gettysburg townspeople elected Stevens to the state legislature, where he initiated much anti-Masonic legislation. He also made fiery speeches in behalf of an act to extend the free school system of Philadelphia to the entire state. His defense of education for all continued as long as he lived. Just a month before his death he introduced a bill in the House of Representatives "to establish a system of schools for the District of Columbia which shall serve as a model for similar institutions throughout the Union."

While still serving in the Pennsylvania legislature, Stevens became active in the antislavery cause, founding a colonization society and presenting a report in favor of abolishing slavery and the slave trade in the District of Columbia. At the state's constitutional convention in 1837 he refused to sign the final version of the constitution because it restricted suffrage to white males. He also acted as lawyer for fugitive slaves from other states hiding in the Pennsylvania hills. He was, by now, widely recognized as one of the state's foremost abolitionists.

In 1842 Stevens found himself at a personal low point. He had lost his seat in the state legislature and was deeply in debt because of business reverses, losses on massive election bets, and the failure of clients and friends to repay loans. To add to his troubles he was faced with a paternity suit brought by the father of an unmarried woman, a man whom he considered a friend. He was eventually cleared of this charge, but was embittered by this betrayal and his experiences in Gettysburg generally. He moved his residence and law offices to Lancaster, where he regained his fortunes and his reputation as the state's most accomplished lawyer. Here he also acquired a mulatto housekeeper, Lydia Hamilton Smith, who worked for him until he died. People speculated about their relationship; his enemies snidely referred to her as "Mrs. Stevens."

In 1848 Stevens was elected to Congress as a Whig. In Washington he immediately gained a reputation as a firebrand. He denounced slavery as accursed, criminal, and shameful, and condemned northerners who permitted its continuance as fiercely as the southerners who practiced it. His House colleagues, from both sections, were often shocked by his abusive and offensive language, believing it better "suited to a fishmarket" than to the halls of Congress. He fought vigorously against both the Compromise of 1850 and the Fugitive Slave Act. After the shattering defeat of Winfield

Scott, the Whig candidate for president in 1852, Stevens left Congress and returned to Lancaster to attend to his legal practice and iron business. Having no legitimate children of his own, he also devoted himself to his nephews, Thaddeus and Alanson.

Though out of Congress, Stevens remained involved in politics, taking an active part in the birth of the Republican party in Pennsylvania. In 1858 he was returned to Congress as a Republican, winning 75 percent of the votes in Lancaster County. In 1860 Stevens was a delegate to the Republican National Convention. He was mentioned for a cabinet post after Lincoln's victory at the polls, but instead stayed in the House, where he became chairman of the powerful Ways and Means Committee. A month after Lincoln's inauguration Confederate troops fired on Fort Sumter, precipitating the War Between the States. Stevens's committee gave the administration staunch support on financial matters. He was largely responsible for the Internal Revenue Act of 1862, which taxed almost every article produced by the Union. He favored the greenback paper currency, issued directly by the United States and backed by the credit of the country rather than by gold.

During the war Stevens was remorseless toward the South. He favored confiscation of captured enemy property and called for war without mercy. Some thought this was in retaliation for the destruction of his iron works during Lee's invasion of Pennsylvania in 1863. He introduced a bill calling for general emancipation, with compensation for loyal slaveholders and the freeing of slaves who wanted to leave their masters or who aided in "quelling the rebellion." Stevens favored generals who opposed slavery, believing that such men fought better. He hated George McClellan for his indecisiveness and was pleased when Lincoln fired him.

It was on Reconstruction that Stevens left his greatest mark. He and Charles Sumner were the two most prominent Radical Republicans—a group that favored strict terms for southern readmission to the Union, strong measures to guarantee the rights of the freedmen, and vigorous federal intervention to further economic progress. The Radicals had not been satisfied with Lincoln's lenient "ten-percent plan" for readmitting the seceded states to the Union. The harsher Wade-Davis Bill pleased Stevens no better; it was still too lenient.

When Andrew Johnson became president after Lincoln's assassination, Stevens hoped he would join the Radicals. On the surface, Johnson looked like an ally. A former senator from Tennessee, he had remained loyal to the Union and had fought against secessionists as military governor of the state. Both Stevens and Johnson had strong sympathies for the underdog, but where Stevens championed blacks, Johnson limited his compassion to poor whites. Less than two months after Johnson took office Stevens was permanently disillusioned with the president, considering his plans dangerous and his actions "insane." When Johnson proceeded to reconstruct the Union according to his own lenient design, Stevens and his fellow Radical Republicans determined to take over Reconstruction themselves.

On December 1, 1865, Stevens called together twenty-five supporters to propose a joint committee of both houses of Congress on Reconstruction. The committee would study the condition of the "so-called Confederate States of America," and no member elected to Congress would be admitted until the committee had made its report. When the full Republican caucus met the next night, it unanimously adopted this proposal. When Congress convened later that month, no southerner was seated and the Joint Committee of Fifteen on Reconstruction was established. As chairman of the House faction, Stevens was the dominant member of the committee. He intended to reduce the South to a "territorial condition" and treat it as a "conquered province" over which Congress would have complete control. He also was determined to guarantee the political and, if possible, the social rights of the freedmen. In 1865 and 1866 Stevens urged confiscation of land owned by rich ex-confederates and the transfer of forty acres of this property to each adult ex-slave. Not only would this provide the freedmen with a secure economic position in the South, it would also humble the proud southern elite that Stevens believed had brought the horrors of a brothers' war on the nation.

Stevens saw Johnson as the chief obstacle to the Radicals' policies and determined to get him. In early 1867 he secured passage of the Tenure of Office Act stripping the president of the authority to remove high officeholders who favored congressional Reconstruction. The Radicals also passed a measure requiring the president to issue orders to the army through the general of the army, Ulysses S. Grant, who could not be dismissed without the Senate's consent. The law was intended to filter all orders concerning Reconstruction through Grant, now a supporter of the Radical position.

This legislation set the stage for the impeachment of Andrew Johnson when the president refused to keep Edwin Stanton, a Radical, in his cabinet and ordered him to resign in February 1868. Stevens was in his middle seventies and in poor health by now, but he actively took part in the impeachment proceedings. He bypassed the Judiciary Committee and reported a resolution out of his own Committee on Reconstruction to impeach the president for violating the Tenure of Office Act. "Old Thaddeus Stevens," wrote a contemporary political commentator, "is still keeping himself alive only by the hope of sometime scalping Andrew Johnson . . . and watches with a feverish and bilious eye from behind the rampart of his Reconstruction laws the least movement of the enemy." The House voted for impeachment 126 to 47, but when the Senate tried Johnson for high crimes and misdemeanors, the necessary two-thirds majority for conviction fell short by one vote.

Stevens lived only ten weeks after the trial. Many said that his disappointment speeded his decline. This was not true, however. In the short period before his death he continued to work for Reconstruction, a free public school system for the District of Columbia, various railroad bills, and the purchase of Alaska. He died in August 1868 and rested in state in front of Lincoln's statue on the Capitol Rotunda, attended by an honor guard of black soldiers from Massachusetts. After his burial in Lancaster, the Republican party, in a grandiose gesture of respect, formally nominated him for Congress. So loyal were his constituents that he won in November!

Stevens made many fierce enemies during his lifetime. For many years after his death their views of him were widely accepted and he was remembered as an ill-tempered, vindictive, and punitive man who set back the course of sectional reconciliation. Now, following the "second Reconstruction" of the 1950s and 1960s, "the old Commoner" appears as a statesman ahead of his times and an often admirable defender of racial justice. He, of course, preferred to be seen as a great egalitarian. The inscription he chose for his tombstone testifies to his deep concern for all humanity, regardless of race:

I repose in this quiet and secluded spot,
Not from any natural preference for solitude
But, finding other Cemeteries limited as to Race by Charter Rules,
I have chosen this that I might illustrate in my death
The Principles which I advocated
Through a long life:

EQUALITY OF MAN BEFORE HIS CREATOR.

17

****

******** A HISTORICAL DOCUMENT ********

Pullman Workers' Grievances

The workers in George Pullman's Palace Car Company went on strike in June 1894 after years of accumulated grievances. These included not only the typical labor issues of wages and hours, but also those involving the community of Pullman, the company town where most of the workers lived. The selection below is from a statement issued by the forty-six-member Pullman employee grievance committee to the American Railway Union, the union many Pullman workers had recently joined. It was designed to explain the Pullman workers' decision to strike and to appeal to the ARU for support.

"In stating . . . our grievances it is hard to tell where to begin. You all must know that the proximate cause of our strike was the discharge of two members of our grievance committee the day after George M. Pullman, himself, and Thomas H. Wickes, his second vice-president, had guaranteed them absolute immunity. The more remote causes are still imminent. Five reductions in wages, in work, and in conditions of employment swept through the shops at Pullman between May and December, 1893. The last was the most severe, amounting to nearly 30 percent, and our rents had not fallen. We owed Pullman $70,000 . . . [on] May 11. We owe him twice as much as today. He does not evict us for two reasons: One, the force of popular sentiment and public opinion; the other because he hopes to starve us out, to break . . . the back of the American Railway Union, and to deduct from our miserable wages when we are forced to return to him the last dollar we owe him for the occupancy of his houses.

"Rents all over the city [of Chicago] . . . have fallen, in some cases to one-half. Residences, compared with which ours are hovels, can be had a few miles away at the prices we have been contributing to make a millionaire a billionaire. What we pay $15 for in Pullman is leased for $8 in Roseland; and remember that just as no man or woman of our 4,000 toilers has ever felt the friendly pressure of George M. Pullman's hand, so no man or woman of us all has ever owned or can ever hope to own one inch of George M. Pullman's land. Why, even the very streets are his. His ground has never been platted of record, and today he may debar any man . . . from walking in his highways. . . .

"Pullman, both the man and the town, is an ulcer on the body politic. He owns the houses, the schoolhouses, and churches of God in the town he gave his once humble name. The revenue he derives from these, the wages that he pays out with one hand . . . he takes back with the other. . . . He is able by this to bid under any contract car shop in this country. His competitors in business, to meet this, must reduce the wages of their men. This gives him the excuse to reduce ours to conform to the market. . . . And thus the merry war . . . goes on, and it will go on, brothers, forever, unless you, the American Railway Union, stop it; crush it out.

"Our town is beautiful. In all these thirteen years no word of scandal has arisen against one of our women, young or old. What city of 20,000 persons can show the like . . . ? We are peaceable; we are orderly. . . . But George M. Pullman . . . is patiently . . . waiting . . . to see us starve. . . .

"George M. Pullman . . . has cut our wages from 30 to 70 percent. . . . [He] has caused to be paid in the last year the regular quarterly dividend of 2 percent on his stock. . . . [He] . . . took three contracts on which he lost . . . $5,000. Because he loved us? No. Because it was cheaper to lose a little money in his freight car and his coach shop than to let his workingmen go, but that petty loss . . . was his excuse for effecting a gigantic reduction of wages in every department of his great works, of cutting men and boys and girls with equal zeal. . . .

"We will make you proud of us, brothers, if you will give us the hand we need. . . . Teach arrogant grinders of the faces of the poor that there is still a God in Israel, and if need be a Jehovah—a God of battles. . . ."

******** A HISTORICAL PORTRAIT ********

Eugene V. Debs

For a generation, Eugene V. Debs was the soul of the socialist movement in America. There were other socialist leaders, but no one else so fired the imaginations and raised the hopes of those who accepted the socialist vision at the beginning of the twentieth century.

Deb's American birth was important for the party and movement he headed. Far too many socialist leaders and followers were foreign-born. With his midwestern twang and rangy build, Debs seemed typically American. Actually, his family roots did not go very deep in American soil. His father and mother were both immigrants from Alsace, the German-speaking province of France, who had arrived at Terre Haute in western Indiana in 1851.

Born in 1855, Eugene enjoyed a moderately prosperous middle-class childhood, attending the local private academy and clerking in his father's grocery store. Though his parents were not needy and opposed his decision, Eugene quit school at fourteen to become an unskilled worker for the Vandalia Railroad.

Over the next four years Debs rose to the rank of fireman, but then lost his job during the depression of the mid-1870s. Fortunately, his father succeeded in getting him placed as a clerk in the prosperous wholesale grocery business of a friend. Debs retained a foot in the blue-collar camp by joining the Vigo Lodge of the recently formed Brotherhood of Locomotive Fireman. Yet the lodge was more a fraternal organization like the Masons or Elks than a modern trade union. It was certainly not a militant, class-conscious organization. In 1878, the year after the violent railroad strikes, Debs would tell an approving Brotherhood convention that the firemen's interests were "closely aligned with those of their employers."

The young man of twenty still believed in social harmony as an ideal. One of his friends was William McKeen, president of the Terre Haute and Indianapolis Railroad. Debs praised McKeen as a benevolent employer. McKeen in turn supported Debs when he ran for Terre Haute city clerk on the Democratic ticket in 1879, and again when he ran for the Indiana State Assembly in 1884. During these years the Republican *Express* called the rising young politician "the blue-eyed boy of destiny." In 1885 Debs capped his worldly success by marrying Kate Bauer, daughter of a prosperous Terre Haute druggist.

Despite his upward mobility, Debs refused to abandon his union work. In 1880 he became national secretary-treasurer of the Locomotive Firemen's Brotherhood. He also served as editor of its journal. His ambitious, status-conscious wife kept urging him to accept various business offers, but Debs continued to travel around the country on Brotherhood business. The marriage was not a happy one. The couple could not have children, and this affliction left a gap. Kate Debs took solace in buying a luxurious house in Terre Haute with the proceeds from an inheritance and furnishing it elaborately. She never liked her husband's union and political associates; they were not respectable. Her obsession with material things would prove embarrassing to the country's leading socialist in later years.

During the later 1880s the increasing impersonality of labor-management relations and the erosion of skilled workers' status by new labor-simplifying technology affected Debs's social views. The event that finally liberated him from his earlier ideal of social harmony was the Firemen's strike in 1888–1889 against the Chicago, Burlington, and Quincy Railroad. The workers were unable to cooperate against an alliance between the railroad and the courts, and they were defeated. The experience convinced Debs that unless working people pulled together, they would never improve their position relative to capital.

In 1893 Debs helped organize the American Railway Union and became its first president. The ARU was soon embroiled in a major strike against James J. Hill's Great Northern Railroad. The following year Debs brought his union into the Pullman strike on the side of the Pullman Palace Car workers. Accused of defying a federal court injunction to stop impeding the mails, Debs and other ARU officials were sentenced to prison terms. The union suffered a blow from which it never fully recovered.

Despite a later myth that Debs himself encouraged, he did not at this time become a socialist. He did emerge from six months in Woodstock prison with a more radical evaluation of American society, yet in 1896 he campaigned for William Jennings Bryan, the Democratic–free-silver candidate for President. Bryan's defeat pushed Debs over the line, however, and in January 1897 he told his associates at the ARU that "the issue is Socialism versus Capitalism. I am for Socialism because I am for humanity." Debs soon maneuvered the remnants of the ARU into forming the Social Democracy of America.

Between 1897 and 1900 Debs came to accept the orthodox socialist class-conflict version of history and politics and became a founding father of the socialist movement. In 1900 the newly formed Social Democratic party nominated him for president, and in 1901 he helped forge the Socialist Party of America out of a collection of socialist splinter groups and factions.

For the next two decades Debs remained the leading figure in the American socialist movement. He was the Socialist party candidate for president in 1904, 1908, 1912, and again in 1920, the last year running his campaign from prison. In the 1912 campaign he received almost a million votes, over 6 percent of the total cast. Debs was a powerful speaker who could hold an audience in his grasp for hours while alternately excoriating capitalism and evoking glowing images of the future Cooperative Commonwealth. Millions, including many who would not "throw away" their votes on a third-party candidate, adored him. To many Americans of the day, he personified the heroic and humane socialist ideal.

Yet within the socialist movement Debs had his critics and opponents. To his right within the party there was Victor Berger of Milwaukee and Morris Hillquit of New York. Both were foreign-born, yet both represented moderate positions. They believed it essential for socialists to work within the existing conservative labor unions, seeking to gain control by influencing members' views. They also believed that socialists must support reform programs in order to appeal to discontented members of the middle class as well as to blue-collar workers.

Debs led the left wing, which endorsed separate radical unions in competition with the American Federation of Labor, was more skeptical of reform, and more "proletarian" in its sympathies than the right wing. Yet Debs had his critics to the left, too. These were people like "Big Bill" Haywood of the Industrial Workers of the World (IWW), who advocated industrial sabotage, the general strike, and overtly confrontationist tactics to bring capitalism to its knees. Debs tried to mediate between these extremes. He did not always succeed, but his charisma and popularity with the rank-and-file members managed to preserve the formal unity of the party.

World War I was a catastrophe for the socialists and for Debs. Some prominent socialists left the party to support the Allied cause even before American entrance into the war, and more resigned when, in April 1917, shortly after America's declaration of war against Germany, the party announced its opposition to the war. During the war the mood of intolerance and superpatriotism led to official repression of socialist publications, government raids on party offices, vigilante actions against socialists, and the arrest and imprisonment of socialist leaders on charges of subversion and attempts to discourage men from registering for the draft. In June 1918, following a speech critical of the United States, Debs was indicted by the federal government for violating the 1917 Espionage Act. He used his trial as an effective forum for his ideas, but he was sentenced to ten years in prison and sent to Atlanta Penitentiary to serve his term.

During the two years Debs actually spent in prison, the party he had helped to found underwent drastic changes. In the decade preceding 1917 more and more of the party membership came to consist of recent immigrants from Finland, Russia, and other parts of eastern Europe. When the Bolsheviks took power in Russia in late 1917, many of these immigrants hailed the event and insisted that the party endorse the Russian Revolution. Before long the "foreign-language federations," with their far-left allegiances, formed a caucus within the party and sought to seize power. In March 1919 the Bolshevik leaders in Moscow ordered the formation of the Third International, with the slogan "Back to Marx" and the name "Communist." One of the first directives issued by the International's leaders was that each of the organized Socialist parties divest itself of any bourgeois, right-wing elements. This encouraged the foreign-language federations to split off from Debs's Socialist party and organize what came to be the American Communist party, leaving behind a depleted and demoralized rump.

At first Debs supported the radicals, but then, while still in prison, he changed his mind. After his release from Atlanta in December 1921, he returned to Terre Haute to be greeted by 25,000 cheering supporters. By this time the early hope that the Socialist party might become a major agent of fundamental change had evaporated. In 1924, recognizing the depleted energies of the party, Debs supported Robert LaFollette's presidential bid on the Farmer-Labor ticket. For this he was bitterly attacked by his former left-wing comrades, now mostly Communists.

Debs had never been a healthy man. Over the years he had suffered numerous breakdowns from mysterious ailments and had taken a series of "cures" at sanitariums. On October 20, 1926, following a massive heart attack, he died in Chicago and his body was brought to Terre Haute. Thousands came to pay their respects, trailing through the parlor of the Debs's house to view the coffin. Eugene's brother Theodore, Theodore's wife and daughter, and other family members greeted the mourners. Debs's widow, Kate, remained upstairs in her room, however. To the very end she could not help expressing her disapproval of her husband's disreputable associates.

18

****

The Boston Poor

Not every city dweller in the Gilded Age, not even every working-class person, was miserably housed, of course. But in this era, when rural Americans and immigrants poured into the country's cities, decent living accommodations were denied many people. For decades following the Civil War few middle-class Americans worried much about the "slums." But then, toward the end of the century, a new urban reform movement appeared, led by men and women who believed that much of the cities' misery could be blamed on the wretched hovels inflicted on the urban poor. One such reformer was Benjamin O. Flower, a Boston journalist and publisher. The following is a description of Boston's North End from a book-length report called *Civilization's Inferno* that Flower wrote in 1893.

"The first building we entered faced a narrow street. The hallway was as dark as the air was foul or the walls filthy. Not a ray or shimmer of light fell through transom or sky-light. The stairs were narrow and worn. By the aid of matches we were able to grope our way along, and also observe more that was pleasant to behold. It was apparent that the hallways or stairs were seldom surprised by water, while pure, fresh air was evidently as much a stranger as fresh paint. After ascending several flights, we entered a room of undreamed wretchedness. On the floor lay a sick man. He was rather fine looking, with an intelligent face, bright eyes, and a countenance indicative of force of character. No sign of dissipation, but an expression of sadness, or rather a look of dumb resignation peered from his expressive eyes. . . . There, for two years, he had lain on a wretched pallet of rags seeing his faithful wife tirelessly sewing, hour by hour and day by day, and knowing full well that health, life and hope were hourly slipping from her. This poor woman supports the invalid husband, her two children and herself, by making pants for leading Boston clothiers. No rest, no surcease, a perpetual grind from early dawn often far into the night. . . . Eviction, sickness, starvation—such are ever-present spectres, while every year marks the steady encroachment of disease, and the lowering of the register of vitality. . . .

"The next place visited was the attic of a tenement building even more wretched than the one just described. The general aspects of these houses, however, are all much the same, the chief difference being in the degrees of filth and squalor present. Here in an attic lives a poor widow with three children, a little boy and two little girls. They live by making pants at starvation wages. Since the youngest child was two and a half years old she has been daily engaged in overcasting the long seams of garments made by her mother. . . . There, on a little stool, she sat, her fingers moving as rapidly and in as unerring a manner as an old experienced needle-woman.

"Among the places we visited were a number of cellars or burrows. We descended several steps into dark, narrow passageways, leading to cold, damp rooms, in many of which no direct ray of sunshine ever creeps. We entered one room containing a bed, cooking stove, rack of dirty clothes and some broken chairs. On the bed lay a man who had been ill for three months with rheumatism. This family consists of father, mother and a daughter in her teens, all of whom are compelled to occupy one bed. They eat, cook, live, and sleep in this wretched cellar and pay over fifty dollars a year in rent. This is a typical illustration of life in this underground world.

"In another similar cellar or burrow, we found a mother and seven boys and girls, some of them quite large, *all sleeping in two medium-sized beds in one room*; this apartment is also their kitchen. . . . Their rent is two dollars a week. The cellar is damp and cold; the air is stifling. Nothing can be imagined more favorable to contagion both physical and moral than such dens as these. Ethical exaltation or spiritual growth is impossible with such an environment. It is not strange that the slums breed criminals, which require vast sums yearly to punish after evil has been perpetrated; but to me it is an ever-increasing source of wonder that society should be so short-sighted and neglectful of the condition of its exiles, when the outlay of a much smaller sum would ensure a prevention of a large proportion of the crime that emanates from the slums; while, at the same time, it would mean a new world of life, happiness, and measureless possibilities for the thousands who now exist in hopeless gloom. . . ."

✶✶✶✶✶✶✶✶ A HISTORICAL PORTRAIT ✶✶✶✶✶✶✶✶

Abraham Ruef

In 1883, Abraham Ruef graduated from the University of California at Berkeley with a senior thesis called *Purity in Politics*. At Hastings Law School he and some friends founded the Municipal Reform League to study city problems and find ways of solving them. Twenty years later, as boss of the San Francisco Republican machine, Ruef pleaded guilty to charges of extortion and spent four years at San Quentin prison.

This reformer-turned-boss was born in San Francisco in 1864, two years after his parents emigrated from France. Though the son of immigrants, Ruef's childhood was affluent. His father became a successful storekeeper on Market Street and a real estate dealer who listed himself in the city directory as "capitalist." Abraham himself was a precocious student who spoke seven languages and graduated from Berkeley with high honors and a major in Greek and Latin.

Ruef stumbled into politics. In 1886 he was admitted to the California bar and opened a law office in the Bay city. Soon after, he found himself at a Republican club meeting in his home district attended by only two others—a boardinghouse owner and a saloonkeeper, the two district leaders. The two men, Ruef later claimed, told him that the large, intelligent crowd that had attended had just left, and they induced him to write a newspaper article describing the successful party gathering. Whether out of appreciation of the young lawyer's literary imagination or his gullibility, they soon made Ruef captain of two Republican precincts and got him elected as delegate to the municipal convention of 1886. Ruef's political career was launched.

San Francisco's leading Republicans soon noticed this bright, cocky lawyer. They may have bridled at his pretensions, but his seniors in the machine found his cultivation and refinement a welcome contrast to the vulgarity and ignorance of the typical machine hack. For his part, Ruef realized the value of the machine in bringing him into contact with public officials, judges, and successful fellow lawyers. Before long he began to dream of becoming United States senator.

Though initially Ruef preferred the good-government faction of the party, he soon judged the reformers "apathetic" and "drifted" to the side of the machine. "Whatever ideals I once had," he later confessed, "were relegated to the background." Ruef quickly became the local Republican boss of San Francisco's Latin Quarter, the raffish, bohemian district of the Bay city.

Boss Ruef displayed all the skills and talents of his breed. He systematically cultivated the different ways to collect votes. He joined every social club he could find. He understood the endless demands of the district's people for charity and bought tickets to every benefit. He made friends with the judges at the police court so he could help his constituents in trouble with the law. He also paid court to the city's tax assessors to help local business people and property owners when tax time came around. He even established useful contacts at the coroner's office so he could get a death report changed to suit a political ally. Ruef understood that every function of government provided an opportunity to do a favor for a constituent. But he also had other political assets. His sense of humor endeared him to the voters. On one occasion at a political rally, he noticed that the audience had a supply of eggs to throw at him when he got up to speak. "Throw all the . . . eggs at one time," Ruef told the crowd, "so that we can get down to business."

In 1901 Ruef founded the Republican Primary League to help influence the course of an important three-way mayoral contest. The city had just weathered a huge dockworkers', sailors', and teamsters' strike that had idled 40,000 workers and tied up 200 ships in the harbor. When Mayor James D. Phelen finally decided to call in the police to protect strikebreakers, a riot had broken out that ended in bloodshed. The strikers, outraged at the use of police, formed a new party of their own— the Union Labor party—to take control of the city government, and received the support of William Randolph Hearst's powerful paper, *The Examiner.*

Ruef allied his League with the new party and then hand-picked his friend and client Eugene Schmitz as its candidate. A violinist, composer, and director of the Columbia Theater orchestra, Schmitz, as president of the local musicians' union, qualified as a friend of organized labor. Meanwhile, the Republicans, dominated by the Southern Pacific Railroad, had picked city auditor Asa Wells as their candidate; the Democrats chose a member of Phelen's entourage, Joseph S. Tobin.

Schmitz's campaign, managed by Ruef, emphasized fair play for labor, public ownership of utilities, and economy in government. Energized by deep working-class resentments against the recent police brutality, the Union Labor party won. Schmitz's fellow musicians expressed their elation at the results by parading around the city playing their instruments with gusto. But no one was more pleased than Ruef. The new party, he wrote, would be "a spark . . . which would kindle the entire nation. . . . [It would be] a throne for Schmitz as Mayor, as Governor—as president of the United States. Behind that throne, I saw myself its power, local, state—nation. . . ." Schmitz, in office, did not actually seek city ownership of public utilities, yet labor did benefit from his friendly attitude. During the streetcar strike in 1902 working people considered his role "fair and fearless." His tight rein on the police allowed labor to win this dispute and many later ones. Under Mayor Schmitz San Francisco would earn the reputation as the "tightest closed-shop town" in the United States. In 1903 the violinist-mayor won a resounding reelection.

As Schmitz prospered, so did Ruef. During the day the "Curly Boss" could be found in his law offices, putting in long hours dealing with clients and constituents. At night he held court at the Pup, a French restaurant downtown. Ruef did not drink or smoke, but he was vain and drove a sporty automobile he called the "Green Lizard." He never married, and his nocturnal headquarters were said by his enemies to be an "institutionalized house of assignation."

Much was also said about his political morals. Both at his office and at the restaurant, Ruef allegedly collected bribes camouflaged as payments for legal services, from the United Railroad, the Pacific State Telephone and Telegraph Company, and the Home Telegraph Company, in exchange for political favors. He and his friends also collected tribute from dairies, real estate brokers, insurance adjusters, auctioneers, produce dealers, and proprietors of restaurants, theaters, gambling houses, saloons, and brothels.

By 1903 the good-government forces, led by Fremont Older, the reformist editor of the *San Francisco Bulletin* and friend of former Mayor Phelen, had resolved to oust Schmitz and break Ruef's grip on the city government. The two men, Older insisted, were false friends of the working people and were utterly corrupt. Soon editorials were appearing in the *Bulletin* almost daily, attacking the "boodlers" and "grafters" who were running the Bay city. Older's denunciations of Ruef spared nothing. Even his legal work for the city's prominent French restaurants was immoral. These establishments, he noted, had family eating rooms with good food on the first floor, but no respectable woman would be seen on the second, with their private dining rooms, or on the third, with their accommodations for prostitutes and their clients.

The campaign of Older, Phelen, progressive reformers, and antilabor city businessmen to dump Schmitz in 1906 failed; the Mayor won a smashing reelection victory. But Older persisted. Later that year he visited President Theodore Roosevelt in Washington and procured the services of Francis J. Heney, special assistant to the United States attorney general. With the support of Rudolph Spreckels, one of the city's most prominent business leaders, Older and his friends raised $100,000 to investigate Ruef's deal to build an electric trolley streetcar line. Aside from their suspicion that it was a corrupt deal, they also objected to the overhead wires that they claimed would mar the city's natural beauty. At the same time they proposed on alternate scheme of their own: streetcars powered by an underground moving cable.

The earthquake and fire that ravaged the Bay Area in April 1906 drove the corruption and transit system issues from people's minds. Schmitz proved to be an able leader in the crisis, and Ruef served on the Committeee on Reconstruction. For the moment it seemed that all hostilities would be suspended. But while the city remained preoccupied with physical reconstruction, Ruef's associates got an ordinance passed authorizing their overhead trolley streetcar. When the public discovered the coup there was a huge outcry amplified by new allegations of money distributed to secure a favorable telephone company franchise. Ruef's plans for building a "greater" San Francisco, charged a city newspaper, were essentially "plans for a greater Ruef."

By this time Older and his associates felt they had enough evidence to proceed to trial. Some of this material had been obtained by a "sting" operation wherein an agent for the reformers had enticed some of the city's supervisors into taking bribes and then promised them immunity in return for testimony against the boss. Ruef tried to forestall the trial, but in November 1906, he, Schmitz, and a flock of their colleagues were indicted for graft.

In exchange for partial immunity, Ruef confessed and implicated several prominent California business leaders in his deals. This did not help him. Chief Prosecutor Heney decided that the confession was entirely self-serving and untrue, and withdrew the immunity offer. The trial was one of the most sensational on record. Prosecution documents were rifled, witnesses suborned, jurors bribed, and incriminating evidence hidden away. A supervisor's house was blown up, and the chief prosecutor was shot in the courtroom by a juror he had revealed to be a former convict. Someone even kidnapped Older and spirited him away to Santa Barbara, but the kidnapper lost his nerve and refused to carry out his commission to kill him. Heney was eventually replaced by a young California lawyer, Hiram Johnson, who later went on to become Governor of the state and a leading progressive in the United States Senate.

In the end the prosecutors obtained only four convictions. Three of these were reversed, and only Ruef ended up going to jail. On March 7, 1911 he entered San Quentin to begin his sentence of fourteen years.

Agitation for his release began almost immediately. Many people felt that with corruption so pervasive in San Francisco, it was unfair to single out Ruef. Foremost among the doubters was Fremont Older, who had been so instrumental in getting Ruef convicted. Older apparently had come to believe that Ruef had been victimized by a corrupt political environment for which all the citizens of San Francisco were to blame. He also felt that by reneging on the promise to grant Ruef partial immunity, the prosecution had used tactics as despicable as those of the defense. A few months after Ruef entered San Quentin, Older visited him, asked his forgiveness, and promised to work for his parole.

As part of his release strategy, Ruef agreed to write his memoirs, which Older would publish in the *Bulletin*. In May 1912, the paper ran the first installment of Ruef's "The Road I Traveled: An Autobiographic Account of My Career from University to Prison, with an Intimate Recital of the Corrupt Alliance between Big Business and Politics in San Francisco." In September, when the account reached the period of the trial, the memoirs stopped. Older had decided that if Ruef's side were published it would raise too many hackles and weaken the public sympathy that had been aroused by the early parts. Instead, Ruef began a new series entitled "Civic Conditions and Suggested Remedies," in which the corrupt boss proposed a series of civic reforms.

Ruef spent three more years in prison. While there Older served as custodian of his estate, and appeared at San Quentin to take him home the day he was released. Ruef left San Quentin in the fall of 1915 and spent the rest of his life in San Francisco, devoting all his time to the real estate business. Although he never reentered politics, his name would appear in the press from time to time in connection with various business schemes, like his project to remove the alcohol from wine without destroying its taste, or his more successful venture, a restaurant at Fisherman's Wharf. At one point he was charged with renting one of his hotel properties to a prostitution ring, but he proved that he had evicted these tenants as soon as he discovered their business.

By the 1920s Ruef had restored most of his fortune. In the Depression, however, he suffered severe business reverses. When he died of a heart attack on February 29, 1936, he was bankrupt.

19

****

******** A HISTORICAL PORTRAIT ********

Sitting Bull

Sitting Bull was the son of Returns-Again, a chief of the Hunkpapa, a tribe of the Teton, the western division of the proud Sioux Nation. Born in 1831 in what is now South Dakota, the young boy was first called Slow. The name described his deliberate way of doing things. Even as an infant, for example, he would examine carefully a piece of food placed in his hand before putting it in his mouth.

Slow got his adult name when he was fourteen. The Sioux were a warlike people. Their clashes with their Indian neighbors were often motivated by their quest for horses. They were also a vital part of Sioux culture with much of the tribe's life taken up with war dances, preparations for war, lamenting for the dead and wounded, and distributing spoils of raids on other tribes.

To the Sioux fighting was a glorious sport. Sioux braves achieved status by striking the first blow, or *coup*, against an enemy in battle, whether the blow was a mere touch with a stick or an actual thrust with a weapon. Yet it was a bloody sport. Once the *coup* had been achieved, the Sioux fought to kill and spared neither men, women, nor children. They often mutilated their victims by removing ears, scalps, fingers, or genitals as souvenirs of their successes.

It was on a raiding expedition against the Crow in 1845 that Slow made his first *coup*, and in recognition he was given the new adult name *Ta-tan'-ka I-yo-ta'-ke*, Sitting Bull. At fourteen the Indian lad was a man.

Thereafter Sitting Bull rose in the esteem and affection of his people as a brave, vigorous, and generous man. His first contact with whites came in 1864 at Kildeer Mountains in present-day North Dakota when the western Sioux clashed with army troops on a punitive expedition following Indian attacks on settlers in Minnesota. Thirty Indians died in a series of skirmishes with the soldiers, but most escaped. Sitting Bull, present in the thick of the fight, was not impressed with the quality of the white fighting men. They did "not know how to fight," he said. "They are not lively enough. They stand still and run straight; it is easy to shoot them."

After the Sand Creek Massacre of 1864, the Sioux joined the Cheyenne for a campaign along the Platte River to avenge Chivington's savagery. During the fighting Sitting Bull proved his prowess against the whites and soon was recognized as a chief not only of his own Hunkpapa, but also of other western Sioux tribes.

For a time in the mid-1860s Sitting Bull directed the aggressive energies of the Sioux against his Indian foes, the Crows, Mandans, Flatheads, Hohe, and Rees. But he did not forget the white danger. Sitting Bull had become a leader of the "hostiles," the Indians who resisted the whites' reservation policy. The Indians, he believed, must be allowed to continue their nomadic, hunting ways, and must never agree to settle down to farm or take the white man's food, blankets, and other handouts. In these immediate postwar years, like other leaders of the northern Plains tribes, he

84

demanded that the whites close their road across the northern Plains, burn and evacuate the forts in the region, stop the steamboats from ascending the Missouri and its tributaries, and expel all white intruders except traders.

The Sioux got much of what they wanted in the Treaty of 1868, a document that reflected the conciliatory mood of the post–Civil War peace policy. Under this agreement the government abandoned its road through the new Great Sioux Reservation, promised to destroy its forts within the Sioux lands and exclude all whites, except those who obtained tribal permission to settle or pass through. But in return the Indians agreed to abandon their nomadic life and settle down on the reservation near the Indian agencies where they were under protection and supervision of the white Indian agent.

Despite the government's concessions Sitting Bull refused to surrender the old ways. In 1869 he led his warriors on raiding expeditions against the Crows and the Flatheads in which many warriors fell. He refused to settle near the Indian agency. In 1872 and 1873 the Sioux skirmished with soldiers escorting Northern Pacific Railroad surveying parties through Sioux lands. After these incidents Sitting Bull and his friend Crazy Horse, of the Oglala Sioux, resolved to adopt a new policy toward whites: "If they come shooting, shoot back."

One of the white officers in these battles was General George Armstrong Custer, a brave, but flamboyant and foolhardy, veteran of the Civil War. In 1874 General Philip Sheridan, of Civil War cavalry fame, sent Custer with a thousand soldiers, along with miners and journalists, to explore the Black Hills region of the Sioux reservation, where, rumors had it, there were rich gold deposits. The Indians protested that this expedition violated the Treaty of 1868, but the authorities refused to yield.

The reconnaissance had tragic consequences. Custer's miners confirmed that there was gold in the Black Hills streams, though not in lavish amounts. The expedition also found fertile, well-watered land, and abundant timber in the region's valleys and mountain slopes. Custer's report, though cautious, was like a lightning bolt in a dry forest. The country was in the midst of a severe business recession with thousands of men seeking jobs and some way of earning a living. News of the Black Hills' resources set off a rush of miners and would-be settlers to the Dakota region.

The influx of whites clearly violated the Treaty of 1868, and the Indians loudly protested. The army made a half-hearted attempt to drive out the miners, but in the end allowed them to stay. In 1875, the government decided to negotiate a new treaty that would remove the Black Hills from Sioux control. The government's incentive was an extension of the period of federal aid and handouts. Under the 1868 agreement this was supposed to last for a limited time while the Indians transformed themselves into settled farmers. The process had failed; the Sioux and other buffalo hunters despised farming as unworthy of true men. Unfortunately, the buffalo on which their nomadic existence had depended were fast disappearing. They found cattle herding more congenial, but it did not provide sufficient food and money for them to become self-supporting. Taking advantage of the Indians' continued need for government largess, federal officials, at a meeting with the Sioux at the Red Cloud agency, offered to give the Indians $400,000 a year for mining rights in the Black Hills or $6 million for their outright sale. Sitting Bull, one of the chiefs present, had already rejected any surrender of Indian lands and the meeting failed to accomplish anything.

The government now decided to use force. In December 1875 the Secretary of the Interior ordered all Indians to report to the reservation agencies or face the government's displeasure. In 1876, after the hostile Sioux had failed to comply, General George Crook sent several expeditions to break their will. Prime target during the spring foray was the camp where Sitting Bull and Crazy Horse had gathered under their command Sioux from almost every tribe as well as hundreds of other Plains Indians who hated both the white man and the reservation policy. In mid-June, Crook's men fought an inconclusive battle at the Rosebud River with Sioux and Cheyenne led by Crazy Horse.

The second punitive expedition produced the greatest military disaster in the long history of the western Indian wars. This foray was led by General Alfred Terry, with Custer second in command. When Terry reached the Tongue River he divided the Seventh Cavalry into two columns, one under Custer, and ordered it to advance on the Indian camp.

Custer did not know that he was about to poke his nose into a hornet's nest. More than 10,000 Indians, including 4,000 fighting men, were encamped near the Little Bighorn River. Custer's force numbered a scant 500 men, and he further weakened his command by placing almost two-thirds of it under other officers, Major Marcus Reno and Captain Thomas Weir.

Early on the afternoon of June 25, 1876, the 140 dismounted cavalrymen of Reno's force approached the Indian encampment. The Sioux and Cheyenne attacked, forcing Reno back. Meanwhile, Custer and his men advanced on the camp from the north. The Indians were desperate to protect their women and children and fell on the soldiers with ferocity. Much of the fighting was hand-to-hand, a whirling confusion of shouts and shots enveloped in a dust cloud stirred up by frantic men and lunging horses. This time the Indians ignored *coups* and fought to kill from the start. Reno heard the sounds and saw the smoke of battle, but he did not come to his superior's rescue. In a brief, savage hour Custer and all 264 of his men lay dead. It was the greatest victory that the Plains Indians had ever won over the white men.

The victory at the Little Bighorn could not alter the fate of the Plains tribes. Though there was some talk of forming an Indian confederacy that would stop the encroachment of the whites, this never came about. Nor would it have made any difference. There were a thousand whites ready to replace every one of Custer's fallen men.

In the wake of "Custer's last stand" another Indian commission forced the Sioux to surrender the Black Hills and accept other onerous revisions of the 1868 Treaty. The original treaty had solemnly promised that there would be no changes unless three-fourths of the adult Indian males had agreed. This provision was simply ignored and the government pronounced the new treaty in effect when the principal chiefs had signed it.

Sitting Bull and his hostiles remained at large and were not a party to this pact. During the winter following the Little Bighorn battle the army continued its campaign to force Sitting Bull and his followers to settle down. At one point General Nelson Miles and Sitting Bull conferred face-to-face and the chief told the general that no white man had ever loved an Indian and that no true Indian had ever failed to hate the white man. Despite Sitting Bull's belligerent response, Miles succeeded in detaching several thousand Indians from the hostile group. Even Crazy Horse defected, but Sitting Bull refused and fled across the border into Canada where the Americans could not touch him.

During the next few years Sitting Bull and his followers remained encamped just north of the international boundary, making occasional raids across the border to hunt buffalo and attack white settlers. Finally, in 1881, their resolve undermined by hunger and exhaustion with incessant fighting, the chief and his remaining followers surrendered to the American authorities.

For a time they were placed under guard at Fort Randall, in South Dakota, and then moved to the Standing Rock agency on the Sioux reservation. During his last years Sitting Bull remained a thorn in the government's side. He demanded extra rations and cattle, even horses and buggies, for himself and his followers. In 1889, when the government once more revised the treaty with the Sioux, further reducing their lands, he again resisted, though this time with words rather than arrows or bullets. Soon after, he took up and encouraged among his people the new Ghost-Dance religion.

As preached by the Paiute Indian prophet Wovoka, the Ghost Dance was a peaceful faith. In Sitting Bull's version, however, the new Indian messiah, when he returned to earth in 1891, would exterminate the white man. It is not clear whether Sitting Bull believed the Ghost-Dance prophecy, or whether he was only seeking to use it to restore his authority among the Sioux, but it frightened the already nervous white authorities.

On December 15, 1890, the reservation police, a force made up of "tame" Indians, came to arrest Sitting Bull for continuing to encourage the Ghost-Dance ceremonies. As he was preparing to accompany them, the old chief shouted "I'm not going. Come on! Take action!" At this signal, Catch-the-Bear, one of his followers, fired a shot that hit Lieutenant Bull Head in the right side. The lieutenant fired back, hitting Sitting Bull. A confused melee followed, and at the end Sitting Bull lay dead.

Scholars often date the end of the nineteenth-century Indian Wars from the Wounded Knee massacre of December 29, 1890. In fact, the wars had really ended two weeks before when the great Hunkpapa chief, Sitting Bull, the fierce defender of his people's heritage, fell before the bullets of the tame Indians wearing the white man's uniform.

✳✳✳✳✳✳✳ A HISTORICAL DOCUMENT ✳✳✳✳✳✳✳

Dawes Act

From the perspective of white reformers, the Dawes Severalty Act of 1887 was an ideal, long-overdue measure that would assimilate the tribal Indians into the mainstream of American life. It would, Amherst College's benevolent president Merrill E. Gates declared, make the Indian "intelligently selfish." It would get him "out of the blanket and into trousers—and trousers with a pocket in them, and with a pocket *that aches to be filled with dollars!*" The actual effects were different, but the measure stands as a monument to the failed good intentions of white reformers toward the country's native American peoples.

"*An act to provide for the allotment of lands in severalty to Indians on the various reservations, and to extend the protection of the laws of the United States and the Territories over the Indians, and for various other purposes.*

"*Be it enacted,* That in all cases where any tribe or band of Indians has been, or hereafter shall be, located upon any reservation created for their use, either by treaty stipulation or by virtue of an act of Congress or executive order setting apart the same for their use, the President of the United States be, and he hereby is, authorized, whenever in his opinion any reservation, or any part thereof of such Indians is advantageous for agriculture and grazing purposes to cause said reservation, or any part thereof, to be surveyed, or resurveyed if necessary, and to allot the lands in said reservation in severalty to any Indian located thereon in quantities as follows:

"To each head of a family, one-quarter of a section;

"To each single person over eighteen years of age, one-eighth of a section; and,

"To each orphan child under eighteen years of age, one-eighth of a section; and,

"To each other single person under eighteen years now living, or who may be born prior to the date of the order of the President directing an allotment of the lands embraced in any reservation, one-sixteenth of a section; . . .

"SEC. 5. That upon the approval of the allotments provided for in this act by the Secretary of the Interior, he shall . . . declare that the United States does and will hold the land thus allotted, for the period of twenty-five years, in trust for the sole use and benefit of the Indian to whom such allotment shall have been made, . . . and that at the expiration of said period the United States will convey the same by patent to said Indian, or his heirs, . . . discharged of such trust and free of all charge or encumbrance whatsoever. . . .

"SEC. 6. That upon the completion of said allotments and the patenting of the lands to said allottees, each and every member of the respective bands or tribes of Indians to whom allotments have been made shall have the benefit of and be subject to the laws, both civil and criminal, of the State or Territory in which they may reside; . . . And every Indian born within the territorial limits of the United States who has voluntarily taken up, within said limits, his residence separate and apart from any tribe of Indians therein, and had adopted the habits of civilized life, is hereby declared to be a citizen of the United States, and is entitled to all the rights, privileges, and immunities of such citizens, whether said Indian has been or not, by birth or otherwise, a member of any tribe of Indians within the territorial limits of the United States without in any manner impairing or otherwise affecting the right of any such Indian to tribal or other property. . . ."

20

****

******** A HISTORICAL PORTRAIT ********

James G. Blaine

James G. Blaine traveled two paths, wrote one of his biographers, "one in the daylight that was straight, one in the dark that was twisted as a ram's horn." An idol to millions in his day, Blaine epitomized to many others all that was venal and corrupt in American political life in the Gilded Age.

Blaine was born in Pennsylvania in 1830 of Irish stock. On his father's side he was descended from a line of Scotch-Irish Presbyterians who came to America from Ulster in the 1740s. His mother's family was Irish Catholic from County Donegal. James himself was raised as a Protestant, though his mother never forsook her Catholic faith. His mixed religious background would affect his career in an age when religion was an important determinant of political preference.

Almost from the outset the young Pennsylvanian exhibited the democratic politician's essential qualities: geniality, eloquence, humor, and an excellent memory for names and faces. At Washington College, which he entered at the startling age of thirteen, both his fellow students and his instructors thought him charming. People were drawn to him in a way that gave meaning to the popular adjective of the day: "magnetic."

After graduation, Blaine became an instructor of mathematics and classical languages at a military academy at Georgetown, Kentucky, where many of his students were as old as he was. It was there that he met Harriet Stanwood, a teacher at the local "female seminary," and married her in 1850. Harriet was a New Englander with family roots in Maine. The connection would prove as important as the marriage was happy.

In 1854, after a short stay in Philadelphia, Blaine was offered an opportunity by Harriet's brothers to edit the *Kennebec Journal*, and he left his native state to spend the rest of his career in Maine. Most ambitious young men went west to seek opportunity; Blaine reversed the direction.

Because all newspapers were then party organs, Blaine's editorship of the *Journal* inevitably thrust him into politics. He had arrived in Maine at the time when the Whigs, his original party, were breaking up. Blaine and the *Journal* soon became ardent Republicans, defending the new party's positions on slavery, the tariff, and the territorial issue. In 1859 he became chairman of the Maine Republican State Committee, a post he retained for over twenty years.

Maine was a small state at a far corner of the continent. But it had advantages for Republican politicians with national ambitions. It was a "rock-ribbed" Republican state and could be counted on to reelect its Republican officeholders over and over again. In Congress this practice guaranteed seniority and national prominence.

In 1862, after three terms in the Maine legislature, Blaine was elected to the United States House of Representatives. He arrived in Washington the following

89

year to take part in the exciting events of the Civil War and Reconstruction eras. Blaine was a Radical Republican who distrusted the "rebels" even after they had laid down their arms. He was not an extremist, however, and frequently clashed with Thaddeus Stevens, leader of the most militantly antisouthern Radical faction. Though Blaine was willing to take strong positions, he kept the respect of his colleagues and in 1869 they elected him Speaker of the House, one of the most powerful positions in the federal government.

Blaine presided over the House with a degree of good nature and fairness that won the respect of even the Democrats. But he did make one enemy: the arrogant, supercilious, opinionated Republican congressman from Utica, New York, Roscoe Conkling. In 1866 Blaine and Conkling got into an argument over a bill to create a permanent provost marshal's office in the army. Conkling was sarcastic about Blaine's views on the issue under discussion. Blaine responded in kind, describing Conkling's "haughty disdain, his grandiloquent swell, his majestic, supereminent, turkey-gobbler strut," and concluding that the New Yorker, compared to the truly eloquent Henry Winter Davis to whom he had been likened, was as "mud to marble, dunghill to diamond, a singed cat to a Bengal tiger, a whining puppy to a roaring lion." Conkling never forgave Blaine, and the two men's enmity would affect the course of Gilded Age politics.

During Grant's administration (1869–1877) Blaine became leader of the Republican "Half-Breeds," along with James Garfield and John Sherman of Ohio, and George F. Hoar of Massachusetts. Slightly younger than the "Stalwarts," led by Conkling, John A. Logan of Illinois, Zachariah Chandler of Michigan, and Simon Cameron of Pennsylvania, the Half-Breeds were also less committed to defending traditional Republican obligations to the freedmen and to invoking the Civil War as the basis of party politics in the post-1865 period. But Half-Breed–Stalwart differences over policy were less important than their battles over patronage and appropriations.

It was during the 1876 presidential campaign that Blaine's reputation for financial honesty suffered its first serious blow. Grant's second term was over and he did not as yet harbor third-term ambitions. The field was wide open for another Republican and many believed Blaine the logical choice. But fate intervened when, in April 1876, a director of the Union Pacific Railroad reported that Blaine had received a permanent loan of $64,000 from the UP against the worthless collateral of some Little Rock and Fort Smith Railroad bonds. In effect, the Union Pacific had given Blaine a large gift of money.

The House committee appointed to investigate the charges soon received information that one James Mulligan had letters by Blaine that implied that the Maine congressman had accepted securities in return for favors to the railroad. When Mulligan came to Washington to testify, Blaine intercepted him at his hotel and walked off with the letters Mulligan had intended to give the committee. The following day Blaine himself wove the letters selectively into a brilliant speech on the House floor that obscured the most incriminating portions. The performance dazzled the public, and convinced his partisans that their hero had thoroughly vindicated himself.

But Blaine never fully cleared his name, and at the Republican convention in Cincinnati he saw the presidential nomination go to the governor of Ohio, the colorless but honest Rutherford B. Hayes. It was at Cincinnati that Robert Ingersoll, in the course of his nominating speech, used the phrase "the plumed knight" to describe Blaine. It became his nickname, often used with irony by his detractors.

In 1877 the Maine legislature sent Blaine to the United States Senate. Here he spent most of his time locked in battle with Conkling and positioning himself for

1880. As the struggle for the nomination began, it seemed like a contest between Grant, with his Stalwart supporters, and the Half-Breeds led by Blaine. In the end the Grant and Blaine forces deadlocked and the nomination—and the election—went to Garfield, a friend of Blaine's.

Blaine had not found the Senate as congenial as the House and he welcomed his appointment by Garfield as secretary of state. In the State Department Blaine was a diplomatic activist who believed that American influence in the Western Hemisphere and elsewhere must be expanded. His aggressive support of American interests abroad earned him the label "Jingo Jim." He also acted as Garfield's chief domestic adviser and used his influence to remove his Stalwart enemies from influential office. In New York this led to wholesale dismissals of Conkling's supporters. Whatever satisfaction Blaine felt at Conkling's discomfiture was short-lived. On July 2, 1881, an embittered Stalwart shot the president, who died two months later, leaving Chester A. Arthur, a New York Stalwart, as his successor. Blaine remained in office for a few months more but then resigned to return to private life and write his political memoirs.

As 1884 approached, the "Blaine legion" of loyal supporters once again prepared to make their idol president. This time they got further than ever before. Blaine won the party nomination at Chicago on the first ballot and, for the sake of party peace, chose Stalwart John Logan as his running mate. His opponent in the contest was Governor Grover Cleveland of New York.

To an unusual extent the race turned on Blaine's honesty. By now a substantial portion of the country's educated class, voters often nominally Republican, were "Mugwumps," who felt that the Republican party had lost its moral bearings and existed only for the sake of patronage and plunder. Cleveland was considered a reformer because as governor he had opposed the New York Democratic machine and conducted an honest state administration. The Mugwumps—led by Carl Schurz, former secretary of the interior; George William Curtis of *Harper's Weekly*; E. L. Godkin of the *Nation*; and others—attacked Blaine as corrupt and a spoilsman. No party, declared Schurz, had any right to expect victory at the polls "without respecting that vital condition of our greatness and glory, which is honest government."

At one point it looked as if the anti-Blaine forces would lose their moral advantage. In July a Buffalo newspaper published an article telling of Cleveland's illegitimate child. This revelation created utter dismay in the reformers' ranks until they rationalized it away as an isolated transgression and one that, in any event, lay in the private rather than the public sphere.

In September the Mugwumps found further ammunition to use against Blaine—a complete, uncensored transcript of the Mulligan Letters, including items not available in 1876. One was a letter from Warren Fisher, Jr., a promoter of the Little Rock and Fort Smith, dictated to Fisher by Blaine, absolving the then Speaker of all blame in the Union Pacific loan incident. Blaine's own letter requesting Fisher to help him had ended with the incriminating phrase "burn this letter." When the Fisher letter and the others were published in the anti-Blaine papers, they confirmed the worst suspicions about Blaine's corrupt relations with the railroads.

In the end Blaine lost the election to Cleveland because the hotly contested state of New York went to the Democrats. Many observers had expected Blaine to carry New York's Irish voters and with them the state. His Catholic lineage, his anti-British attitudes, and his personal warmth and charm were all supposed to be particularly appealing to Irish-Americans. Unfortunately, he failed to reprove the disparaging "Rum, Romanism, and rebellion" charge made against the Democrats by the Reverend Samuel Burchard and consequently lost Irish votes. He had also offended many working men by appearing at "Balshazzar's Feast" in New York, a banquet given in his honor by some of the nation's best-hated "money kings." The two mistakes clearly lost him more than the 1,200 votes that gave the Empire State and the election to the Democrats.

Blaine was not finished with public life. Though his health was poor, he accepted the post of secretary of state once again when it was offered him by Benjamin Harrison in 1889. His second stint as secretary represents America's resumption of a vigorous foreign policy, now more in tune with the public mood. Blaine was especially interested in displacing Great Britain from economic leadership in Latin America, and to this end sought to create an informal "Pan-American" union with the United States as "elder sister."

Though his three years in the State Department under Harrison stand out from the low plain of nineteenth-century American diplomacy, the period was not personally fulfilling. The Blaines resided during the winters in a house close to the State Department, formerly owned by William Seward. They escaped the Washington summer heat at their home in Bar Harbor on the Maine coast. The Blaine's marriage remained happy, but tragedy struck when their eldest son, Walker, died of pneumonia at only thirty-five. Soon after, their eldest daughter, Alice, also died, and in a little over a year their second son, Emmons, was dead as well. Nor did Blaine find much satisfaction in his relations with his chief. Harrison was a distant and aloof man whose personality clashed with that of the outgoing, genial Blaine. In June 1892 Blaine resigned his post in a brief, cool letter. Harrison's acceptance was equally brief and formal. Neither man expressed any personal esteem for the other.

Blaine's health had been fast declining and he did not have many months left. The Blaines went to Bar Harbor for the summer of 1892 and then, in the fall, returned to the Seward House in Washington. Suffering from gout and Bright's disease, Blaine took to his bed. Bulletins about his health appeared in the newspapers and the faithful Blaine legion, who had worshiped the man for thirty years, gathered before his house to express their loyalty. He died on January 27, 1893, three days short of his sixty-third birthday. His life had indeed followed two paths, "one in the daylight" and "one in the dark."

21

****

******** A HISTORICAL PORTRAIT ********

Alfred T. Mahan

No single person, of course, was responsible for American expansionism at the end of the nineteenth century. The events that culminated in the war with Spain in 1898 and the acquisition of an American empire are bound up in an intricate criss-cross of forces, institutions, values, personalities, and accidental circumstances. Yet no explanation of the nation's post–Civil War outward thrust can ignore the role of a tall, balding, intellectual naval captain, Alfred Thayer Mahan.

Mahan's father was an army officer and engineering professor at the military academy at West Point when Alfred was born in 1840. If Alfred's story had been typical, he would have become an army officer himself. But Professor Mahan and his wife did not believe that a military life was desirable for their son and sent him to Columbia College in New York for a conventional education. Alfred, for his own part, had developed a fascination for the sea from his boyhood reading and defied his parents' wishes. In 1856 he convinced his local congressman to appoint him to the United States Naval Academy at Annapolis.

Acting Midshipman Mahan, with two years of college, was ahead of most of his classmates and was therefore given advanced standing at the academy. This advantage alone would have made him unpopular with his classmates, but in addition, Mahan was a reserved young man more interested in reading than in the rough games of the typical Annapolis cadet. He also had a priggish streak. Upperclassmen were expected to report lowerclassmen for infractions of the rules. However, they exempted themselves from the practice. Mahan insisted on treating his fellow seniors like everyone else, and was soon on speaking terms with few of them.

In June 1859 Mahan graduated from the academy and was assigned to the frigate *Congress* for his first long tour of sea duty. His experience on the *Congress* taught him much about ships and navies in the age of sail, knowledge that would be invaluable to him when he undertook his histories of sea power. While on station off the coast of Brazil, the crew of the *Congress* learned of the secession of the southern states and the ship quickly returned home.

Lieutenant Mahan spent most of the next four years on blockade duty off the Confederate coast. Though vital for Union victory, the duty was routine and monotonous. One event of the war stood out for Mahan, however. In December 1864, while serving with Admiral Dahlgren's squadron off Georgia, he was able to present his father's greeting to William Tecumseh Sherman, Professor Mahan's former student at "the Point," when his army reached Savannah after their march to the sea.

The end of the war was followed by the precipitous decline of the U.S. Navy. Appropriations were drastically cut and thousands of officers and men left the service. Ships were neither repaired nor replaced. By 1874, a military publication noted, the navy was "a heterogeneous collection of . . . trash."

During these years of retreat Mahan served aboard a succession of creaky vessels in Europe, the Far East, South America, and other places. In June 1872 he married Ellen Evans of New York. Like all navy wives, Mrs. Mahan was forced to accept her husband's long absences at sea, punctuated by leaves and occasional longer periods of shore duty. She was not happy with the arrangement, but she kept busy raising the Mahan children and serving as hostess when the captain was at home.

In these early postwar years Mahan was opposed to expansion and an aggressive foreign policy. During the 1884 Blaine–Cleveland presidential campaign, he thanked God that the jingoistic Blaine was not president. "If that magnetic statesman were in office," he wrote a friend, "I fancy that American diplomats would be running around in the [ships'] with lighted candles."

But American attitudes toward expansion, including Mahan's, would soon change. In 1885 Admiral Stephen Luce induced the navy to establish the United States Naval War College to help revitalize the service. This would be a sort of graduate school for commissioned naval officers where they would study naval history and tactics. Many "old sea dog" types opposed the scheme, and for its first decade the War College, located in Newport, Rhode Island, was under constant attack. But Luce prevailed and appointed Mahan to his faculty to teach naval tactics.

Mahan took most of a year off to prepare for his new task. During these months he read widely in naval and general history and took extensive notes for his forthcoming lectures. These notes his wife typed up until he had a large volume of 400 pages. The course proved a success. Mahan's own lectures at the War College were supplemented by talks of visiting scholars. One of these was the young civil service commissioner, Theodore Roosevelt, who had written a scholarly history of the naval War of 1812. The Mahan-Roosevelt encounter brought together two men who would become leaders in the new expansionism.

Despite the War College's success, its enemies managed to cut its budget and merge it with the adjacent Torpedo Station. Fortunately the emerging "new navalism" soon rescued both the War College and Mahan. In 1889 Harrison's secretary of the navy, Benjamin Tracy, induced Congress to make the War College a permanent navy installation with a new building for its own use at Newport. The supervisor of construction would be Captain Mahan.

Over the next few years, while Mahan was overseeing this project and giving lectures, he published the book that brought him fame. It was a study of how sea power had governed history during the years when Britain was establishing its overseas empire through its domination of the seas. *The Influence of Sea Power upon History, 1660–1783* made an implicit plea not only for a powerful American navy but also for colonies. The road to glory for the United States, Mahan suggested, was the route that Britain had pioneered.

By this time Mahan had become an unabashed expansionist. He had formerly believed, he later noted, that colonies required large standing armies and that these in turn made free government difficult. But his study of Britain's experience had convinced him that great empires were created by navies, not armies, and this was not incompatible with democratic rule. He had also come to believe that the British Empire had benefited the peoples it had governed and ultimately the world. Surely a similar venture by the United States would have similar benevolent results. During the early 1890s, in a succession of articles and letters to newspapers, Mahan endorsed the construction of the new "dreadnought" type battleships, American annexation of Hawaii, the conversion of the Caribbean into an American lake, the construction of an isthmian canal across Panama, and other policies that became vital parts of the expansionist platform.

In 1892 Mahan completed a sequel to his first sea power book, *The Influence of Sea Power upon the French Revolution and Empire*, which recounted the effect of navies on the momentous events in Europe between 1793 and 1812. This work was even more influential than the first. Widely praised in the United States by the advocates of a bigger navy, it also evoked a strong response elsewhere. The young, headstrong German emperor Wilhelm II considered it a masterpiece and had copies in translation placed in German naval libraries. Mahan's ideas helped to inspire the German naval expansion that so frightened and antagonized the British in the closing years of the century.

In 1893, despite the efforts of his many political friends and admirers to keep him ashore where he could pursue his scholarly studies, Captain Mahan was ordered to sea as commander of the cruiser *Chicago* under Admiral Henry Erban, head of the European station. The three-year tour of duty turned into a personal triumph. Wherever the ship docked, Mahan was feted. In England banquets, attended by members of the royal family, were given in his honor. Erban felt slighted and responded by submitting a negative report on his chief subordinate. The captain, he declared, was not interested in "ship life or matters," and he was "therefore not a good officer." Mahan protested against this evaluation, but in truth it was accurate.

The European tour was Mahan's last sea duty. He returned to the United States in 1895, and the following year retired from the navy to devote the remainder of his life to scholarship. In 1898 he returned to active duty for a short while to head the strategy board supervising naval operations in the war against Spain. The board actually had little influence on the course of events that led to the great American naval victories in the Philippines and off Cuba, but Mahan could take satisfaction in his part in the naval revival that had provided the country with the modern vessels that made the victories of Dewey and Sampson possible. In the debate over the peace Mahan was also an influential voice on the side of those who wanted to keep what America had seized from Spain.

Mahan spent his last years in New York City. He continued to lecture at the Newport War College and to write. In 1902 he was elected president of the American Historical Association, the historical guild's highest honor. Four years later, though on the retired list, he was promoted to the rank of rear admiral. In 1914 Mahan was induced by J. Franklin Jameson, a noted historian, to come to the Carnegie Institution of Washington as scholar-in-residence. This last chapter in his life did not last long. Mahan had been ill with a weak heart for some time, and on December 1, at the Washington naval hospital, he died.

The tributes and assessments quickly poured in. His friend, former president Theodore Roosevelt, called him "one of the greatest and most useful influences on American life." A foreign newspaper labeled him "the greatest naval historian of the nineteenth century." But the most pithy, and in some ways the most accurate, evaluation was one by a small-town paper: "The super-dreadnoughts are his children, and the roar of the 16″ guns are but the echoes of his voice."

******** A HISTORICAL DOCUMENT ********

Anti-Imperialism

America's outward thrust during the last years of the nineteenth century did not go unchallenged at home. A sizable portion of the American people saw it as a violation of the country's most precious traditions and a dangerous precedent. In June 1898, people of this persuasion met in Chicago and formed the Anti-Imperialist League to fight what they considered the jingoism and aggressiveness of the expansionists. The following is the core of the Anti-Imperialist League platform adopted at the League's October 1899 Chicago convention.

"We hold that the policy known as imperialism is hostile to liberty and tends toward militarism, an evil from which it has been our glory to be free. We regret that it has become necessary in the land of Washington and Lincoln to reaffirm that all men, of whatever race or color, are entitled to life, liberty, and the pursuit of happiness. We maintain that governments derive their just powers from the consent of the governed. We insist that the subjugation of any people is 'criminal aggression' and open disloyalty to the distinctive principles of our Government. . . .

"The United States have always protested against the doctrine of international law which permits the subjugation of the weak by the strong. A self-governing state cannot accept sovereignty over an unwilling people. The United States cannot act on the ancient heresy that might makes right.

"Imperialists assume that with the destruction of self-government in the Philippines by American hands, all opposition there will cease. This is a grievous error. Much as we abhor the war of 'criminal aggression' in the Philippines, greatly as we regret that the blood of Filipinos is on American hands, we more deeply resent the betrayal of American institutions at home. The real firing line is not the suburbs of Manila. The foe is of our own household. The attempt of 1861 was to divide the country. That of 1899 is to destroy its fundamental principles and noblest ideals. . . .

"We propose to contribute to the defeat of any person or party that stands for the forcible subjugation of any people. We shall oppose for reelection all who in the White House or in Congress betray American liberty in pursuit of un-American gains. . . .

"We hold, with Abraham Lincoln, that 'no man is good enough to govern another man without that man's consent. When the white man governs himself, that is self-government, but when he governs himself and also governs another man, that is more than self-government—that is despotism. . . . Those who deny freedom to others deserve it not for themselves, and under a just God cannot long retain it.'

"We cordially invite the consideration of all men and women who remain loyal to the Declaration of Independence and the Constitution of the United States."

22

★★★★★★★★★★★

★★★★★★★★ A HISTORICAL DOCUMENT ★★★★★★★★

Social Darwinism

Conservatives justified the inequalities of the social order in late-nineteenth-century America in several ways. One of the more popular was recourse to "social Darwinism," a theory that held that in human society, as in the natural world, the struggle for survival was the only way that progress was achieved. The theory was drawn from the "evolutionary" ideas of Charles Darwin, the eminent English naturalist, as spread through the writings of the English philosopher Herbert Spencer. Among Spencer's disciples in the United States, none was more forceful than William Graham Sumner, an Episcopal priest-turned-college professor, whose 1883 book, *What Social Classes Owe to Each Other*, is excerpted below.

"The humanitarians, philanthropists, and reformers, looking at the facts of life as they present themselves, find enough which is sad and unpromising in the condition of many members of society. They see wealth and poverty side by side. They note great inequality of social position and social chances. They eagerly set about the attempt to account for what they see, and to devise schemes for remedying what they do not like. In their eagerness to recommend the less fortunate classes to pity and consideration they forget all about the rights of other classes; they gloss over all the faults of the classes in question, and they exaggerate their misfortunes and their virtues. They invent new theories of property, distorting rights and perpetuating injustice. . . . When I have read certain of these discussions I have thought that it must be quite dishonest to own property, quite unjust to go one's own way and earn one's own living, and the only really admirable person was the good-for-nothing. The man who by his own effort raises himself above poverty appears, in these discussions, to be of no account. . . .

"We owe it to the other [person] to guarantee rights. Rights do not pertain to *results*, but only to *chances*. They pertain to the *conditions* of the struggle for existence, not to any of the results of it; to the *pursuit* of happiness, not to the possession of happiness. It cannot be said that each one has a right to have some property, because if one man had such a right some other man or men would be under a corresponding obligation to provide him with some property. . . .

"The only help which is generally expedient . . . is that which consists in helping a man to help himself. . . . Now, the aid which helps a man to help himself is not in the least akin to the aid which is given in charity. If alms are given, or if we 'make work' for a man, or 'give him employment,' or 'protect' him, we simply take a product from one and give it to another. If we help a man to help himself, by opening the chances around him, we put him in a position to add to the wealth of the community by putting new powers in operation to produce. . . .

97

". . . The class distinctions [in society] simply result from the different degrees of success with which men have availed themselves of the chances which were presented to them. Instead of endeavoring to redistribute the acquisitions which have been made between the existing classes, our aim should be to *increase, multiply, and extend the chances*. Such is the work of civilization. . . ."

✱✱✱✱✱✱✱✱ A HISTORICAL PORTRAIT ✱✱✱✱✱✱✱✱

William James

Few men epitomize the American spirit at its best so well as William James, the philosopher and experimental psychologist. Optimistic, tolerant, generous, liberal, practical, and forward-looking, he transformed these attitudes into a major philosophical approach that we call *pragmatism*. Though at times expressed in the technical jargon of academic philosophy, pragmatism was a distillation of the American experience of subduing a continent, creating a people, and conferring wide abundance.

William James was the grandson of a Scotch-Irish immigrant, also named William, who arrived in America in 1789 and made a fortune in business in Albany, New York. His son, Henry, was afforded the leisure of a gentleman by his father's wealth, but he rejected his father's dour Presbyterian Calvinism. Henry James the elder devoted his life to literature, conversation, social reform, and the pursuit of spiritual fulfillment. The young William, his first child after his marriage to Mary Robertson Walsh, grew up in a household where Emerson, Thoreau, Bryant, Greeley, Tennyson, Carlyle, and Mill were frequent guests, and the great theories and ideas of the age were discussed more often than the price of eggs or the best way to remove a clothing stain.

William's father was physically as well as intellectually and spiritually restless. The family never seemed to settle down anyplace. The Jameses traveled often, and William and his younger siblings, including Henry Jr., the future novelist, lived for long periods in Albany, New York, Boston, London, Paris, Berlin, Geneva, Florence, and other places. The children attended schools of many different kinds, for their father had advanced ideas about the proper nurture of young people and was constantly trying out new schemes. It was an unusually cosmopolitan experience for a young American, but it never undermined William's quintessentially American values.

When William reached adulthood he was forced to consider a profession. His father favored science; William preferred painting. For a time William studied under the artists William M. Hunt and John La Farge in Newport, but after a year concluded that he was not greatly gifted as a painter and in 1861 entered the Lawrence Scientific School at Harvard. Here he studied chemistry and physiology and in 1864 entered the Harvard Medical School. He did not earn his M.D. degree until 1869.

The delay was caused by indecisiveness and poor health. In 1865 William took nine months off to join an expedition to the Amazon region to collect plant and animal specimens. Back at Harvard, he met the young war veteran Oliver Wendell Holmes, Jr., then resuming his law studies after three years fighting the Confederates. James thought "Wendell" a "first rate article," but disagreed with his friend's overemphasis on thought. "Feeling counts," he retorted, thus announcing a principle that would remain fundamental to his philosophy throughout his life.

Another major delay in his formal education occurred soon after. James was attracted to the scientific side of medicine, but did not like bedside visits with patients and daily hospital rounds. He found the work dull and tiring, and began to suffer severe back pains. He became deeply depressed and thought at times of suicide. In April 1867 he took another leave of absence from Harvard and sailed for Europe to "take the baths" at the German and Austrian spas and immerse himself in German science to rest his troubled spirit.

The year and a half abroad neither improved his health nor resolved his career uncertainties. He returned to Cambridge and obtained his medical degree, but found it impossible to settle down as a doctor. For almost three years James drifted, still depressed and beset by physical maladies. He also began to experience fierce attacks of dread and panic. He finally achieved a psychological breakthrough when he read an essay by the French philosopher Charles Renouvier, on the freedom of the will, that cut through his despair and made him feel it was possible to mold one's life as one wished; the human being was not simply a woodchip tossed about aimlessly by the currents of the world.

James's emotional recovery coincided with a renaissance at Harvard under its new president, Charles W. Eliot, one of James's old teachers. In 1872 Eliot appointed James to an instructorship in physiology at the college, and for the next ten years James taught comparative anatomy, hygiene, and physiology to Harvard undergraduates. But he did not teach his subjects in a conventional way. By this time he had become convinced that there was no easy way to separate body from mind. His own experience had taught him that thoughts and feelings had a profound influence on bodily functions. Out of this came a growing interest in psychology, then a new subject in the college curriculum. In 1875 he offered a course on the "Relations Between Physiology and Psychology." The course was soon transferred to the department of philosophy, and in 1880 James himself joined that department.

The 1870s and 1880s were decades of growing satisfaction for James personally and professionally. In 1878 he married Alice Howe Gibbens, an intelligent, competent, and interesting Boston schoolteacher, the daughter of a country doctor. The marriage was a rare success. They had five children, four of whom lived to maturity. Alice proved a supportive, though not infinitely tolerant, wife. She had saved him from hopeless neurasthnia, he later declared. William also took great pleasure in the literary success of his brother, Henry, who during this decade achieved fame as a novelist.

During the 1880s James's major intellectual preoccupation was a psychology text he had contracted for in 1878. He did not intend to supply a mere rehash of the accepted principles, though the publisher would have been content with that. Instead, he hoped to break new ground. Writing such a work, however, proved to be a gigantic task, and *The Principles of Psychology* did not appear until 1890, when it attracted wide acclaim as a new view of the way the mind worked.

James saw the mind as essentially a tool with which the individual dealt with his or her environment. It was not some mystical entity; it had a biological basis and, like all biological appurtenances, had evolved over time. In divorcing the idea of mind from older concepts, James went so far as to declare that what we perceive as emotions are really only the biological responses—rapid pulse, thumping heart, churning stomach, sweaty palms, and so forth—that are *associated* with emotions. Some of James's readers felt that he had reduced human beings to unfeeling robots, but that was never his intention. To the end of his life he refused to accept this sort of crude materialism because it seemed deterministic, suggesting a closed universe and the impossibility of human beings changing things or mastering their own fate.

During the decade following the publication of the *Principles* James made philosophy his field, with the issue of "how we know" his special interest. Here he encountered two competing philosophical schools. The first, *rationalism*, held that we know first principles instinctively because they are emanations from God. We then ultimately deduce from these all the other aspects of reality. The second, *empiricism*, rejected deduction from first principles and held instead that all knowledge comes from observation of discrete events and phenomena. James liked the empiricists' skepticism of grandiose systems that purported to explain everything, but he was impatient with their refusal ever to generalize. Empiricism's rejection of principles left the world a buzzing confusion and seemed both cold and arid. It was from a desire to preserve the best of both theories that James evolved his pragmatism. In the process he borrowed much from his Harvard colleague, the philosopher Charles Pierce, who had made "everything is to be tested by its practical results" his philosophical guide.

James's first big philosophic project was a book on religion. He could not accept traditional religious views as the exact truth. But he also found atheism and agnosticism unacceptable because they deprived the individual of the comfort of religion. In the essays collected in *The Will to Believe* in 1897, he asserted that individuals had the right to accept any view of the universe, whether "provable" or not, that provided the emotional support they needed. James himself followed this principle. However much the scientist, for example, he was also a spiritualist who believed it possible to communicate through "mediums" with the dead.

At the end of the nineteenth century James found himself drawn into political controversy. He was a democrat who had enormous respect for the free and egalitarian institutions of his native land. He deplored the seizure of the Philippines after the Spanish-American War as a repudiation of American traditions of self-rule for all people. These views drew him into the anti-imperialist movement, which was dedicated to keeping the United States from joining the Western nations' race for empire.

James's major contribution to philosophy came in the last decade of his life, though it was foreshadowed many years earlier. In a series of lectures given in 1907 he elaborated the theory of pragmatism associated with his name. James expressed impatience at many of the age-old controversies about the "truth" of particular ideas or propositions. These would never be settled. But that was irrelevant, for what was important was not whether some concept was true in some supposedly final, ultimate way, but whether believing it *made a difference* and whether it was useful in human terms. As a Darwinian, James linked this view to the idea of an evolving universe, one that never reached a final, static form, but was perpetually open to change. Truths, then, were working hypotheses that we could use for our purposes. Critics charged that this reduced truth to personal opinion and made any view, any belief, as good as any other. James responded that it merely required that each person's view meet the test of workability, that it have "cash value." In the hands of a younger group of philosophers associated with John Dewey at the University of Chicago, pragmatism became a system called "instrumentalism," of subjecting social ideas to the scientific method.

James's last years were marked by both sunlight and shadow. His books and lectures were enormously popular and successful and he received international recognition. Frequent trips to Europe and to California, visiting professorships and lectureships, generous praise by much of the world's intellectual community, brought variety and satisfaction. Distinguished men and women from all over the Western world came to visit the Jameses in Cambridge or at their summer places in the Adirondacks and New Hampshire. His family life was happy. Alice, as always, was warm and supportive, and his children brought him pleasure. But for the last decade of his life James was afflicted with a severe heart condition; in 1909 he began to suffer serious chest pains. As a doctor, he knew how serious his condition was, but he could not relax or slow his pace. In early 1910 the Jameses sailed for Europe to visit Henry, now living permanently in England. William was sick during much of the time and the Jameses returned home in August, with William failing, and made their way to their New Hampshire summer house. On the evening of August 26 Alice recorded in her diary: "William died just before 2:30 in my arms. I was coming in with milk and saw the change. No pain at the last and no consicousness. . . . Poor Henry, poor children."

23

****

******** A HISTORICAL PORTRAIT ********

Ida Tarbell

Ida Tarbell could never decide whether she was a muckraker or a historian. Today her contributions to history are largely forgotten; we remember her only as a muckraker. She may have been, in fact, the first of the muckrakers.

Tarbell belonged to that special breed of journalists and writers who shaped the way early twentieth-century Americans perceived their society. Their exposés of corrupt municipal governments, patent medicine deception, the revolting conditions in meat-packing plants, the unscrupulous business practices of trusts, the exploitation of child workers, and the venality of the American Senate, among other issues, produced the agenda for the reform movement we call progressivism.

Ida Tarbell was born during the financial crisis of 1857 in a log cabin in northwestern Pennsylvania. Her mother, Esther, a descendant of Sir Walter Raleigh, was a schoolteacher whose own mother insisted she give up her career when she got married. Her father, Franklin, was a farmer who, at the time of his first daughter's birth, was in Iowa looking for promising land on which to settle down with his family. The panic closed the bank where the Tarbell savings were deposited and compelled Franklin to return home on foot without buying the farm, teaching to earn money as he traveled across Illinois, Indiana, and Ohio. By the time he arrived home, Ida was already eighteen months old and greeted the father she had never seen by telling him, "Go away, bad man."

Franklin Tarbell still intended to move the family to Iowa, and for the next three years he saved his money. Then came the oil strikes in Erie County and all thought of moving ceased.

With "rock oil" gushing from the ground in vast amounts, storage space was in short supply. A skilled carpenter, Franklin constructed a new kind of wooden tank that could hold over a hundred barrels of oil without seepage. By the summer of 1860 he had established a profitable shop for building such tanks near the well that gave him his first order. He also built a house adjoining the shop, and it was there that Ida and her baby brother, Will, spent the next ten years. The log cabin where she had been born was near trees, streams, and flowers; the new house was encircled by oil pits and derricks and smelled of gas. Ida was often scolded and spanked for exploring her surroundings and climbing on the derricks in the front yard. After a few months she tried to run away, but could not find the road to her grandmother's farm. Her new home made her a rebel. "This revolt," she confessed in her autobiography, "was a natural and righteous protest against having the life and home I had known, and . . . loved, taken away without explanation and a new scene, a new set of rules which I did not like, suddenly imposed." This spirit of defiance remained with her throughout her life.

Her questing and independent personality was reinforced by her family environment. Her parents were ardent antislavery Republicans who followed the Civil War closely in *Harper's Weekly, Harper's Monthly*, and the *New York Tribune*. Her earliest memory of concern for things outside her own world, as well as her first "realization of tragedy," occurred when President Lincoln died. Her father and mother sobbed on hearing the news, shut up their house, and put black crepe on all the doors. Her parents also welcomed to their home reformers and crusaders, whether prohibitionists, women's suffragists, or independent oilmen fighting Rockefeller. Her mother, who had never reconciled herself to the loss of her own teaching career, was also deeply concerned with improving the lot of the poor and hungry, and for a while felt drawn to socialism. A further boost to Ida's doubting nature came in high school when she developed a strong scientific curiosity. She was then faced with the problem of trying to reconcile her religious beliefs with the contradictions she found in studying science. In an age when only a handful of women went to college, her father and mother encouraged her to get the higher education she needed to become a biology teacher.

In 1876 Ida went to Allegheny College in nearby Meadville, Pennsylvania. Although the institution was nominally coeducational, Ida was the only girl in the freshman class. The head of the natural science department was impressed with her dedication and allowed her to use the college microscope. He also permitted her to experiment with the electrical apparatus in the laboratory. When she graduated four years later, she found that there were few opportunities for women in science and took a teaching post at the Poland Union Seminary in Ohio. There she taught foreign languages as well as geology, botany, geometry, and trigonometry—on both high school and college levels. After two tiring years that left her no time to use her beloved microscope, she left teaching and went back to her parents' house.

Though she wanted to go on to further study, her father was now in financial trouble. Standard Oil, the biggest refiner, had made an arrangement with the railroads. In exchange for all of Standard's enormous business, they would give the company a secret rebate on freight rates. This reduced Standard's overhead and allowed it to sell its oil at cut-rate prices. Standard's competitors, particularly the independents like Franklin Tarbell, could not market their oil because they could not obtain the cheap freight rates. Many oilmen simply gave in to the inevitable and sold out to the larger company. Ida's father resisted, but in 1882 he was forced out of business. "It was not the economic feature of the struggle in the Oil Region which deeply disturbed . . . me," Ida wrote many years later. "It was what it was doing to people themselves, . . . to my father and mother and their friends. It was the divided town, the suspicion and greed and bitterness and defeats and surrenders." At twenty-four, Ida was discouraged, feeling that she was faced with only two choices: marriage or becoming resident spinster in the family home. Neither appealed to her.

At this point her luck changed. Reverend T. L. Flood, publisher of a monthly magazine, offered her a job on his staff. *The Chatauquan* had a circulation of 40,000 and the right views on government, temperance, labor, monopoly, and feminism. Ida immediately accepted and moved back to Meadville, where the monthly was put out. Although she was hired on a temporary basis, she soon became a permanent staff member, doing everything from copy editing to advertising. Before long she was writing unsigned columns on current events as well. Her first byline appeared in 1886 under the title "The Arts and Industries of Cincinnati." Unfortunately Flood wanted her to stick to editing, and Ida, by now tired of the circumscribed world of western Pennsylvania, decided to resign and move to Paris. When she told the publisher she was going to France to write, he told her rudely: "You're not a writer; you'll starve."

Undaunted, in 1891 Ida and two friends left for Paris, where they took inexpensive rooms in the Latin Quarter. She went to lectures at the Sorbonne, did research at the Bibliothèque Nationale on women's role in the French Revolution, began a biography of the female revolutionary Madame Roland, and wrote columns for Pittsburgh, Chicago, and Cincinnati newspapers. She was thrilled when *Scribner's Magazine* bought one of her stories for $100. In the summer of 1892, S. S. McClure visited Paris and interviewed Tarbell. He immediately hired her to translate French newspaper articles into English and write her own stories when needed by his publishing syndicate and his new magazine. McClure was particularly interested in scientific discoveries, and Ida had a field day interviewing Pierre Janssen, the builder of the Mont Blanc observatory; Alphonse Bertillon, the inventor of a criminal identification system; and Louis Pasteur, the famous French bacteriologist. In 1893 McClure asked her to return to the United States and commissioned her to write a lengthy biography of Napoleon, to be serialized in his magazine. After her first installment appeared (the full-length biography was eventually issued in book form), McClure assigned her to do a biography of Abraham Lincoln. By 1896 the popularity of Tarbell's series on Napoleon and Lincoln had raised the magazine's circulation and helped assure its success.

By the beginning of the century the magazine had acquired a permanent staff of young and talented reporters and writers. Reform was already in the air and McClure was prepared to unleash them on the abuses that seemed to flourish everywhere. But he insisted that his staff be factual, accurate, and fluent. With the advantage of weekly, rather than daily, publication, there was no reason why journalists could not be held to high standards. McClure's reporters included Tarbell, Ray Stannard Baker, Lincoln Steffens, and William Allen White. This was the core of the influential group whom Theodore Roosevelt would soon dub the "muckrakers."

McClure knew that business monopoly was one of the problems that already troubled the American public. The huge business conglomerations frightened and confused people. The reporters thought it would be timely to pick out one industry to analyze—its origins, its growth, its strong-arm tactics, its combinations, "and so on, until it is finally absorbed into a great Trust." After a great deal of discussion the staff finally decided that they would choose the "greatest [trust] of them all—the Standard Oil Company." Tarbell was picked for the assignment, partly because of her family's experiences with Standard Oil, partly because she was such an assiduous collector of facts, and partly because Ray Baker declined the job.

In 1901 Tarbell started her research. The work was designed to be impartial, with material both favorable and critical, and Tarbell insisted that she had an open mind. "We were neither apologists nor critics," she wrote in her autobiography, "only journalists intent on discovering what had gone into the making of this most perfect of all monopolies." But as she got deeper into the project, important documents in the company's archives vanished, her father's former colleagues refused to speak to her, and she was physically threatened. One pamphlet that she tried to locate was *The Rise and Fall of the South Improvement Company*, published in 1873, that detailed how the company, under an earlier name, had conspired with railroads to get payments for each barrel of oil shipped by its competitors, and illicit information about shipments by its rivals. All the copies in circulation had abruptly disappeared. Finally Ida found one in the New York Public Library and learned how Rockefeller had actually bought the charter of the South Improvement Company to secure the enormous range of business powers granted it by the state of Pennsylvania. The only right he was not given was that of banking, and he soon rectified this by buying the National City Bank of New York.

Tarbell's additional research included interviews with the Industrial Commission, the Interstate Commerce Commission, and Henry Rogers, a Standard Oil partner. She went to services at the Euclid Avenue Baptist Church in Cleveland to get a look at Rockefeller in person, and was amused to see that he wore a skullcap to cover his baldness. The project, which took five years to complete, was published in nineteen articles in *McClure's* and then as a two-volume book in 1904. Much of what Tarbell wrote has been confirmed by more recent scholarship.

By the time the Standard Oil series concluded, Ida Tarbell was famous and sought after. She was insulted, however, at being excluded from the Periodical Publishers' Dinner, an all-male affair that McClure, Baker, and Steffens, as well as other colleagues, attended. "It is the first time . . . ," she wrote, "that the fact of petticoats has stood in my way and I am half inclined to resent it." Although she researched and wrote about the status of women and chose a career over marriage, she never became a women's rights or suffrage activist. In fact, in two separate series on women she publicly opposed giving the vote to women on the grounds that suffrage would not cure all of society's ills, as the activists claimed, and that women did not pay enough attention to the values of home and family. When pressed by feminist critics, she finally confessed her position as "a kind of instinct. It is no logic or argument. . . ."

In 1906 Tarbell helped lead a staff revolt at *McClure's* over the founder's management policies, business practices, and personal philandering. The upshot was that she, Baker, Steffens, White, and Finley Peter Dunne left *McClure's* and bought a competitor, *The American Magazine*. It was for this latter publication that she wrote her series on tariff abuses. She also shifted from a negative to a positive attitude toward business after she visited Henry Ford's factories and was impressed by his mass-production techniques, his fair wages, and his benevolent treatment of his workers. In 1914 and 1915 she wrote a series in *The American Magazine* in favor of Frederick Taylor's scientific management methods in industry. In the same year she published a series on women in *Women's Home Companion*, and this ended her full-time affiliation with *American Magazine*.

In 1916 Tarbell, dividing her time between her New York apartment and her Connecticut farm, became a free-lance writer, and continued this career until the end of her life. She served on the Women's Committee of the Council of National Defense in World War I, and as a member of President Wilson's Industrial Conference. In 1919 she covered the Paris Peace Conference and published her only novel. Throughout the 1920s she wrote on Lincoln and his family, and on Elbert H. Gary, the founder of United States Steel. She also visited Italy to observe Mussolini's regime. In 1930 she was elected the first woman member of the Authors' Club. She was a supporter of the New Deal, endorsing the National Recovery Administration and social security. She contributed a volume, *The Nationalizing of Business*, to the distinguished *History of American Life* series. In 1939 she published *All in the Day's Work: An Autobiography*. Five years later, at the age of eighty-seven, still in full possession of her mental faculties and working on *Life After Eighty*, she died of pneumonia. Ida Tarbell was buried in the Pennsylvania oil country in a cemetery in Titusville near her forebears.

24

★★★★★★★★★★★

★★★★★★★★ A HISTORICAL DOCUMENT ★★★★★★★★

The Great War

Many months before President Woodrow Wilson, Robert Lansing, Bryan's successor as secretary of state, had come to the conclusion that imperial Germany was a menace to America and to democracy. Lansing was not shy about presenting his views. In the selection below he tells the president how he perceives Germany under the Kaiser and how the United States should respond. The date of the memo is July 11, 1915, almost twenty months before the American declaration of war.

"I have come to the conclusion that the German Government is utterly hostile to all nations with democratic institutions because those who compose it see in democracy a menace to absolutism and the defeat of German ambition for world domination. Everywhere German agents are plotting and intriguing to accomplish the supreme purpose of their government.

"Only recently has the conviction come to me that democracy throughout the world is threatened. Suspicions of the vaguest sort only a few months ago have been more and more confirmed. From many sources evidence has been coming until it would be folly to close one's eyes to it.

"German agents have undoubtedly been at work in Mexico arousing anti-American feeling and holding out false hopes of support. The proof is not conclusive but is sufficient to compel belief. Germans also appear to be operating in Haiti and San Domingo and are probably doing so in other Latin American Republics.

"I think that this is being done so that this nation will have troubles in America and be unable to take part in the European War if a repetition of such outrages as the *Lusitania* sinking should require us to act. It may even go further and have in mind the possibility of a future war with this Republic in case the Allies should be defeated.

"In these circumstances the policies we adopt are vital to the future of the United States and, I firmly believe, to the welfare of mankind, for I see in the perpetuation of democracy the only hope of universal peace and progress for the world. Today German absolutism is the great menace to democracy. . . .

"The remedy seems to me to be plain. It is that Germany must not be permitted to win this war or to break even, though to prevent it this country is forced to take an active part. This ultimate necessity must be constantly in our minds in all our controversies with the belligerents. American public opinion must be prepared for the time, which may come, when we will have to cast aside our neutrality and become one of the champions of democracy.

"We must in fact risk everything rather than leave the way open for a new combination of powers, stronger and more dangerous to liberty than the Central Allies are today."

George Creel

World War II came abruptly with death from the sky over Pearl Harbor; the Civil War arrived with a bombardment of the United States fort in Charleston Harbor. Both attacks shocked the American people and united them at least temporarily behind the effort to defeat the enemy.

In 1917 war came only after two and a half years of debate that left a nation unsure of itself and its goals. Millions of Americans had little reason to love Britain or Russia, two of our chief allies; many others had strong reason to love Germany, their *Vaterland*, our chief enemy. Thousands of Americans opposed all wars; thousands more opposed all "capitalist wars." Given these facts, many influential pro-war Americans feared that the nation would be unable to mobilize itself for the hard struggle ahead. It was for this reason that on April 13, 1917, just a week after the war declaration, President Woodrow Wilson issued an executive order creating the Committee on Public Information (CPI) and appointed George Creel of Denver to head it.

Creel was a good choice, a man with the experience and the values that the task seemed to require. His father was a former Confederate officer who never got over the South's defeat and, while his wife supported the family by running a boardinghouse, slowly drank himself to death. George Creel became a journalist as a teenager and for a while published a small crusading newspaper in Kansas City. In 1909 he moved to Denver to edit first the flamboyant *Denver Post*, and then the *Rocky Mountain News*.

Creel was a full-fledged progressive who used his journalism to advance the "people's cause" against the "interests." At one point he got into trouble by recommending that eleven Colorado state senators with close ties to exploitive business groups be lynched. Creel also had liberal social views. Elected police commissioner in 1912, he applied the legal theories of the famous Denver judge, Benjamin Lindsey, to the evil of urban prostitution. Rather than arrest the women or merely drive them from the city, he organized a rehabilitation center for them, headed by a sympathetic woman.

In 1916 Creel wrote a book, *Wilson and the Issues*, that became a major item in the president's reelection effort. The work depicted Wilson as nobly struggling to avoid war, yet always determined to protect the interests of the United States. It "mightily pleased" the president and he rewarded Creel with the appointment to head the CPI.

As director of the new agency, Creel tried to avoid encouraging hysteria or abandonment of America's liberal and humane values. In March 1918 he wrote to a progressive Democrat: "I shall support every necessary measure directed to the supreme end of defeating . . . the unholy combination of autocracy, militarism, and predatory capitalism that rules Germany and threatens liberty and self-government everywhere. . . . [But] I ask and expect support only of those who believe that for the sake of political liberty and social progress, America must win this war while it consolidates at home every position won from the forces of reaction and political bigotry." Creel's hopes would be disappointed.

Even before the CPI began to beat the drums of patriotism, Americans had been gripped by a spasm of intolerance and irrational fear. Between 1914–1916, when the

United States had become a major supplier of munitions to the Allies, German agents had been active on this side of the Atlantic. Once the United States entered the war, among the unthinking, it was easy to equate the antiwar opposition of German-Americans, pacifists, and socialists with espionage. Some conservatives seized on the socialist issue to stigmatize all political views left of center, including progressivism, as anti-American. Congress encouraged the fearful mood by passing a series of repressive measures including the Espionage Act and the Trading-with-the-Enemy Act. These made aiding the enemy, obstructing military recruitment, or preaching disloyalty crimes punishable by stiff sentences. They established a Censorship Board to screen messages between United States citizens and citizens of foreign countries, and imposed severe penalties on anyone who uttered, wrote, or published "disloyal, profane, scurrilous, or abusive language about the form of government of the United States, or the Constitution of the United States, or the military or naval forces of the United States, . . . or any language intended to bring the form of government of the United States . . . into contempt, scorn, contumely, or disrepute." One of Wilson's appointees to the Censorship Board was George Creel.

A chief function of the CPI was to distribute government releases. Officials saw this as a way of keeping the public well informed, but inevitably the CPI held back as much information about the war as it disseminated. Besides this indirect censorship, the CPI laid down prohibitive guidelines for news that should not be published under any circumstances and news of dubious propriety. Though the CPI had no power to punish, its rebuke to papers that violated its guidelines was inevitably coercive and a damper on the free flow of information to the American public. Creel's interference with the free operation of the press made him the target of countless attacks. Some of these he deserved, but often he was merely the scapegoat for administration opponents who feared to attack the president himself.

Far more important than censorship was the CPI's work as a propaganda agency. Creel hoped to clarify the nation's war goals and mobilize the public to achieve them. He solicited free space from newspaper and magazine publishers and filled it with patriotic articles, advertisements for Liberty Bonds, and attacks on the "Prussianism" that would sweep the world if the Kaiser was not stopped. The CPI created a Division of Pictorial Publicity with the illustrator Charles Dana Gibson in charge. Gibson and his recruits from the art world created hundreds of posters, cartoons, and magazine illustrations depicting heroic American soldiers and sailors, patriotic American housewives, and bestial-looking German "Huns."

One of Creel's most inspired schemes was the Four-Minute Men. These were 75,000 volunteers who delivered short rousing speeches urging such patriotic acts as bond purchases, food conservation, and donation of binoculars to the navy. They laid out American war aims, explained the workings of the draft, and told their audiences how to sustain morale. They often described German atrocities against civilians in Belgium. The volunteers spoke in school auditoriums, movie theaters, and opera houses, in every language current among the polyglot American population.

Two of the CPI's most powerful allies in molding public opinion were the movie industry and academe. Anxious to demonstrate their patriotism, the movie moguls quickly offered their services to the CPI. Creel was happy to take up the offer, and during the war the CPI and Hollywood collaborated on a series of documentaries and feature films. One of these was *Our Colored Fighters*, designed to appeal to black audiences. Another was *The Kaiser, the Beast of Berlin*, a no-holds-barred anti-German attack that attracted long lines to the theaters where it played. In addition, the CPI employed stars like Mary Pickford, Douglas Fairbanks, and Theda Bara to sell Liberty Bonds.

The nation's scholars and academics lent themselves to Creel's goals. The CPI's Division of Civic and Educational Cooperation, headed by Dean Guy Stanton Ford of the University of Minnesota Graduate School, employed some of the nation's most prominent historians and social scientists to churn out hundreds of pages of war propaganda in the guise of scholarship. Like almost all the wartime propaganda, this material glorified the American cause and disparaged imperial Germany, its values, and its institutions. The division's most widely circulated pamphlet was the German-language version of *American Loyalty by Citizens of German Descent*, a work that testified to the patriotism of the German-American population. Yet much of the CPI's effort to avert ethnic bigotry within the country failed. In the end the anti-German propaganda encouraged the intolerance that was sweeping the United States.

After the war Creel defended Wilsonian internationalism and the League of Nations. He moved to San Francisco in 1926 and became a member of the city's cultural elite. During the New Deal period he held posts with the WPA and other government agencies, but he broke with Roosevelt during World War II. The president and his colleagues, he believed, were too lenient toward the enemy. In his old age Creel became an intense anticommunist. For most of his life he had tried (though not always successfully) to avoid simplistic ways of thinking. But now he lost his sense of balance and came to exemplify the intolerance his enemies had, on the whole unfairly, ascribed to him many years before when he headed the Committee on Public Information.

25

****

******** A HISTORICAL DOCUMENT ********

The "Red Scare"

More than once in our history Americans have been seized by a wave of hysteria over the danger of internal subversion. One such occasion was shortly after World War I, when the success of the Bolsheviks in Russia raised the specter of radical revolution in many Western countries.

The "red scare" of 1919–1920 was fed by the chief legal officer of the United States government, Attorney General A. Mitchell Palmer. Under Palmer, the Justice Department imprisoned thousands of suspected radicals and began deportation proceedings against those who were not citizens. In the selection below Palmer justifies his actions in terms that appealed to the intolerant mood of the day.

"Like a prairie-fire, the blaze of revolution was sweeping over every American institution of law and order a year ago. It was eating its way into the homes of the American workman, its sharp tongues of revolutionary heat were licking the altars of the churches, leaping into the belfry of the school bell, crawling into the sacred corners of American homes, seeking to replace marriage vows with libertine laws, burning up the foundations of society.

"Robbery, not war, is the ideal of communism. This has been demonstrated in Russia, Germany, and America. As a foe, the anarchist is fearless of his own life, for his creed is a fanaticism that admits no respect of any other creed. . . .

"Upon these two basic certainties, first that the 'Reds' were criminal aliens, and secondly that the American Government must prevent crime, it was decided that there could be no nice distinctions drawn between the theoretical ideals of the radicals and their actual violations of our national laws. . . .

"My information showed that communism in this country was an organization of thousands of aliens, who were direct allies of [Leon] Trotsky [a leader of the Bolshevik Revolution]. Aliens of the same misshapen caste of mind and indecencies of character . . . were making the same glittering promises of lawlessness, of criminal autocracy to Americans that they had made to the Russian peasants. . . . How the Department of Justice discovered upwards of 60,000 of these organized agitators of the Trotsky doctrine in the United States, is the confidential information upon which the Government is now sweeping the nation clean of such alien filth. . . . In my testimony before the sub-committee of the Judiciary Committee of the Senate . . . I had fully outlined the conditions threatening internal revolution in the nation that confronted us. . . .

"One of the chief incentives for the present activity of the Department of Justice against the 'Reds' has been the hope that American citizens will, themselves, become voluntary agents for us, in a vast organization for mutual defense against the sinister agitation of men and women aliens, who appear to be either in the pay or under the criminal spell of Trotsky and Lenin. . . .

"... [W]hat will become of the United States Government if these alien radicals are permitted to carry out the principles of the Communist Party as embodied in the so-called laws, aims and regulations? ... There wouldn't be any such thing left. In place of the United States Government we should have the horror and terrorism of bolshevik tyranny such as is destroying Russia now. Every scrap of radical literature demands the overthrow of our existing government. All of it demands obedience to the instincts of criminal minds, that is, to the lower appetites, material and moral. The whole purpose of communism appears to be a mass formation of the criminals of the world to overthrow the decencies of private life, to usurp property that they have not earned, to disrupt the present order of life regardless of health, sex or religious rights. By a literature that promises the wildest dreams of such low aspirations, that can occur in only the criminal minds, communism distorts our social law. ...

"These are the revolutionary tenets of Trotsky and the Communist Internationale. Their manifesto further embraces the various organizations in this country of men and women obsessed with discontent, having disorganized relations to American society. These include the I.W.W.s [Industrial Workers of the World, a radical trade union], the most radical socialists, the misguided anarchists, the agitators who oppose the limitations of unionism, the moral perverts and the hysterical neurasthenic women who abound in communism. The phraseology of their manifesto is practically the same wording as was used by the Bolsheviks for their International Communist Congress."

******** A HISTORICAL PORTRAIT ********

Edna St. Vincent Millay

My candle burns at both ends;
It will not last the night;
But ah, my foes, and oh, my
    friends—
It gives a lovely light!

This quatrain became a rallying cry for the "flaming youth" of the 1920s, young men and women who experimented with new patterns of living, drinking, dressing, and sexual expression. Its author was Edna St. Vincent Millay, and her poem caught the essence of her own tempestuous life.

Edna St. Vincent Millay was born in Rockland on the Maine coast, on February 22, 1892. The poet's mother, Cora Buzzelle Millay, was an unconventional woman in her own right and set the stage for the drama of her daughter's life. A New Englander with literary and musical inclinations, she was determined that her three daughters, Edna, Norma, and Kathleen, be given the opportunity to fulfill themselves in a way that she was unable to. "My frustration," she declared, "was their chance." In 1900 she scorned custom by divorcing her husband, Henry, a school principal, and moved to Camden, Maine, a resort town on Penobscot Bay, where she supported her children by working as a district nurse.

When her daughters were little, Cora worked only at night so that she could be with them during the day. By the time Edna was twelve, her mother began to take on "live-in" cases, which meant she was away for days or weeks at a time. Edna was made responsible for all the household chores and her sisters' upbringing. She tried to prepare nutritious meals, but sometimes when there was no money, supper would consist of milk and the wild blueberries they had just picked. The three girls washed the dishes singing Edna's composition, "I'm the Queen of the Dishpans." At night Edna would play the piano or tell her sisters stories she made up. The three girls depended on one another and were particularly affectionate and close-knit throughout their lives.

Though often absent, when she returned, Cora worked feverishly to get her house and children in order. She baked, cooked, preserved, gardened, made new clothes or mended old ones, and caught up on the girls' progress in school and music lessons. Edna remembered her childhood as extraordinarily happy. "Meseems it never rained in those days," she wrote later. The absence of a father, however, probably contributed to Edna's later distrust of men and her doubt of love's permanence, a motif that often appeared in her poetry.

At thirteen, having skipped eighth grade, Edna entered Camden High School and immediately joined the literary magazine, which published her autobiographical essay "The Newest Freshman," as well as her poems. In her senior year she became editor. When she graduated from high school she had no intention of going to college. There was little money to pay for an education, and her mother disapproved of college for creative "genius." Instead, using her typing and shorthand skills, Edna worked part-time as a secretary for tourists and spent the rest of her time keeping house for her sisters.

In 1912 Edna entered a poem about nature and survival in a poetry contest. She came in fourth. The poem was published with the others and many readers and critics wrote in claiming that Millay's work was the best in the collection. During the following summer she read it at a party at the Whitehall Inn, a large resort hotel in Camden. One of the listeners was Caroline Dow, head of the National Training School of the Young Women's Christian Association, who was so impressed that she convinced Edna to consider college and promised to obtain the necessary financial aid.

Edna spent the winter of 1913 in New York City, preparing for her entrance into Vassar College the following fall. Although she lived in the protected environment of the National Training School, she plunged into New York's cultural life. She attended the controversial Armory Show of avant-garde art, watched Sarah Bernhardt in *Camille*, and was invited to meetings, teas, and luncheons at the Poetry Society of America. She rode the double-decker New York buses with poet Sara Teasdale and explored the city with Salomon de la Selva, a young Nicaraguan poet teaching poetry at Columbia. "Recuerdo," written many years later, commemorates her trips on the Staten Island ferry and picnics with de la Selva.

Millay entered Vassar in Septem-ber 1913, four years older than most of the incoming students. Already acclaimed for her literary talents, and unusually independent and self-reliant as a result of her unsupervised childhood, she chafed at Vassar's strict rules of conduct for its young ladies. The college limited absences and cuts, required attendance at chapel, and prohibited smoking. It permitted young men on campus only on Sundays, and closely chaperoned them until they departed. "I hate this pink-and-gray college." Edna wrote to an older male friend. "They trust us with everything but men. . . . [A] man is forbidden as if he were an apple." A few months later, however, she wrote home that she was "crazy about the college." Although Edna made good use of her four years at Vassar, she broke every college rule she could. She cut classes regularly, came late to those she attended, missed chapel frequently, and smoked in a nearby cemetery. Just before her graduation she went for a car ride with some friends, and did not get back the same night. The faculty voted to suspend Millay indefinitely, forcing her to postpone her degree. This meant that she would have to miss graduation, though she had already composed the music and words for the Baccalaureate Hymn. Fortunately, the senior class circulated a petition on her behalf and the liberal president, Henry MacCracken, lifted the suspension, enabling her to graduate and attend the ceremonies.

With her B.A. in hand, Millay moved to New York in 1917, where she rented a tiny apartment in Greenwich Village. The Village had already become America's bohemia. Here lived the sculptors, the painters, the poets, the playwrights, the actors and actresses, the political radicals, and those who just wanted to escape conventional society. These people drew up their own codes of sexual and social mores. "We held the same views of literature and art," reminisced Floyd Dell, the popular Village novelist and playwright, "we agreed in hating capitalism and war. And, incidentally, of course, we agreed in disbelieving in marriage. We considered it a stupid relic of the barbaric past. . . ."

Edna was determined to find work as an actress to support her writing. She auditioned for Dell's play, *The Angel Intrudes*, then being rehearsed by the Provincetown Players, a theater group established to perform radical, controversial, and noncommercial plays. Dell was so charmed by the "slender little girl with red-gold hair" that he not only gave her that part, but others in subsequent plays. He also became the first of her many lovers and, in spite of his declarations against marriage, wanted to make his relationship with her legal and permanent. Claiming she was "nobody's own," Millay refused on the grounds that marriage would tie her to one person. Women, she insisted, should have the right to love as freely and casually as men. She was also afraid that if she married and got involved with babies and domestic responsibilities, she would not have time for her poetry. The love affairs that came after Dell were similar in pattern. They started quickly and intensely and were followed by a period of idyllic companionship. The promising beginning ended, however, in bickering and fighting, possibly fueled by Edna's fear of being hemmed in. In this stage she cast around for a new flame, before the old had been entirely extinguished.

By 1920 every Villager knew Edna St. Vincent Millay, as the "beautiful young actress at the Provincetown" or "America's leading woman poet." She brought her popular and pretty sisters and her mother down to the Village to live with her. Not only did she continue acting, but the Provincetown Players produced her own poetic drama, *Aria da Capo*, with her sister, Norma, playing the lead. Most of her income, however, came from stories and poems that she published under the pseudonym Nancy Boyd. In 1920 she met Edmund Wilson, a rising young literary critic, who fell in love with her and got her work printed in the prestigious *Vanity Fair*. In the same year Millay published her first book of sonnets, twenty poems that expressed love from a woman's viewpoint, but without the sentimentality or romanticism that usually characterized female love poetry. *A Few Figs from Thistles*, with the "burning candle" quatrain, also appeared that year and established her as the spokesperson of the convention-flaunting postwar generation. During this period Millay was burning her own candle at both ends. She was working hard, eating irregularly, getting little sleep, drinking too much, and under emotional strain from pursuing and being pursued.

That same momentous year Edna and her family moved to Cape Cod for a summer of plain living, good eating, sea breezes, and sun. Edmund Wilson came to Truro to ask her to marry him. Edna, confessing that she was worried about money and the future, for a while considered it. In the end, however, she accepted an offer from *Vanity Fair* that took her to Europe. Millay sailed for Paris on the *Rochambeau* on January 21, 1921, forsaking, at least temporarily, her family, her theatrical career, and her importuning suitors. She joined the flood of young American literary expatriates—including Hemingway, Fitzgerald, Ezra Pound, and Gertrude Stein—who believed that Europe offered a kind of creative excitement and cultural freedom missing even from Greenwich Village.

Millay spent two years in Europe traveling and writing, but she could not escape the men who found her irresistible. Not only did she have to fend off a new flock of European lovers, but Wilson appeared in Paris to resume his marriage campaign. News reached her of both her sisters' weddings, and despite her many suitors, she felt unbearably lonely. In 1922 she received an advance for a novel and used it to bring her mother to Paris to keep her company. At this point, after years of eating poorly, Edna's stomach began to trouble her. Her mother took her to England to nurse her. There she worked on her novel, ate well, and exercised both on horseback and on foot. She still felt ill, and in the winter of 1923 she and her mother returned to the United States.

Millay was living in a small apartment in the Village when she won the Pulitzer Prize for poetry, based on *Figs*, eight new sonnets, and a long poem, "The Ballad of the Harp Weaver," on the impermanence of love. The prize made her America's foremost woman poet and she was soon a celebrity whose activities were followed at every step like a movie star's. Thousands of young Americans who read about her in the gossip columns quoted her and tried to imitate her. All this notoriety exhausted her and she continued to feel sick. With gratitude, Edna accepted the invitation of a friend to visit at her country house in Croton-on-the-Hudson.

Croton was then a sort of "suburb of Washington Square" where a group of political liberals and radicals had homes, including John Reed, Max Eastman, Stuart Chase, and Doris Stevens, a militant suffragist author. It was at a party at Stevens's that Edna was reintroduced to Eugen Boissevain, a Dutch coffee and sugar importer, whose former wife had been the beautiful Inez Milholland, a lawyer and suffragist. Boissevain, now a widower, loved the company of creative people and was himself a feminist.

He and Millay fell instantly in love, and Boissevain resolved to spend the rest of his life taking care of the poet and nurturing her creativity. "Anyone can buy and sell coffee," he declared, "but anyone cannot write poetry." At last Edna had met the right man. The newspapers had a field day with the decision of a confirmed "free spirit of romance" to wed. "Has Happiness Come to Repay/Fair Edna St. Vincent Millay?" asked the title of a five-column article in the *Chicago Times*. It was subtitled "She Married As She Lived—On a Moment's Impulse." The moment's impulse lasted twenty-six years, until Boissevain's death in 1949.

Eugen's first concern was Edna's health. He took her to doctors to diagnose her fatigue and illness. When they decided an operation was necessary, he insisted she marry him before going to the hospital. They were married by a justice of the peace in Croton and then drove to New York for Edna's operation. Before she went into surgery she declared: "If I die now, I shall be immortal." After she recuperated, Eugen and Edna moved into a narrow brick house at 75½ Bedford Street, in the heart of the Village.

In November 1923 Millay appeared at a rally commemorating the seventy-fifth anniversary of the Senaca Falls Equal Rights Meeting. At the unveiling of a statue in honor of Mott, Anthony, and Stanton, she read "The Pioneer," a poem written for the occasion and dedicated to Inez Millholland. During the winter of 1924 Millay toured the United States, reading her poems to audiences who came to see what the "bohemian poetess" looked like and how many of her more scandalous poems she would read. When the tour was over, she and Eugen visited the Orient and Hawaii, returning to Bedford Street early in 1925.

On Bedford Street they were constantly sought after by admirers and friends. On May 1, 1925, the Ashcan Cats, a group of students from Barnard, including future anthropologist Margaret Mead and poet Leonie Adams, brought Millay a May basket made up of moss, wild flowers, and twigs from Bronx Park. After they placed the basket on the doorstep, they shouted: "We want Edna!" and were delighted when she opened the door, dressed in a long bathrobe. She shook hands with each of them and asked their names, which she then diligently repeated. Much as she enjoyed this sort of attention and admiration, however, she began to feel that life in New York was too hectic for her to work.

In 1925 the Boissevains bought a farm in the Berkshire foothills at Austerlitz, New York, which they named "Steepletop." Here they planned to spend the rest of their lives, Millay writing and Eugen farming and landscaping as well as cooking, cleaning, and doing the laundry. The only problem was that Steepletop was not near the sea, which they both loved. To remedy this lack, in 1933 they bought Ragged Island in Casco Bay in Maine, and spent part of every year on their island. It is obvious that this woman who epitomized the frenetic Jazz Age also had a deep yearning for tranquility.

At Steepletop Edna worked on the libretto for an opera commissioned by the Metropolitan Opera Company, with music by Deems Taylor. *The King's Henchman* premiered on February 17, 1927, before an audience glittering with celebrities from every field. Enthusiastic applause followed each act, and when the opera finally ended, the ovation lasted twenty minutes. "I thank you," responded Edna, "I love you all." Afterward critics called it "the best American opera we have ever heard," and one reviewer said she was the "young sovereign of the written word."

Later that year Edna went to Massachusetts to protest the impending execution of Sacco and Vanzetti, two Italian anarchists accused of robbery and murder. Like many other American intellectuals of the day, she believed that they were the victims of prejudice against both Italians and radicals. The execution was set for August 23, 1927, and Massachusetts Governor Alvan Fuller had earlier denied an appeal for clemency. On August 22 thousands of protesters began to gather on Boston Common. Millay and John Dos Passos led a demonstration of writers and poets. Millay was picked up by the police, thrown into a patrol wagon, and taken to a police station, where she was formally charged with "sauntering and loitering." Her husband arrived in time to bail her out. Later that day she made a personal appeal for clemency in an audience with Governor Fuller. At night she read a poem called "Justice Is Denied in Massachusetts" to a crowd in the shadow of Old North Church. Just before the execution at midnight, Millay wrote a letter to Fuller, which was hurriedly delivered to the statehouse. "There is need in Massachusetts of a great man tonight," she pleaded. "It is not yet too late for you to be that man." The electrocution took place as scheduled, and the next day Edna was fined $10 for her part in the demonstration.

Over the next ten years Edna and Eugen spent most of their time at Steepletop or Ragged Island. Edna was in poor health and probably drinking too much, but she continued to write and publish her poetry. In 1929 she was elected to the prestigious National Institute of Arts and Letters; in 1931 she received a national prize for a collection of poems. Throughout the thirties she was active at her craft and also worked on a translation from the French of Baudelaire's decadent *Flowers of Evil*. By the middle of the decade her feverish life had truly begun to catch up with her and she felt ill much of the time. In addition, although her poetry continued to sell and receive critical acclaim, reviewers began to criticize her work and her popularity diminished. In 1936 a manuscript of a play she had written was destroyed in a hotel fire on Sanibel Island. During the summer she injured the nerves of her back in an automobile accident. Her last years were full of unwelcome drama and worries. Both Edna and Eugen drank too heavily and their friends became very concerned for them.

During World War II Edna wrote nothing but propaganda poetry. She was no mere apologist for America, however, and warned that when the soldiers returned, they must beware of "the very monster which they sallied forth to conquer and quell." During the summer of 1944, weakened by years of frail health and worried about money because of her husband's financial setbacks, she had a nervous breakdown. She was confined to Doctors Hospital for a long time and could not write for two years. In August 1949 her husband died after a stroke following an operation for lung cancer. Millay started drinking relentlessly after the funeral and once again suffered a nervous collapse, spending many more months in the hospital. On her release, she resumed her writing, but she had little time left. In October 1950 she collapsed of a heart attack at Steepletop. A friend found her there the next afternoon, halfway up the stairs, a glass of wine and a page of poetry nearby. Her epitaph might have been her own beautiful lines:

Down, down, down into the
    darkness of the grave
Gently they go, the beautiful, the
    tender, the kind;
Quietly they go, the intelligent, the
    witty, the brave.
I know. But I do not approve. And I
    am not resigned.

26

****

******** A HISTORICAL DOCUMENT ********

Hoover Hits Back

Roosevelt and the New Dealers succeeded in creating a political coalition that included broad segments of the American people. They did not convince all Americans that they had found the correct formulas for national health, however. One of the outspoken dissenters was former president Herbert Hoover. Here, speaking on the eve of the Roosevelt landslide of 1936, Hoover attacks the New Deal and his opponent of four years before, and expounds the Republican philosophy of "freedom" against what he portrays as the New Deal doctrines of centralized power and "personal government."

"Through four years of experience this New Deal attack upon free institutions has emerged as the transcendent issue in America. All the men who are seeking for mastery in the world today are using the same weapons. They sing the same songs. They all promise the joys of Elysium without effort.

"But their philosophy is founded on the coercion and compulsory organization of men. True liberal government is founded on the emancipation of men. This is the same issue upon which men are imprisoned and dying in Europe right now. . . .

"I gave the warning against this philosophy of government four years ago from a heart heavy with anxiety for the future of our country. It was born from many years' experience of the forces moving in the world which would weaken the vitality of American freedom. It grew in the four years of battle as President to uphold the banner of free men.

"And that warning was based on sure ground from my knowledge of the ideas that Mr. Roosevelt and his bosom colleagues had covertly embraced despite the Democratic platform.

"Those ideas were not new. Most of them had been urged on me. . . .

"I rejected the notion of great trade monopolies and price-fixing through codes. That could only stifle the little business man by regimenting him under the big brother. That idea was born of certain American Big Businesses and grew up to be the NRA.

"I rejected the scheme of 'economic planning' to regiment and coerce the farmer. That was born of a Roman despot 1,400 years ago and grew up into the AAA.

"I refused national plans to put the government into business in competition with its citizens. That was born of Karl Marx.

"I vetoed the idea of recovery through stupendous spending to prime the pump. That was born of a British professor.

"I threw out attempts to centralize relief in Washington for politics and social experimentation. I defeated other plans to invade States' rights, to centralize power in Washington. Those ideas were born of American radicals. . . .

"I rejected all these things not only because they would not only delay recovery but because I knew that in the end they would shackle free men. . . .

"It was not until after the [1932] election that the people began to awake. Then the realization of intended tinkering with the currency drove bank depositors into the panic that greeted Mr. Roosevelt's inauguration.

"Recovery was set back for two years, and hysteria was used as the bridge to reach the goal of personal government. . . .

"The people knew now the aims of the New Deal philosophy of government.

"We propose instead leadership and authority in government within the moral and economic framework of the American system.

"We propose to hold to the Constitutional safeguards of free men.

"We propose to relieve men from fear, coercion, and spite that are inevitable in personal government.

"We propose to demobilize and decentralize all this spending upon which vast personal power is being built. We propose to amend the tax laws so as not to defeat free man and free enterprise.

"We propose to turn the whole direction of the country toward liberty, not away from it. . . .

". . . [D]o not mistake. Free government is the most difficult of all government. But it is everlastingly true that the plain people will make fewer mistakes than any group of men no matter how powerful. But free government implies vigilant thinking and courageous living and self-reliance in a people.

"Let me say to you that any measure which breaks our dikes of freedom will flood the land with misery."

✦✦✦✦✦✦✦✦ A HISTORICAL PORTRAIT ✦✦✦✦✦✦✦✦

Fiorello H. La Guardia

The New Deal was a political upheaval that resounded through the whole of America, affecting the politics of cities and states as well as the nation's. In New York, the country's largest metropolis, it was personified not by the patrician Democrat in the White House, but by a Republican of Italian-American ancestry, Fiorello H. La Guardia.

The Little Flower (his first name in Italian) was, as one of his biographers says, Brotherhood Week all by himself. His father, Achille, was a lapsed Catholic from Foggia in southern Italy; his mother, Irene Luzatto Coen, was a moderately observant Jew from Trieste on the Adriatic. Fiorello was born in New York's Greenwich Village in 1882, two years after his parents arrived in the United States. He grew up in western military posts, where his father served as army bandmaster. He always considered Arizona his native state, and throughout his career as a New York political leader wore western string ties and a high-crowned Stetson hat.

The young La Guardia imbibed his democratic political principles from an improbable source: the pages of Joseph Pulitzer's *World*. Though the paper arrived in Prescott, Arizona, almost a week late, young Fiorello avidly read its socially conscious columns and editorials and absorbed Pulitzer's sincere concern for the underdog. His years in the West were formative for La Guardia, but they ended in 1898 when Sergeant Achille La Guardia set off to fight the Spaniards, only to be struck down by the "embalmed beef" that the Quartermaster Corps served the troops. Discharged from the army as unfit for service, Achille took his family to Trieste, where they moved in with Irene's widowed mother. There, in the Italian-speaking part of Austria-Hungary, and later in Budapest, Fiorello got a job as a U.S. consular representative and learned seven languages.

La Guardia returned to the United States in 1906 and for a while worked as an interpreter for the immigration service at Ellis Island. He went to night law school and opened a law office in New York. The experience did not enhance his views of lawyers or judges. The ones he met were invariably associated with Tammany Hall, the New York Democratic machine, and were invariably dishonest, ignorant, or stupid. La Guardia himself stayed free of the machine and its corrupting patronage by establishing ties with the Italian-Jewish garment worker unions. In 1909–1910 he helped to settle a major garment industry strike and received much favorable attention.

In 1914 Fiorello, a Republican out of hatred for Tammany, received his party's nomination for Congress. The choice meant little; no Republican had ever won in the 14th District, and the weak Republican organization gave him no help. He lost, but his impressive showing won him appointment as deputy state attorney general by the Republican governor. Two years later he won the same congressional seat, largely through the votes of Italian-Americans who resented the Irish-dominated Democratic machine and wanted to see one of their own in office.

The first Italian-American ever to sit in Congress, La Guardia arrived in Washington in time to vote for war against Germany and Austria-Hungary. During the war the young congressman took a leave and joined the air corps. He was sent to Italy to learn to fly and to establish liaison with America's Italian ally. La Guardia never became a very good pilot, but he utterly charmed the Italians with his American bumptiousness and exuberance. He returned home a decorated hero in 1918, in time to win reelection for a second term, but then resigned to run successfully for president of the New York Board of Alderman. In 1921 he sought the Republican nomination for mayor but was defeated. The following year, however, he was returned to Congress from a new Manhattan district, and then reelected to three more terms.

La Guardia was a political maverick in every way. At a time when the country as a whole had become conservative, he retained his skepticism of big business and joined with Senator George Norris of Nebraska to prevent sale of the Muscle Shoals waterpower site to private utility companies. When the country turned isolationist, he fought for the League of Nations. When most Americans were still convinced that Prohibition was a "noble experiment," he sought to have the Volstead Act repealed. La Guardia was considered a troublemaker by his colleagues. The practice of the day allowed congressmen to introduce bills on Wednesdays to benefit constituents under "unanimous consent." It was understood that these would not be challenged. La Guardia had no patience with such boondoggles at the taxpayers' expense and regularly raised objections, thereby forcing a vote. He did not endear himself to his fellow representatives.

During the boom years of the 1920s men like Norris, Robert La Follette, and La Guardia were ignored. Though he served seven terms in Congress, La Guardia never received coveted committee chairmanships, and never was entirely happy with his job in Washington. In 1929 he ran for mayor of New York against the Democratic incumbent, Jimmy Walker. Walker spent more time in nightclubs than in his City Hall office. He was a heavy drinker and a womanizer who had left his wife for a showgirl mistress. He was also politically corrupt. But he suited the devil-may-care spirit of the Jazz Age, and he swamped the gadfly little congressman by almost half a million votes.

The Crash and the Depression abruptly changed the fortunes of the country's political insurgents. In the liberal Congress elected in 1930 La Guardia joined with western progressives to push through important legislation. He jointly sponsored the Norris–La Guardia Anti-Injunction Act outlawing "yellow-dog" contracts (agreements by employees, signed as conditions of employment, not to join unions) and forbidding federal court injunctions in labor disputes except when they threatened to become violent. The new law eliminated a major weapon that management had for years wielded against organized labor.

The Depression irreparably tarnished the luster of "Beau James," the playboy mayor of New York. In 1931 a commission under the patrician judge Samuel Seabury revealed Mayor Walker as an unvarnished crook who had taken thousands from people doing business with the city. The mayor had stored $1 million of his illegal gains in a safety deposit box. When the Seabury investigation finished its work, Walker abruptly resigned and sailed off to Europe.

Walker was gone, but Tammany remained. To challenge the machine, the good-government forces, composed primarily of upper-middle-class professionals and business leaders, organized a Fusion party. Their natural candidate was Seabury himself, but the judge, anxious to preserve the objectivity of his continuing investigation, refused to run. Seabury instead endorsed La Guardia, who also received the support of the New York City Republicans and of the president, Franklin Roosevelt. Though a Democrat, Roosevelt liked La Guardia and despised Tammany.

La Guardia won with a 250,000-vote majority. On January 1, 1934, in the oak-paneled study of Judge Seabury's luxurious Upper East Side townhouse, the Little Flower took the oath as ninety-ninth mayor of New York.

His first task was to save the city from bankruptcy. New York, like almost all American cities in this the fifth year of the Great Depression, confronted intolerable burdens with drastically reduced means. A million unemployed people depended on the city Department of Public Welfare for food and shelter, but the city was broke. Five hundred million dollars of short-term city obligations were past due, and the bankers would not lend New York another dime. As the new mayor began his term, over 140,000 city teachers, firefighters, police, and sanitation workers faced the prospect of payless paydays.

La Guardia got the state legislature to grant the city fiscal autonomy and allow it to consolidate departments to cut expenses. The arrangement reassured the bankers, and New York was able to borrow again at reasonable rates. The mayor's friendship with FDR also paid off. Federal money soon began to flow into the city's coffers.

With the financial crisis past, La Guardia could devote his energies to reform. The Little Flower was the best mayor the city ever had. He was compassionate, dynamic, honest, candid, amusing, and effective. He made it clear right off who was boss. "In this administration," he told the Tammany-dominated Board of Aldermen, "I am the majority." He rejected all patronage appointments, even of Fusionists who had worked for his election. Merit alone counted. There was not, he said, "a Republican or a Democratic way to collect garbage." His appointees to high city office were almost invariably the top people in their field, and he never let them relax their vigilance. On one occasion he telephoned his sanitation commissioner at 3 A.M. to find out if he had a snow-alarm plan in place. "Sure," the startled official replied. "I'm called as soon as the first flake falls." "Wonderful," the mayor responded. "Stick your head out of the window." The commissioner did; there was a raging blizzard under way. Like other officials who committed boners, the commissioner got a polished sheep shank as a trophy.

La Guardia was a ruthless anti-vice and anti–crime crusader. He cracked down on illegal gambling and, to the dismay of some, drove burlesque from the city. He imprisoned hoodlums who preyed on legitimate business people, and he supported the efforts of New York's crusading district attorney, Thomas Dewey, to break the power of racketeers. He told the city police at one point: "I want you to put so much fear into the heart of every crook in New York that when he sees a cop he'll tip his hat."

The mayor carried into his office the same sensitive social conscience he had shown as a congressman.

La Guardia procured millions of dollars of federal money for public housing to replace the most squalid of New York's slums. During the bitterly cold winter of 1934 he opened the city's armories to the homeless and heatless. He established a large covered market in the city for the hundreds of pushcart peddlers who had to face inclement weather and police harassment. He was also a master builder. He and his parks commissioner, Robert Moses, often with federal aid, built dozens of bridges, scores of schools, hundreds of playgrounds and parks, and the city's two major airports.

The mayor was a newspaper reporter's delight. He was funny. When, in 1945, New York newspaper deliverers went on strike, the mayor turned up at the city's municipal radio station to read the comics over the air to the city's children. It was a memorable performance. "Ahh! what do we have here? The gardener! Stabbed! . . . But Dick Tracy is on the trail!" When the city was legally forced to allow the pro-Nazi German-American Bund to stage a rally in Madison Square Garden, the mayor assigned only Jewish policemen to maintain order. When Commissioner Moses had tried the tactic of resigning to force concessions from him once too often, the mayor had a pad of forms printed reading: "I, Robert Moses, do hereby resign as _____, effective _____." The next time Moses swept into his office with a resignation threat, La Guardia handed him the pad and said: "Here, just fill in the blanks." La Guardia was theatrical. He was always at the scene of the crime, the fire, or the disaster—often wearing the hat of the city service in charge.

La Guardia's three terms as mayor (1934–1946) coincided almost exactly with FDR's reign. The two political leaders worked closely together. La Guardia seldom came back from Washington without some spoils for the city in his pocket. Roosevelt could always count on Fiorello to use his popularity to win votes for New Deal measures in Congress and for himself every four years at the polls. FDR was also grateful for the mayor's effective neutralizing of Tammany, always an embarrassment to him. In many ways, what La Guardia accomplished in New York was a little New Deal that helped to bind the city's voters to the new Democratic coalition.

By the time his third term ended, La Guardia had lost interest in the mayor's office. After FDR died in 1945, his successor, Harry Truman, appointed La Guardia head of the United Nations Relief and Rehabilitation Administration, the agency for rescuing and resettling the millions of Europeans made homeless by the war. The work was not congenial, and he soon resigned. Though only sixty-three, his health was now poor. In the spring of 1947 his severe back pain was diagnosed as cancer of the pancreas, a virtually incurable disease.

On September 20 Fiorello La Guardia died. When they opened his safety deposit box, they found $8,000 in war bonds. The only other asset he could pass along to his wife, Marie, and their two adopted children was a heavily mortgaged modest house in the Bronx. The Little Flower had lived the exemplary life he preached after all!

27

******** A HISTORICAL DOCUMENT ********

Price Controls

The first economic effect of the outbreak of war in December 1941 was to put every-one back to work. Before long, however, the flood of federal war spending began to produce enormous pressures on prices. By mid-1942 prices and wages were being closely regulated by the government through the Office of Price Administration to prevent runaway inflation.

Not every American accepted the regimentation that this system entailed. One of the objectors was John L. Lewis, president of the powerful United Mine Work-ers' Union. Lewis believed that his men's wages had been fixed *after* prices had already risen, thus depriving them of considerable income. On the other hand, he charged, nothing was being done to limit business profits. Roosevelt responded to Lewis's attempt to scuttle price-and-wage controls by the Executive Order below, issued in early April 1943. (His proposal, at the end of the order, to increase taxes, was never adopted by Congress.)

"The Executive order I have signed today is a hold-the-line order.

"To hold the line we cannot tolerate further increases in prices affecting the cost of living or further increases in general wage or salary rates except where clearly necessary to correct substandard living conditions. The only way to hold the line is to stop trying to find justifications for not holding it here or not holding it there. . . .

"All items affecting the cost of living are to be brought under control. No fur-ther price increases are to be sanctioned unless imperatively required by law, . . . any further inducements to maintain or increase production must not be allowed to dis-turb the present price levels; such further inducements, whether they take the form of support prices or subsidies, must not be allowed to increase prices to con-sumers. . . .

"On the wage front the directions in the order are equally clear and specific.

"There are to be no further increases in wage rates or salary scales beyond the Little Steel formula [a 15 percent increase authorized in 1942], except where clearly necessary to correct substandards of living. Reclassifications and promotions must not be permitted to affect the general level of production costs or to justify price increases or to forestall price reductions. . . .

"Some groups have been urging increased prices for farmers on the ground that wage earners have unduly profited. Other groups have been urging increased wages on the ground that farmers have unduly profited. A continuance of this conflict will not only cause inflation but will breed disunity at a time when unity is essential. . . .

"We cannot stop inflation solely by wage and price ceilings. We cannot stop it solely by rationing. To complete the job Congress must act to hold in check the excess purchasing power. We must be prepared to tax ourselves more—to spend less and save more. The details of new fiscal legislation must be worked out by the appropriate committees of the House and of the Senate. The executive department stands ready to submit suggestions whenever the committees desire."

******** A Historical Portrait ********

George S. Patton

General George S. Patton once wrote: "War is very simple, direct and ruthless. It takes a simple, direct and ruthless man to wage war." Everyone who knew Patton recognized that he was describing himself.

Patton was destined to be a soldier. One of his ancestors had been a Revolutionary War general; his grandfather, the first George Patton, had commanded a regiment of Virginia infantry during the Civil War and had died of battle wounds in 1864. His father attended the Virginia Military Institute (VMI), though he became a California lawyer and politician rather than a regular army officer. As a child, George was fascinated by military history and military heroes and read about them voraciously while growing up on his father's ranch near Pasadena. He eventually developed the strange sense that he had been a soldier in many previous incarnations—with Caesar in Gaul, with the English at Crécy, and with Napoleon at Jena and Austerlitz.

The young Patton spent his childhood riding horses and learning the classics by heart. In 1904 he entered West Point. Though bright—even intellectual—he was poor in mathematics and took five years to graduate, and then only in the middle of the class. Fortunately, he had money, both through his own family and through his wife, Beatrice Ayer, a New England heiress, and this would help the young second lieutenant's army career despite his undistinguished record at "the Point." While other young officers in the peacetime army were forced to get ahead on their merits, Lieutenant Patton entertained lavishly and often provided his superiors with mounts from his stable of thoroughbreds.

But Patton had more than generous hospitality to offer. He was well-read, literate, and charming. He was also colorful and impetuous. In 1916 he served as aide to John ("Black Jack") Pershing, commander of the army expedition sent into northern Mexico to capture Pancho Villa, and attracted wide attention by killing three of Villa's bodyguards in a Wild West–type shootout.

Patton liked to dress the part of military hero. Tall and erect, he wore high, shiny cavalry boots, starched cavalry breeches, a well-tailored khaki wool shirt, and a tie neatly tucked into his shirt between the second and third buttons. Strapped to his hips in open holsters, he carried two pearl-handled revolvers.

In 1917 Patton fought with the American Expeditionary Force in France in a new military branch, the tank corps. He won several medals, and was promoted to the rank of colonel, but was severely wounded before the final drive against the Germans. He returned to the boredom of peacetime army service in 1919, and during the next twenty years occupied himself largely with polo, riding, writing articles on the art of war for military journals, and attending every army school available. During the late 1930s he attracted the attention of George C. Marshall, the army deputy chief of staff.

Marshall regarded Patton as hot-tempered and insubordinate, but also as brave and aggressive. When America began to rearm to meet the growing German and Japanese threats, he saved Patton from oblivion by assigning him a prominent role in the revival of the army's tank force.

When war broke out Marshall gave Patton command of the First Armored Corps, and in October 1942 he and his men landed in North Africa to wrest the region from the Vichy French and their German masters. Patton's own men, though green and half-trained, fought well. But other American troops, pitted against the veterans of Erwin Rommel's Afrika Korps, were whipped badly at Kasserine Pass in Tunisia. Hoping to restore morale, General Dwight Eisenhower, in overall command of the British-American forces, sent Patton to the Tunisian front. He performed as expected. Taking command from his beaten predecessor, he clamped down on the lax practices previously allowed. Because too many officers were reporting late to duty each morning, he closed the officers' mess at 7:30 A.M. He also insisted that all personnel under his command, including the nurses, wear their steel helmets at all times. Patton did not leave compliance to chance. He personally gathered up violators and, after chewing them out en masse, told them they could either pay a $25 fine or be court-martialed. It was even rumored that he peeked into unit latrines to see if men answering the call of nature did so with their helmets firmly on their heads. Patton's tactics were not always appreciated, but they were effective in restoring morale and infusing fighting spirit into the Tunisian front troops.

In July 1943 Patton led the American forces in the invasion of Sicily from North Africa. His superior in the campaign was British Field Marshal Bernard Montgomery, a cautious man whose indecisiveness angered and frustrated the American. Patton's pent-up rage boiled over in August when, on a series of visits to Sicilian military hospitals, he slapped and kicked several American soldiers awaiting evacuation for what he considered malingering and cowardice. Eisenhower forced Patton to apologize when he got wind of these incidents, but he tried to keep them from the American people. In November, however, the story was leaked by the radio commentator Drew Pearson and produced a storm of public outrage. Americans who felt that citizen-soldiers of a democracy should not be abused by their officers demanded that Patton be relieved of command. Eisenhower thought Patton too good a soldier and refused, but he also denied Patton the coveted command of the great cross-Channel invasion of France being prepared for 1944.

In March 1944 Patton was assigned to command the U.S. Third Army in England as a subordinate of Omar Bradley, the American general in charge of the invasion. He and his men did not land on the beaches of Normandy on D-Day, June 6, 1944, but arrived weeks later, when the Anglo-American forces were penned up in the Cotentin Peninsula, unable to break out of the pocket and sweep south and east to destroy the Nazis and liberate Europe. On August 1 Patton's tanks punched through the German line at Avranches and burst out into open country. The Third Army rolled up the enemy into Brittany to the west and simultaneously sliced through the German lines to the south and east. The triple-pronged tactic was probably a mistake. Though made worse by the caution and tardiness of the British and Canadians on the eastern end of the Normandy front, the thrust into Brittany slowed the American advance eastward and prevented the encirclement at Falaise of most of the German army in France.

By mid-September Patton's army had dashed to the east as far as the Franco-German border, but then ground to a halt for lack of supplies and gasoline, much of which had been commandeered by Montgomery for *his* drive eastward. Patton was forced to mark time while the Germans themselves prepared a counterblow. At this point—if the supplies had been available and if Bradley and Eisenhower had given him the go-ahead signal—the war could probably have been quickly won. Instead, just before Christmas, having squeezed every available man, gun, tank, and plane, from their depleted resources, the Germans attacked the Americans in the Ardennes Forest.

The Battle of the Bulge was Germany's last gasp on the Western Front, but it produced a near disaster for the American army. The blow fell on General Courtney Hodges's First Army, which reeled back fifty miles and threatened to crack. At Bastogne 18,000 Americans were surrounded by the German forces. They refused to surrender, though greatly outnumbered. Eisenhower called on Patton for help, scarcely believing he could turn his Third Army, oriented eastward toward Germany, northward in time to aid Hodges and save the besieged American troops. But Patton shifted direction in a few days and launched a powerful counterattack against the Germans from the south that lifted the Bastogne siege and broke the Wehrmacht's offensive.

This was the last major military effort the Germans were capable of. They were now too exhausted by five years of war against half the world to continue more than a token fight. By March 1945 Patton and his colleagues had driven to the Rhine. Soon after, the Anglo-American troops were slicing through Germany virtually without opposition, while the Russians, coming from the opposite direction, were steam-rolling over the few ill-equipped troops the Germans could still muster. Patton was one of those American officers who hoped that American troops could drive on to Czechoslovakia and exclude the Russians. But on April 16 he was ordered to turn south to prevent the Nazis from retreating to a supposed "redoubt" in the mountains, where, it was feared, they would hold out to the bitter end. In the end the Soviets liberated the Czechs from Nazi control and ultimately made the country into a Soviet satellite.

The Third Army's last day of fighting was May 6, 1945. It was also George Patton's. Following the German surrender Patton was placed in charge of the program in Bavaria to uncover and punish ex-Nazi leaders, but he was now convinced that the Russians were a greater danger to America and urged a German-American alliance to drive the Russians back across the Soviet border. It is not surprising that the Bavarian denazification program was a conspicuous failure. Patton was soon at the eye of a storm over his seemingly pro-Nazi position, and shortly after was removed from his command and placed in charge of a largely paper army as punishment.

In December, scarcely six months after the war's end, Patton suffered a broken neck in an automobile accident. Twelve days later, at the army hospital at Heidelberg, he died of a blood clot on the lungs. He was buried at the big American military cemetery at Hamm in Luxembourg, alongside 6,000 other men of the Third Army that had done so much to destroy the power of Hitler's savage empire.

28

****

******** A HISTORICAL DOCUMENT ********

Joe McCarthy

The career of Senator Joseph R. McCarthy of Wisconsin was a Cold War artifact. McCarthy was an undistinguished member of the upper house faced with a stiff fight for reelection when he happened on the anti-Communist issue in 1950. Thereafter, he became a power in the land, winning reelection handily in 1952, and striking fear into the hearts of his political enemies by his grip on the imaginations and loyalties of millions of Americans. The following is the heart of McCarthy's famous Wheeling, West Virginia, Lincoln Day speech of February 1950 wherein he first broached the issue of "treason" in high places.

"Six years ago, at the time of the first conference to map out the peace—Dumbarton Oaks—there was within the Soviet orbit 180,000,000 people. Lined up on the antitotalitarian side there were in the world at that time roughly 1,625,000,000 people. Today, only 6 years later, there are 800,000,000 people under the absolute domination of Soviet Russia—an increase of over 400 percent. On our side, the figure has shrunk to around 500,000,000. In other words, in less than 6 years the odds have changed from 9 to 1 in our favor to 8 to 5 against us. This indicates the swiftness of the tempo of Communist victories and American defeats in the cold war. As one of our outstanding figures once said, 'When a great democracy is destroyed, it will not be because of enemies from without, but rather because of enemies from within.'

"The truth of the statement is becoming terrifyingly clear as we see the country losing each day on every front. . . .

"The reason why we find ourselves in a position of impotency is not because our only powerful potential enemy has sent men to invade our shores, but rather because of the traitorous actions of those who have been so well treated by this Nation. It has not been the less fortunate or members of minority groups who have been selling this Nation out, but rather those who have had all the benefits that the wealthiest nation on earth has had to offer—the finest homes, the finest college education, and the finest jobs in Government we can give.

"This is glaringly true in the State Department. There the bright young men who are born with silver spoons in their mouths are the ones who have been worst. . . .

"When Chiang Kai-shek was fighting our war, the State Department had in China a young man named John S. Service. His task, obviously, was not to work for the communization of China. Strangely, however, he sent official reports back to the State Department urging that we torpedo our ally Chiang Kai-shek and stating, in effect, that communism was the best hope of China.

"Later, this man—John Service—was picked up by the Federal Bureau of Investigation for turning over to the Communists secret State Department information.

Strangely, however, he was never prosecuted. However, Joseph Grew, the Under Secretary of State, who insisted on his prosecution, was forced to resign. Two days after Grew's successor, Dean Acheson, took over as Under Secretary of State, this man— John Service . . . was not only reinstated . . . but promoted. . . .

"Then there was a Mrs. Mary Jane Kenny, from the Board of Economic Warfare . . . , who was named in an FBI report and in a House committee report as a courier for the Communist Party while working for the Government. And where do you think Mrs. Kenny is—she is now an editor in the United Nations Document Bureau.

"This, ladies and gentlemen, gives you somewhat of a picture of the type of individuals who have been helping to shape our foreign policy. In my opinion the State Department . . . is thoroughly infested with Communists.

"I have in my hand 57 cases of individuals who would appear to be either card-carrying members or certainly loyal to the Communist Party, but who nevertheless are still helping to shape our foreign policy. . . .

"As you know, very recently the Secretary of State proclaimed his loyalty to a man [Alger Hiss] guilty of what has always been considered the most abominable of all crimes—of being a traitor to the people who gave him a position of great trust. The Secretary of State in attempting to justify his continued devotion to the man who sold out the Christian world to the atheistic world, referred to Christ's Sermon on the Mount as a justification and reason therefore, and the reaction of the American people to this would have made the heart of Abraham Lincoln happy.

"When this pompous diplomat in striped pants, with a phony British accent, proclaimed to the American people that Christ on the Mount endorsed communism, high treason, and betrayal of a sacred trust, the blasphemy was so great that it awakened the indignation of the American people.

"He has lighted the spark which is resulting in a moral uprising and will end only when the whole sorry mess of twisted, warped thinkers are swept from the national scene so that we may have a new birth of national honesty and decency in Government."

******** A HISTORICAL PORTRAIT ********

Jack Kerouac

Jean-Louis ("Jack") Kerouac would be a hero to young rebels trying to escape the stifling conformity of the 1950s. He was also a "mamma's boy" who invariably returned from his misadventures to the safety and comfort of Gabrielle Lévesque Kerouac ("Mémêre").

Jack Kerouac always believed that his ancestors were noble Celts from Cornwall who later settled in France. The truth is more prosaic. Jack's parents, Leo and Gabrielle, were both born in Quebec of peasant stock and emigrated with their families to New England as small children. They were part of the flood of French Canadians who crossed the U.S. border seeking better livelihoods than afforded by the thin soils of the St. Lawrence Valley. When Jack was born in 1922 his parents were living in the old mill town of Lowell, Massachusetts, where Leo ran a print shop.

The three formative influences of Jack's childhood and youth were the death of his older brother, Gerard, when Jack was four, his discovery of the novels of Thomas Wolfe when he was fifteen, and football at Lowell High School. Gerard's tender, long-suffering character left his little brother with an image of saintly purity that would always attract one pole of his personality. Wolfe's sprawling, disorderly style would be Jack's literary inspiration. Varsity football at Lowell High in his teens would be his ticket of escape from the narrow world of immigrant Massachusetts.

In 1939 Columbia University offered Kerouac a football scholarship, and he arrived in New York in the fall to attend Horace Mann, a Columbia-affiliated prep school, to make up deficient academic credits and put on some weight. Kerouac's college football career was short-lived. In 1940 he played for the Columbia freshman squad but broke his leg and spent the rest of the year on campus in a cast. When he returned to school the following September he played briefly for the varsity, but quit the team when Coach Lou Little relegated him to a line position. Meanwhile, the United States had entered World War II, and Kerouac joined the merchant marine as a cook's galley helper and went on one trip to Greenland. He returned for a brief stint at Columbia and then quit for good. In early 1943 he was inducted into the navy but was discharged for psychiatric reasons: He could not obey orders.

Kerouac learned little from Columbia, but New York would become a major focus of his life. In 1943 the elder Kerouacs moved to New York, where Leo and Mémêre both got jobs. Jack divided his time between their apartment in Queens and that of Edie Parker, an attractive art student from Michigan, who lived in the Columbia neighborhood. At Edie's he met a crowd of young bohemians, including Lucian Carr, a Columbia freshman from St. Louis, and his friend, Allen Ginsberg, another Columbia student from Paterson, New Jersey. Through Carr, Kerouac also met an older man, William Burroughs, who, like Ginsberg, was physically attracted to Carr.

His new friends were different from anyone Kerouac had encountered before. They were cultural rebels with a streak of surrealism in their nature. On a visit to Burroughs's Greenwich Village apartment, Carr, imitating André Gide's *acte gratuit*, chewed up a beer glass. To continue the game, host Burroughs served his guests a plateful of razor blades. Burroughs also introduced Kerouac to Oswald Spengler's celebration of Western civilization's decay, *The Decline of the West*. Nineteen forty-five was also the year that Jack married Edie (the marriage was brief and unhappy); started to take Benzedrine, a powerful stimulant; and discovered Bop, the new, "cool" form of jazz that black musicians such as Dizzy Gillespie, Charlie Parker, Miles Davis, and Thelonious Monk were beginning to play in New York. It was from the "hipster" fans of Bop—young people who despised the "square world" of postwar America—that Kerouac and his friends borrowed the term "beat" to describe their cultural stance.

Toward the end of that momentous year Leo Kerouac was diagnosed as having stomach cancer. Jack came back to Queens to help his mother nurse him. His father's death in May 1946 plunged Jack into gloom, but shortly after he began to write *The Town and the City*, his first novel. An even more important event of the first full postwar year was Jack's meeting with Neal Cassady, a young man who came to represent heroic freedom and inspired the book that made Kerouac famous.

Cassady was essentially a juvenile delinquent. He had been raised by a wino father in a Denver flophouse. He began to steal cars at fourteen, and by the time he reached twenty had stolen over 500. After reform school in New Mexico he decided that he wanted to write and came to New York in the fall of 1946, determined to enter Columbia.

To Kerouac, Cassady represented the vital life force and liberation from conventional morality. Jack admired his friend's sexual freedom, his western openness, his physical fearlessness. He seemed a "mad genius of jails and raw power." The two planned a car trip west together, but then, in March, Cassady suddenly returned to Denver with his sixteen-year-old wife and a stolen typewriter. That summer both Kerouac and Ginsberg turned up in Denver. The visit with Cassady was not a success, and Kerouac went on to San Francisco after a few weeks for his first stay of many in that lively, creative city. In July he returned to Mémère in Queens, finished his 1,100-page novel, and met John Clellon Holmes, another aspiring writer. The two young men got along well, and it was in a discussion of their generation that Kerouac would remark, "I guess you can call us a beat generation," one weary "with all the forms, all the conventions." Holmes later wrote a novel about Kerouac and "the Beats" called *Go*.

While *The Town and the City* made the rounds of the publishers, Kerouac took courses in literature at the New School and began a novel about a long-distance car trip. In October Cassady turned up in New York with a brand-new silver-colored Hudson Hornet, and he and Kerouac set off on a marathon drive that took them south to visit Burroughs in Louisiana, across Texas to Tucson, and on to San Francisco. The two young men hurtled across the landscape of fifties America, exhilarated by the sheer joy of moving fast. The impressions collected on this trip, when merged with the earlier car manuscript, became the building blocks of Kerouac's most famous novel, *On the Road*.

By the mid-1950s, in isolated pockets across America, young men and women were declaring their independence of their society's conventionality and timidity. Few of them were "creative." Most were merely consumers of culture, but this culture was intensely antagonistic to middle-class fifties values. "Beatniks" sought a particular personal style. They assumed a "natural" look. They dressed in working-class style: jeans, open-necked plaid shirts, workshoes. They led freer sex lives; they often smoked marijuana; they listened to Bop; they struck poses of personal "coolness"— uninvolvement—including indifference to politics.

There were also more creative Beats. In New York, Los Angeles, and especially San Francisco, small clusters of young, cool poets and novelists gathered together to provide mutual support for their writing. In San Francisco, a refuge for mavericks and bohemians ever since Gold Rush days, the Beat poets reached a critical mass under the aegis of a former Chicagoan, Kenneth Rexroth, and Lawrence Ferlinghetti, a San Francisco poet who ran a combined bookstore–publishing house called City Lights that became a haven for the city's Beats. Both Kerouac and Ginsberg were in the Bay Area in October 1955, just in time to be included in a Rexroth-sponsored poetry reading at the Six Gallery in an old San Francisco garage. Jack himself was only a spectator, but it was here that Ginsberg first read his long poem "Howl," a work that became the anthem of the cultural left for a generation and made Ginsberg famous.

Jack was soon to make his own very large literary splash. In September 1957 Viking Press published *On the Road* to rave reviews in *The New York Times* and other leading newspapers and magazines. Written on a continuous roll of typewriter paper in a twenty-day burst of creative energy fueled by oceans of coffee, the novel recounted the adventures of "Dean Moriarty" and "Sal Paradise" as they rolled frenetically across the continent in Moriarty's tail-finned behemoth, drinking in the essence of American vitality. Soon after, following articles on them in *Harper's Bazaar, The New York Times, Evergreen Review*, the *Nation*, and other publications, the Beats became culture heroes to the rebellious young and curiosities to their conventional elders of fifties America.

Kerouac spent much of the remaining 1950s as a restless wanderer shuttling among New York, San Francisco, North Carolina, Mexico, Florida, Long Island, and Tangier in Morocco. He was often in the company of Cassady, Ginsberg, Burroughs, or one of the new Beat poets. At least half the time he stayed with Mémère in several different places. Kerouac became a devotee of Zen Buddhism and wrote about his Zen friend Gary Snyder in *The Dharma Bums*, a book finished in ten mammoth typing sessions. He wrote a flock of other works in the 1950s and early 1960s, but few were taken seriously by the critics.

As Kerouac's stock fell, Allen Ginsberg's rose. Ginsberg became a prophet who, as the sixties unfolded, adapted to the new political rebelliousness of the young. Unlike Kerouac, who grew more conservative and misanthropic as he got older, Ginsberg moved politically left and became a gentle, nonviolent guru-radical. He also became an apostle of the new "psychedelic" drug culture, while Kerouac's mind-bender of choice remained alcohol—and ever larger quantities of it. In 1967 Kerouac moved with his mother and third wife back to Lowell, and then to St. Petersburg, Florida. In 1968 Neal Cassady collapsed and died in Mexico after overindulging in liquor and drugs. By now Kerouac's own health had deteriorated. The former varsity football player had become, at forty-six, a bloated, seedy alcoholic. On October 20, 1969, as he sat in front of his TV set with a can of tuna fish and a small bottle of whiskey, Jack suffered a massive intestinal hemorrhage. Eighteen hours later he died in surgery.

When they heard the news, reporters rushed to interview Allen Ginsberg at his upstate New York farm. Ginsberg started to quote William Blake's lines, "The days of my youth rise fresh in my mind," but he was too choked to finish. When the journalists left, he inscribed on a tree with a hunting knife: "Jack Kerouac, 1922–1969."

29

****

******** A HISTORICAL PORTRAIT ********

Martin Luther King, Jr.

The birthdays of only three Americans have become national legal holidays. One is that of George Washington, father of his country; another that of Abraham Lincoln, preserver of the Union. The last is the birthday of a black American, Martin Luther King, Jr., the most powerful and effective leader of the post–World War II civil rights revolution.

King was born in Atlanta, Georgia, in 1929 at a time and in a place not favorable for a young black male. Racism and its legal reflection, segregation, permeated every corner of southern life. Martin escaped almost all of this. The Kings belonged to the small black elite of Atlanta. Martin's father, Martin Luther King, Sr., was a respected, influential Baptist minister, the pastor of one of Atlanta's richest and most prestigious black churches, Ebenezer Baptist. Martin's family lived in a large house provided with all the most modern amenities. He and his small circle of equally prosperous friends—the children of doctors, lawyers, academics, morticians, and small business people—attended the best black schools in the city, and many, including Martin, went on to Morehouse College, the liberal arts school affiliated with the black community's greatest symbol of achievement, Atlanta University.

Yet even such a sheltered life could not spare King or his parents the cruel snubs, insults, and penalties of being black in racist, segregated Atlanta. When Martin was eleven a white woman walked up to him in a local department store and, without warning, slapped his face. "The little nigger stepped on my foot," she later explained. It was a small incident but it revealed the depth of white contempt for blacks in the 1940s South.

"Daddy" King wanted Martin to enter the ministry and become co-pastor at the Ebenezer Church and eventually succeed him. But Martin demurred. He wanted to expand his intellectual horizons before settling down comfortably as head of a large and prosperous southern congregation. In 1948 he went to Crozier Theological Seminary in Pennsylvania and earned his Bachelor of Divinity degree, graduating first in his class. In 1955 he earned his Ph.D. at Boston University with a dissertation comparing the concepts of God in the thinking of two contemporary Protestant theologians. In Boston Martin met and married the beautiful Coretta Scott, a young Alabama woman then training as a singer at the New England Conservatory of Music.

Before getting his doctorate, Martin accepted a parish. The Kings moved to Montgomery, Alabama, where Martin became pastor of the Dexter Avenue Baptist Church. He and Coretta had been in the Alabama capital only a year when they found themselves thrust into the middle of a momentous struggle over segregation that would make Dr. King the most famous and powerful civil rights leader in America.

Like all southern cities, Montgomery was thoroughly segregated along racial lines. All public facilities had white and black sections. Almost without exception

131

the facilities available to blacks were inferior to those provided whites. Any black person who refused to obey the city ordinances prescribing the racial divisions was committing a misdemeanor and subject to fine and imprisonment.

Then, on Thursday afternoon, December 1, 1955, Rosa Parks, a dignified black woman, boarded a Montgomery city bus to return home after a day's work as a seamstress in a downtown department store. She took her seat, as prescribed, in the black section at the rear. But when more whites got on, the blacks in the front row of their section were asked to surrender their seats, as prescribed by law, to the new white passengers. Rosa Parks refused to move. The bus driver called the police and Mrs. Parks was arrested and fingerprinted.

The arrest triggered a strong reaction among Montgomery's black leaders. Ever since the *Brown* school desegregation decision in 1954 they had determined to challenge the city's Jim Crow system. The arrest of Mrs. Parks, a respectable middle-aged lady, promised to make an excellent case. In a matter of hours Montgomery's civil rights activists had decided on a boycott of the bus company until all black bus riders were treated as the equals of whites. Though King was a newcomer to Montgomery and just settling into his new duties and responsibilities, he was elected chairman of the Montgomery Improvement Associa-tion, the group formed to run the boycott, with the Reverend Ralph Abernathy of the First Baptist Church as his chief lieutenant.

Planned for a single day, the boycott lasted for almost thirteen months. Black passengers, the chief users of the buses, walked to work or made do with the Improvement Association's car pools. The bus company and the city authorities fought back. They procured injunctions; they harassed King and the other boycott leaders with minor traffic violation charges and threw them into jail; they invoked an ordinance to prevent black taxi drivers from transporting passengers at the same low rates charged by the bus company. At the end of January someone bombed King's home, and Mrs. King and the children barely escaped death. Despite the provocation, the young minister admonished blacks not to resort to violence. "We want to love our enemies," he told a black audience. "We must love our white brothers no matter what they do to us." Though inspired primarily by the Christian concept of charity, these words contained a trace of Mohandas Gandhi's nonviolent civil disobedience philosophy, *Satyagraha*, that King had encountered at Crozier Seminary.

Victory at Montgomery was ultimately won by the courage and sacrifices of the city's black citizens. But it was also helped immeasurably by the Supreme Court decision of November 1955 declaring that Alabama's state and local laws upholding segregation in transportation were unconstitutional. On Friday, December 21, the Montgomery city buses were officially desegregated. The long battle was over.

The Montgomery victory made Martin Luther King a national leader. He was soon in demand wherever black activists needed his eloquence, his leadership, and his ability to attract media attention to their plight. A literate man, he wrote widely for the national press on the goals of the civil rights movement and, despite a killing schedule of speaking engagements and personal appearances, authored several eloquent books. In 1957 he helped to found the Southern Christian Leadership Conference (SCLC), and for the remainder of his life this organization, located in Atlanta, was his chief base of operations. In 1959 King's Gandhian convictions were powerfully reinforced by a trip to the places in India where the saintly Mahatma had actually practiced his nonviolent precepts.

Montgomery proved to be only one of a hundred battles to dismantle the huge edifice of segregation that loomed over the South. During the 1960s the civil rights movement that King helped lead could count on wide liberal support in the North and in Washington. John F. Kennedy owed black voters a debt for his hairline election victory in 1960. Yet relations between the Kennedy administration and King were, at best, touchy. During 1961–1962 King and the SCLC sponsored a series of "Freedom Rides" in conjunction with the militant Congress of Racial Equality (CORE) and the equally militant Student Nonviolent Coordinating Committee (SNCC) to test the compliance of southern towns with court rulings desegregating bus terminals. Once beyond the border states, the Freedom Riders were met by angry white mobs who burned the buses and beat many of them mercilessly. King and the other civil rights leaders demanded that federal marshals intervene to ensure the Freedom Riders' safety, and were deeply disappointed when the attorney general, the president's brother, Robert, was slow to respond.

King had his share of failures. In Albany, Georgia, the authorities were able to blunt the drive he led to end segregation and improve the job opportunities of black workers by a policy that combined evasion and careful avoidance of police brutality. By the time King left the small city little had changed. King and his colleagues had greater success in Birmingham, the New South's industrial showcase. Here the city's safety commissioner, T. Eugene ("Bull") Connor, was a hothead racist who used brutal tactics against the protest marchers organized by King and his colleagues to dramatize the discrimination practiced against the city's black population. Connor's police attacked marchers and demonstrators with night-sticks, cattle prods, vicious dogs, and high-pressure hoses. The most shocking attack was directed against a thousand black children marching from the Sixteenth Street Baptist Church to downtown. Public outrage forced the active intervention of the Kennedy administration and much of the business community. Powerful men in Washington and in New York corporate offices contacted friends and associates in Birmingham and demanded that the scandal be stopped. On May 10 the city capitulated and signed an agreement with the civil rights leaders desegregating department stores, promising accelerated hiring of black workers, establishing a biracial committee to plan additional desegregation, and dropping charges against all those arrested in the demonstrations.

The Birmingham victory was capped by the mass march on Washington of August 1963. Organized by CORE, SCLC, SNCC, and the National Urban League, and co-sponsored by white liberal organizations, the march was the biggest civil rights demonstration of all time. Over a quarter of a million people, white and black, came to the nation's capital for the purpose of supporting a major civil rights bill pending in Congress. The high point of the enormous rally was King's ringing "I Have a Dream" address at the Lincoln Memorial, which lifted the hearts of everyone present with its vision of a democratic society where "all God's children, black men and white men, Jews and Gentiles, Protestants and Catholics," would "be able to join hands and sing in the words of that old Negro spiritual, 'Free at last! Free at last! Thank God almighty, we are free at last!'"

Though he would achieve international recognition when he was awarded the Nobel Peace Prize in 1964, never again would Martin Luther King come so close to personifying black America's aspirations. By this time rifts had appeared within the civil rights movement. To King's right were the conservative NAACP, which emphasized lawsuits to end discrimination, and the Urban League, which favored education and persuasion. Both believed that street demonstrations and marches were dangerous and unproductive. To King's left was SNCC, which had accepted nonviolence as a tactic, but not as a principle. Blacks, the young SNCC workers believed, could not be expected to turn the other cheek when brutalized by white supremicists. Still further left were the Black Muslims, who demanded complete withdrawal from any association with "white devils," and proclaimed the superiority of blacks over whites. King also had little appeal for the unorganized militants in the northern cities, who saw nothing to recommend in a Christian nonviolent approach to the frustrations of ghetto life. Besides ideological differences, many in the civil rights movement resented King's eminence and believed that he and his associates encouraged the view that Martin Luther King, Jr., *was* the civil rights movement. Some of these people called King "de Lawd" behind his back.

After 1963 King and SCLC began to slip in influence. SCLC played only a secondary role in the voter registration drives and freedom schools organized by SNCC and CORE in the Deep South during the summer of 1964. It recouped somewhat when King helped lead the voter registration drive at Selma, Alabama, in early 1965. King's adversary this time was Sheriff Jim Clark, a man as hot-tempered as Birmingham's Bull Connor. He wore a big badge on his lapel with the word "Never." Clark's men shocked the nation when they used tear gas and clubs against 500 blacks crossing the Pettus Bridge on their way to the Alabama state capital to present their grievances to Governor George Wallace. Seventeen of the marchers were seriously hurt and forty were hospitalized. The violence at Selma brought a wave of white liberals to the city for a second march in defiance of a court order. This time, faced with state troopers, King stopped the marchers just after they crossed the bridge. For this he was criticized by many militants. But the Selma Campaign had done its work. In its wake President Johnson announced that he was sending a tough, new voting rights bill to Congress.

After Selma SCLC ran into increasing difficulties. In the summer of 1965, beginning with Watts in Los Angeles, the northern black ghettoes began to explode. King deplored the violence but could neither prevent it nor repudiate the rioters. He also found it difficult to deal with the growing separatism of black militants who rejected the integrated society he envisioned and, under the banner of "black power," repudiated the nonviolence he preached. Finally, there was the Vietnam War. King was appalled by the war, but felt that to join SNCC and other leftists civil rights groups in demanding that the United States leave Vietnam would risk destroying his ties with the Johnson administration. Ultimately, he took the principled course and in 1967 proclaimed the folly and injustice of Vietnam.

When the end came, King was shifting his focus from segregation and voting rights—issues primarily relevant to the South—to poverty, job discrimination, and substandard housing—issues primarily of concern to the northern urban ghettoes. In 1966 and 1967 SCLC launched a campaign to force the city of Chicago to improve the housing of the city's black poor. In early 1968 King and his colleagues drew up plans for a march on Washington to demand a $12 billion "economic bill of rights" from Congress. But before the Poor People's Campaign could be launched, King was induced to come to Memphis to lend support to a sanitation workers' strike against the city.

King visited the city several times during the early spring of 1968 to help the predominantly black garbage collectors. On the evening of April 4, as he prepared to go to dinner, he stepped out on the balcony of his motel. A shot rang out and King fell dead. The killer was a white escaped convict whose motives have never been fully explained.

Martin Luther King was buried under a marble tombstone inscribed: "Free at Last, Free at Last, Thank God Almighty, I'm Free at Last."

Port Huron Statement

The major organized expression of the radical student movement during the 1960s was SDS, Students for a Democratic Society. Formed in 1959 as the student auxiliary of the old socialist League for Industrial Democracy, it eventually broke away from the staid parent organization and eventually became a byword for campus radicalism. By the end of the sixties it had evolved into the urban guerrilla group called the Weathermen.

In 1962, long before its final violent stage, SDS issued a manifesto expressing the new mood of dissent among young college students. The document, composed largely by Tom Hayden, then a recent University of Michigan graduate, was adopted at an SDS convention at Port Huron, Michigan. It catches the spirit of SDS when it was still young and more strongly influenced by Jefferson than by Marx. The selection below is the Port Huron Statement's preamble.

"We are people of this generation, bred at least in modest comfort, housed now in universities, looking uncomfortably to the world we inherit.

"When we were kids the United States was the wealthiest and strongest country in the world; the only one with the atom bomb, the least scarred by modern war, an initiator of the United Nations that we thought would distribute Western influence throughout the world. Freedom and equality for each individual, government of, by, and for the people—these American values we found good, principles by which we could live as men. Many of us began maturing in complacency.

"As we grew, however, our comfort was penetrated by events too troubling to dismiss. First, the permeating and victimizing fact of human degradation symbolized by the Southern struggle against racial bigotry, compelled most of us from silence to activism. Second, the enclosing fact of the Cold War, symbolized by the presence of the Bomb, brought awareness that we ourselves . . . might die at any time. We might deliberately ignore, or avoid, or fail to feel all other human problems, but not these two, for these were too immediate and crushing in their impact, too challenging in the demand that we as individuals take the responsibility for encounter and resolution.

"While these and other problems either directly oppressed us or rankled our consciences and became our own subjective concerns, we began to see complicated and disturbing paradoxes in our surrounding America. The declaration 'all men are created equal . . .' rang hollow before the facts of Negro life in the South and the big cities of the North. The proclaimed peaceful intentions of the United States contradicted its economic and military investments in the Cold War status quo.

"We witnessed, and continue to witness, other paradoxes. With nuclear energy whole cities can easily be powered, yet the dominant nation-states seem more likely to unleash destruction greater than that incurred in all wars in human history. Although our own technology is destroying old and creating new forms of social organization, men still tolerate meaningless work and idleness. While two-thirds of mankind suffers under-nourishment, our own upper classes revel amidst superfluous abundance. Although the world population is expected to double in forty years,

135

the nations still tolerate anarchy as a major principle of international conduct and uncontrolled exploitation governs the sapping of the earth's physical resources. Although mankind desperately needs revolutionary leadership, America rests in national stalemate, its goals ambiguous and tradition-bound instead of informed and clear, its democratic system apathetic and manipulated rather than 'of, by, and for the people.'

"Not only did tarnish appear on our image of American virtue, not only did disillusion occur when the hypocrisy of American ideals was discovered, but we began to sense that what we had originally seen as the American Golden Age was actually the decline of our era. The worldwide outbreak of revolution against colonialism and imperialism, the intrenchment of totalitarian states, the menace of war, overpopulation, international disorder, supertechnology—these trends were testing the tenacity of our own commitment to democracy and freedom and our abilities to visualize their application to a world in upheaval.

"Our work is guided by the sense that we may be the last generation in the experiment with living. But we are a minority—the vast majority of our people regard the temporary equilibriums of our society and world as eternally functional parts. In this is perhaps the outstanding paradox: we ourselves are imbued with urgency, yet the message of our society is that there is no viable alternative to the present. Beneath the reassuring tunes of the politicians, beneath the common opinion that America will 'muddle through,' beneath the stagnation of those who have closed their minds to the future, is the pervading feeling that there simply are no alternatives, that our times have witnessed the exhaustion not only of Utopias, but of any new departures as well. Feeling the press of complexity upon the emptiness of life, people are fearful of the thought that at any moment things might be thrust out of control. They fear change itself, since change might smash whatever visible framework seems to hold back chaos for them now. For most Americans, all crusades are suspect, threatening. The fact that each individual sees apathy in his fellows perpetuates the common reluctance to organize for change. The dominant institutions are complex enough to blunt the minds of their potential critics, and entrenched enough to swiftly dissipate or entirely repel the energies of protest and reform, thus limiting human expectancies. Then, too, we are a materially improved society, and by our own improvements we seem to have weakened the case for further change.

"Some would have us believe that Americans feel contentment amidst prosperity— but might it not better be called a glaze above deeply-felt anxieties about their role in the new world? And if these anxieties produce a developed indifference to human affairs, do they not as well produce a yearning to believe that there is an alternative to the present, that something *can* be done to change circumstances in the schools, the workplaces, the bureaucracies, the government? It is to this latter yearning, at once the spark and engine of change, that we direct our present appeal. The search for truly democratic alternatives to the present, and a commitment to social experimentation with them, is a worthy and fulfilling human enterprise, one which moves us and, we hope, others today. On such a basis do we offer this document of our convictions and analysis: as an effort in understanding and changing the conditions of humanity in the late twentieth century, an effort rooted in the ancient, still unfulfilled conception of man attaining determining influence over his circumstances of life."

136

30

****

******** A HISTORICAL DOCUMENT ********

Roe v. Wade

In 1973 the United States Supreme Court issued a momentous decision striking down a Texas statute making abortion a crime. A pregnant unmarried woman, given the name Jane Roe to protect her identity, who wanted an abortion had sued the Dallas district attorney in 1970, claiming that the Texas antiabortion law was a violation of her right to privacy under the federal Constitution. The case was finally decided in the Supreme Court by an opinion written by Associate Justice Harry Blackmun.

Justice Blackmun not only struck down the Texas law but all others with similar provisions, arguing that they were medically out of date, that they no longer expressed the common view of the community, and that they did indeed violate the constitutional rights of pregnant women to privacy. Though the decision did not make all abortions legal, it did open the door to widespread use of abortion to limit births and thereby created a major social controversy that still roils the nation.

"In view of all this, we do not agree that, by adopting one theory of life, Texas may override the rights of the pregnant woman that are at stake. We repeat, however, that the State does have an important and legitimate interest in preserving and protecting the health of the pregnant woman, whether she be a resident of the State or a nonresident who seeks medical consultation and treatment there, and that it has still *another* important and legitimate interest in protecting the potentiality of human life. These interests are separate and distinct. Each grows in substantiality as the woman approaches term and, at a point during pregnancy, each becomes 'compelling.'

"With respect to the State's important and legitimate interest in the health of the mother, the 'compelling' point, in the light of present medical knowledge, is at approximately the end of the first trimester. This is so because of the now-established medical fact, referred to above . . . , that until the end of the first trimester mortality in abortion may be less than mortality in normal childbirth. It follows that, from and after this point, a State may regulate the abortion procedure to the extent that the regulation reasonably relates to the preservation and protection of maternal health. Examples of permissible state regulation in this area are requirements as to the qualifications of the person who is to perform the abortion; as to the licensure of that person; as to the facility in which the procedure is to be performed, that is, whether it must be a hospital or may be a clinic or some other place of less-than-hospital status; as to the licensing of the facility; and the like.

"This means, on the other hand, that, for the period of pregnancy prior to this 'compelling' point, the attending physician, in consultation with his patient, is free to determine, without regulation by the State, that, in his medical judgment, the patient's pregnancy should be terminated. If that decision is reached, the judgment may be effectuated by an abortion free of interference by the State.

"With respect to the State's important and legitimate interest in potential life, the 'compelling' point is at viability. This is so because the fetus then presumably has the capability of meaningful life outside the mother's womb. State regulation protective of fetal life after viability thus has both logical and biological justifications. If the State is interested in protecting fetal life after viability, it may go so far as to proscribe abortion during that period, except when it is necessary to preserve the life or health of the mother.

"Measured against these standards, Art. 1196 of the Texas Penal Code, in restricting legal abortions to those 'procured or attempted by medical advice for the purpose of saving the life of the mother,' sweeps too broadly. The statute makes no distinction between abortions performed early in pregnancy and those performed later, and it limits to a single reason, 'saving' the mother's life, the legal justification for the procedure. The statute, therefore, cannot survive the constitutional attack made upon it here."

✦✦✦✦✦✦✦✦ A HISTORICAL PORTRAIT ✦✦✦✦✦✦✦✦

Yo-yo Ma

Asian-Americans have achieved renown in science, technology, medicine, and music. In the international musical world few, however, have won such universal acclaim as the Paris-born cellist of Chinese ancestry, Yo-yo Ma, who now makes his home in Winchester, Massachusetts.

Yo-yo Ma's paternal grandparents were landowners in Ningbo, a city south of Shanghai, but his father, Hiao-tsiun Ma, loved music and chose it as his profession. Ma senior learned to play the violin and became a professor of music at Nanjing University. In 1936, troubled by the increasing cultural and political instability in China, he emigrated to Paris. Yo-yo Ma's mother, Marina, a mezzo-soprano from Hong Kong, and a former student in Hiao-tsiun Ma's music-theory class at Nanjing, moved to Paris in 1949. They were married there soon after and in 1951 had a daughter; in 1955, they had a son. In Chinese tradition, all family members from the same generation share the same written character in their names, in this case Yo, which means "friendship." Their daughter was named Yeou-cheng and their son Yo-yo. Ma means "horse."

Yo-yo Ma describes his parents as two very different people. His father was the rational, systematic, and intellectual parent; his mother the more passionate one. They even spoke two different dialects of Chinese. Hiao-tsiun instructed his children in French history, Chinese mythology, and calligraphy. Naturally, he also taught them music, using a system for teaching very young children to play by intense short practice stints rather than long hours at their instruments. Yeou-cheng learned the violin but later gave up her musical career to become a pediatrician. Yo-yo Ma selected the cello and at the age of four he amazed his teacher by playing a Bach suite. At five, the little boy, playing both cello and piano, gave his first public recital at the University of Paris.

In 1962, the Ma family moved to New York, where Hiao-tsiun took a job at a school for musically talented children and shortly after established the Children's Orchestra of New York. Meanwhile, his son kept astounding the critics with his

138

extraordinary talent and ended up studying with two acclaimed cellists, Leonard Rose of the internationally famous Juilliard School of Music, and Janos Scholz. In 1963, Leonard Bernstein, the composer and then conductor of the New York Philharmonic, invited Yo-yo to appear on the nationally televised *American Pageant of the Arts*, a money-raiser for the future John F. Kennedy Center for the Performing Arts in Washington, D.C. Yo-yo made his Carnegie Hall debut at nine years of age. At fifteen he performed the Saint-Saens concerto with the San Francisco Symphony. In 1968, he entered the Professional Children's School, skipping two years and graduating from high school when he was fifteen.

Enrolling in Juilliard's college division for the fall, Yo-yo Ma spent the summer at Meadowmount, a music camp in the Adirondacks. This was his first experience away from home and he went wild, missing rehearsals, leaving his cello outside in the rain, drinking, painting graffiti, and going for midnight swims. Yo-yo Ma attributes his rebellion partly to the strain of growing up with two contradictory cultures. At home, like other Chinese children, he had to obey family rules, live within a rigidly structured framework, and submerge his individuality. At school, he was free to explore his identity. At home, he spoke only Chinese and was constantly reminded of his Chinese ancestry and traditions. "But I was also American," Yo-yo told an interviewer for the *New Yorker* magazine, "growing up with American values." Today, he is embarrassed by his teenage escapades. In America they would have been considered standard adolescent pranks; they were taken much more seriously by his Chinese parents.

Rather than focusing exclusively on his musical career, Yo-yo decided to go to college. He entered Columbia University, while continuing to study at Juilliard, and lived at home. This arrangement seemed too much like high school to him, however, and after visiting his sister at Radcliffe, he transferred to Harvard. There he kept up his musical career, while undertaking a full-time academic program, studying history, anthropology, literature, science, sociology, and math. He explains his ability to combine both academic courses and music by his fitful work habits. He worked in waves, sometimes staying up far into the night to write a paper, at other times practicing more diligently than usual if a concert was in the offing. During this period, he later admitted, his standards for both his studies and his performances were not as high as they should have been. On the other hand, he says, going to Harvard was the "best decision" he ever made because it expanded his education and his world in a way that no musical conservatory could have done.

While at Harvard, Yo-yo continued to do concerts, playing on campus as well as accepting professional engagements elsewhere. He gave solo recitals and performed in chamber music and orchestral concerts with student and faculty musicians. He formed a student trio with pianist Richard Kogan and violinist Lynn Chang. On many weekends he performed in the Boston suburbs where he often tried out new musical compositions, and for four summers he went to the Marlboro Festival in Vermont where he met the legendary cellist Pablo Casals, then in his mid-nineties. He played in the orchestra with Casals conducting and says it was "an inspiration for a lifetime." During his college years, he also made his debut in London with the Royal Philharmonic as the soloist in the "Elgar Cello Concerto." He was soon getting so many requests to perform that he realized he could make a good living as a cellist and considered dropping out of Harvard. His father exhorted him to stay and insisted that he limit the number of engagements to one a month. As a good Chinese son he obeyed. He graduated from Harvard with a B.A. in humanities in 1976 and in 1991 the university awarded him an honorary doctorate in music. Yo-yo also spent three years as an artist-in-residence at Harvard's Leverett House.

Though dedicated to his music and his career, Yo-yo had a personal life as well. The first summer at Marlboro, he renewed his acquaintance with Jill Hornor, a sophomore at Mount Holyoke, who had signed on as a festival administrator. That summer's friendship evolved into love on Yo-yo's part. But when he first worked up the courage to tell her how he felt, she told him she considered him a cherished younger brother. By the time Yo-yo entered Harvard, Hornor had gone to Paris for her junior year abroad. The infatuated young man wrote her every day and ran up exorbitant bills as he burned up the transatlantic telephone wires. His unceasing efforts changed her feelings and soon his love was reciprocated. After Mount Holyoke, Jill went to graduate school at Cornell, in Ithaca, New York, studying German literature, while Yo-yo was finishing up at Harvard. In the spring of 1977, he bought a wedding ring. Then he called Jill and told her to be at her house at seven that evening but he did not tell her why. He took the next bus to Ithaca, rang her doorbell, got down on his knees and proposed. She agreed to marry him.

The year 1978 was a momentous one for Yo-yo Ma. He won the Avery Fisher Prize, one of the most prestigious in classical music. Ever since the prize had been established three years earlier it had been awarded to multiple winners. But Yo-yo seemed so far ahead of any of his competitors that the honor was accorded to him alone. Designed to give outstanding young instrumentalists the chance to perform with major orchestras, the prize included commitments to play with the New York Philharmonic and the Chamber Music Society of Lincoln Center.

On May 20, 1978, Yo-yo married Jill, his long-time love. The marriage to an American woman from New England created strains between Yo-yo and his parents. They did not disapprove of Jill personally, but they feared that her Western upbringing would conflict with the Chinese family structure, where obedience to the wife's in-laws is part of the heritage. They also worried that the children of a Chinese-American intermarriage would drift even further from the Chinese heritage. Hiao-tsiun was particularly upset and was alienated for a while from his son. By the time the couple's children, Nicholas and Emily, were born, however, Yo-yo's parents had come to appreciate Jill and accept the situation. When Yo-yo and Jill celebrated their tenth anniversary, Yo-yo's parents, then living in Taiwan part of the time, came back to the United States to join the festivities.

When Yo-yo was twenty-four he had an operation on his spine. He had been suffering from scoliosis for many years, and this condition, a curvature of the spine, was probably worsened by the position in which a cellist plays his instrument. The medical procedure was anything but routine. If certain nerves were damaged during the operation he might be unable to play. Still, he had little choice; his spine was so bent that if allowed to worsen it would press on internal organs.

For six months afterward the operation, Yo-yo was in an upper-body cast to keep his spine completely rigid. Happily, his wife brought his cello to the hospital and the doctors found a way to cut the cast so he could practice. During his recuperation, while the results were still uncertain, Yo-yo contemplated what he would do with his life if his musical career were terminated. One of the things he considered was social work because of his great love for people. Luckily for both him and the music world the operation was a success; his fingers were not affected and his cello playing was as accomplished as ever.

When he fully recovered, his concert career took off and soon he was playing all over the world in solo recitals, chamber music performances, and duets with his good friend, the pianist Emanuel Ax, whom he had met at Marlboro. Yo-yo Ma has been on the road almost continuously since then. In 1986 and 1987 he went to

China where he spent hectic days playing concertos and meeting his father's colleagues from forty years before. He was made an honorary professor at the Shanghai Conservatory where he gave a master class. By the mid-1980s he had achieved "superstar" status, selling out concert halls for his performances and winning eight Grammy Awards. He is acclaimed internationally as a spokesman for classical music and its essential place in society.

Concertizing is only one ingredient in Yo-yo Ma's musical life. He finds it fulfilling to teach and nurture young musicians. One of his favorite haunts is Tanglewood in Lenox, Massachusetts, the summer home of the Boston Symphony Orchestra where he invariably gives one or two performances in July and August. At Tanglewood he also teaches the cello to young musicians from all over the country who compete to earn places in the Tanglewood Music Center. His performing and teaching activities at Tanglewood during the summer of 1989 were televised in a documentary seen on the Arts and Entertainment Network and BBC Television. When he travels to other cities, he is willing, if his schedule is not too hectic, to give master classes, where he does not insist that the students use his particular technical or interpretative methods. He also likes to play concerts with young, unknown soloists.

Yo-yo Ma is not just a virtuoso performer. He is also a partisan of his instrument, seeking constantly to add to the rather limited classical cello repertory, by adapting music originally meant for other instruments to the cello and by playing a great deal of twentieth-century music, including new works by recent composers. In January 1993, playing with the New York Philharmonic, he performed Oskar Moravetz's "Memorial to Martin Luther King," with its large cello part, in honor of the slain black leader's birthday. In May 1992 he presented the world premiere of Tod Machower's composition "Begin Again Again" for cello and live computer hyperinstruments. This performance involved four computers and three engineers, and Yo-yo used both an electric cello and his own eighteenth-century Italian-made instrument. He has also experimented with jazz in recent years, giving concerts in which he plays both written-out parts and his own improvisations.

Yo-yo Ma, with his sparkling dark brown eyes and expressive face, is still boyish-looking at the age of thirty-eight in spite of his frenetic schedule. He is universally liked for his openness, charm, and puckish sense of humor. He regrets the time spent on the road and away from his wife and children, but he has trouble turning down requests for concerts and engagements. He has tried very hard to make time to be at home and prevent his obligations from encroaching on his family life. In recent years, he has become more identified with his origins, studying China's history and culture and the Confucian ethic. Still, he is a man divided. As he admitted in a recent interview, "It's hard for me to say just who or what I am. I'm a person of various influences; sometimes they connect, sometimes they don't." Yet, taken together, the mixture of cultures has produced an extraordinary performer and a compassionate man.

31

****

******** A HISTORICAL DOCUMENT ********

Reagan and Labor

Ronald Reagan, though at one time a trade-union leader himself, was not organized labor's closest friend. His coolness toward the trade-union movement showed itself in many ways, but one of the most dramatic was his firing of all the members of PATCO, the Professional Air Traffic Controller Organization, for striking against the government. The strike was indeed illegal, but it is hard to believe that a pro-labor president would not have shown more forbearance.

The following is a record of a press conference held August 3, 1981, in which Reagan and his attorney general announced their plans to clamp down on the striking air controllers.

The President. This morning at 7 A.M. the union representing those who man America's air traffic control facilities called a strike. This was the culmination of 7 months of negotiations between the Federal Aviation Administration and the union. At one point in these negotiations agreement was reached and signed by both sides, granting a $40 million increase in salaries and benefits. This is twice what other government employees can expect. It was granted in recognition of the difficulties inherent in the work these people perform. Now, however, the union demands are 17 times what had been agreed to—$681 million. This would impose a tax burden on their fellow citizens which is unacceptable.

I would like to thank the supervisors and controllers who are on the job today, helping to get the nation's air system operating safely. In the New York area, for example, four supervisors were scheduled to report for work, and 17 additionally volunteered. At National Airport a traffic controller told a newsperson he had resigned from the union and reported to work because, "How can I ask my kids to obey the law if I don't?" This is a great tribute to America.

Let me make one thing plain. I respect the right of workers in the private sector to strike. Indeed, as president of my own union, I led the first strike ever called by that union. I guess I'm maybe the first one to ever hold this office who is a lifetime member of an AFL–CIO union. But we cannot compare labor-management relations in the private sector with government. Government cannot close down the assembly line. It has to provide without interruption the protective services which are government's reason for being.

It was in recognition of this that the Congress passed a law forbidding strikes by government employees against the public safety. Let me read the solemn oath taken by each of these employees, a sworn affidavit, when they accepted their jobs: "I am not participating in any strike against the Government of the United States or any agency thereof, and I will not so participate while an employee of the Government of the United States or any agency thereof."

It is for this reason that I must tell those who fail to report for duty this morning they are in violation of the law, and if they do not report for work within 48 hours, they have forfeited their jobs and will be terminated.

Q. Mr. President, are you going to order any union members who violate the law to go to jail?

The President. Well, I have some people around here, and maybe I should refer that question to the Attorney General.

Q. Do you think that they should go to jail, Mr. President, anybody who violates this law?

The President. I told you what I think should be done. They're terminated.

The Attorney General. Well, as the President has said, striking under these circumstances constitutes a violation of the law, and we intend to initiate in appropriate cases criminal proceedings against those who have violated the law.

Q. How quickly will you initiate criminal proceedings, Mr. Attorney General?

The Attorney General. We will initiate those proceedings as soon as we can.

★★★★★★★ A HISTORICAL PORTRAIT ★★★★★★★

Bill Richardson

The twenty-second United States Ambassador to the United Nations, Bill Richardson, qualified for a place in the *Guinness Book of World Records* for having shaken 8,871 hands in a single day while campaigning for a congressional seat in New Mexico. Though he lost that election, he went on to win the next eight, many by landslides.

Richardson, unlike some of his predecessors for whom foreign policy was a deadly serious proposition, is known for his relaxed approach to diplomacy, his easy smile, his eagerness to talk to the press, and his love of all kinds of food. His first day on the job he introduced himself not only to the dozens of UN employees and emissaries eating in the cafeteria but also to the cooks and the busboys. "There is a new era in the relationship between the United States and the United Nations," said the new ambassador. "I want to symbolize that. We care about all UN employees, not just the ambassadors and the high level people."

Richardson is proud of his Hispanic roots. Speaking at the fifteenth annual Hispanic leadership conference in Chicago in 1997, he exhorted the listeners to "start thinking of ourselves as Hispanics" and talked about the likelihood of "a first Hispanic president."

William Blaine Richardson was born in Pasadena, California on November 15, 1947 to Maria Luisa Zubiran, a native of the southern Mexican state of Oaxaca, and William Richardson, an American banker from Massachusetts. His father represented Citibank in Mexico City where young Bill and his sister, Vesta, spent most of their childhood. Since Citibank was then the only American bank operating in Mexico, the senior Richardson held an elite position as one of the leaders of the American business community there.

Bill was a talented pitcher who traveled to the United States with a Mexican Little League Team to compete in the finals for the World Series. Observing him pitch in Williamsport, Pennsylvania, the baseball coach at the Middlesex School in Concord, Massachusetts encouraged him to enroll. Entering in the eighth grade at Middlesex, he was their starting pitcher until he finished high school.

When Bill graduated from Middlesex in 1966, he was drafted by the then-Kansas City Athletics, but his father persuaded him to go to college instead. Disappointed at not being able to play major league baseball, the following year his elbow went out. Bill had to concede that attending Tufts University, his father's alma mater, had been the right choice. At Tufts he majored in French and political science, but remained a jock until he got to graduate school. In 1971 he earned an MA from the university's Fletcher School of Law and Diplomacy.

Richardson's future career was profoundly influenced by the Democratic Senator from Minnesota, Hubert Humphrey, when on a Fletcher field trip to Washington, Bill listened to a speech he gave in the Senate. When I heard him "talking about Africa," he reminisced, "he turned me on. . . . I can still hear him bellowing, and I said, 'I want to be part of that.'" After his graduation, he returned to the capital, joining the State Department as a Congressional liaison person. In 1972, he married Barbara Flavin, a young woman he had met several years before while hitchhiking in Massachusetts. Three years later he began working for Hubert Humphrey on the Senate Foreign Relations Committee.

Tired of being a mere political staffer for someone else, he decided to run for elective office himself. In 1978, he moved to New Mexico, where his background, in the voter mix of Hispanics, Anglos, and Native Americans, would help him become a serious political player. But first he took the job of executive director of the state Democratic party offered him by the governor of New Mexico. Two years later, he ran for Congress against a very popular Hispanic Republican, Manuel Lujan Jr. Though his opponents charged he was a carpetbagger, partly because his mother, still living in Mexico City, helped finance his campaign, his charm and his tireless campaigning brought him within 5000 votes of victory. In 1981, New Mexico created a new and ethnically mixed congressional district in the northern regions of the state, including the cities of Santa Fe and Taos, the Los Alamos nuclear labs and a large section of the Navajo Reservation. Richardson campaigned in all the Hispanic and Native American villages promising to pay special heed to their concerns and bring more jobs to the district. He won, and went to Congress where he was appointed to the Energy and Commerce Committee, a significant assignment for a congressman from a state with major petroleum and natural gas resources.

One of Richardson's greatest talents is interpersonal relations and it was in Congress that he first discovered his diplomatic flair. To stay in office, he had to navigate among the various squabbling interests in his district. Some of the issues had to be resolved on the spot, according to Richardson, who explained: "We have disputes over land and water between native American tribes, the Hispanic population, and the local Anglo population." To please his constituents, he held over two thousand town meetings. If he voted for or against a bill that he knew would make one faction unhappy, he would immediately arrange a town meeting with them. First he would "open up," and then he would "take the abuse from people." He was reelected each time he ran by sixty percent or more of the vote.

Though he maintained cordial relations with all the ethnic groups in his district, he became a special spokesman in Congress for the Hispanic and Native American blocs. In 1985, he became chairman of the Congressional Hispanic Caucus. In 1986, however, he voted for a modified version of the Simpson-Mazzoli Act which, although it granted legal status to thousands of "undocumented" immigrants already in the United States, also penalized employers for hiring aliens without papers. Most Hispanics opposed the bill, claiming that it would lead to discrimination against foreigners in general. Richardson's vote caused a rupture in the Hispanic caucus and he resigned as its head. Trade with Mexico was also one of his major interests and he became a passionate proponent of NAFTA—the international agreement to link Canada, Mexico and the United States in the world's largest tariff-free trade zone. At the same time, he worked tirelessly to better the quality of life for his Native American constituents, sponsoring over twenty bills that improved job-training programs and health case resources for the tribes. During the 103rd Congress, he became Chairman of the Native American Affairs Committee.

As second-ranking Democrat on the Select Committee on Intelligence, Richardson was able to travel around the world on fact-finding missions that enable him to polish his skills in the international arena. He began to undertake missions to countries with governments hostile to the United States as an informal representative. He clearly was favored by the Clinton administration, but he also had the advantage of operating as a free agent. The State Department found it useful to send in "someone with credibility through the back door." Recognition as an influential but unofficial diplomatic force came when he led an international delegation to Myanmar to bring a personal message of support from President Clinton to Aung San Suu Kyi, a Nobel Peace Prize winner who had been placed under house arrest by the ruling military junta. This was the first time that anybody had seen her other than her family since 1989. He also met with the junta's leader and though nothing happened immediately, she was released seventeen months later.

The next trip took him to Haiti in July 1994. The Clinton administration wanted the leader of the military regime, General Raoul Cedras, to give up control and let Haiti's elected President Bertrand Aristide assume his rightful position. Richardson told Cedras that he was mistaken if he thought he had any friends in Congress and "that unless he made a move of some kind, he was going to be faced with an invasion." Two months later, Cedras stepped down, working out the terms of his surrender with an American delegation led by former President Jimmy Carter.

In November 1994, the Republicans won control of the House of Representatives, chilling the ambitions of aspiring Democratic Congressmen. Richardson was one of these who felt the shivers, but luckily he now had another option. He was gaining a solid reputation for expertise in foreign policy. In December 1994, he went to Pyongyang to haggle over implementation of the United States-North Korean deal to freeze North Korea's nuclear weapons program. Shortly after he arrived, North Korea shot down an American military helicopter which had ventured slightly north of the demilitarized zone. One pilot, David Hilemon, was killed, the other, Bobby Hall, captured. For five days, Richardson insisted that Hall be freed and the remains of the dead pilot be released, refusing to discuss the nuclear agenda until these matters were cleared up. North Korean officials asked him to leave the country but he refused. Running up a $10,000 phone bill to Washington to get further instructions, he finally secured what he wanted. He left North Korea with Hilemon's body and a promise by the communist government to release Hall.

Securing the release of Americans imprisoned in foreign countries became Richardson's specialty. Nineteen ninety-five and 1996 found him all over the globe. In July 1995, he went to Iraq, meeting with the Saddam Hussein, the brutal Iraqi dictator, to see about freeing two hapless American engineers who had been languishing in a Baghdad jail after mistakenly crossing the border from Kuwait to Iraq after getting lost in the desert. Richardson inadvertently offended Hussein by crossing his legs and revealing the sole of his shoe, a sign of insolence in some Arab countries. Hussein stalked out but returned later and, after a lengthy discussion, turned the captives over to Richardson.

The next stop was Cuba where he got Castro to reduce the paperwork fee charged for immigration to the United States. The following month, after talking with Castro a second time, three political prisoners were allowed to fly to Florida with Richardson on an American Air Force plane. He then went to Bangladesh where he sprang from prison a young woman from Texas who was serving a life sentence for drug smuggling. The next stop was North Korea again, to secure the freedom of Evan Hunziker, an American who swam into North Korean territory after becoming drunk. Though the State Department had been conducting behind the-scenes negotiations, Richardson went and brought Hunziker back.

One of his most colorful exploits was in the Sudan in December 1996. Surrounded by buzzing flies and with a vulture perched on the top of an adjacent hatched roof, Richardson shared a meal of goat-meat oozing some unknown green liquid under a mango tree, with rebel leader Kerubino Kwanyin Bol. Richardson talked the Sudanese leader into giving up three Red Cross workers by emphasizing his Hispanic roots and his aide's American black background. "We understand sometimes," he told Kerubino, "not being part of the mainstream." Richardson wheedled Bol into liberating the hostages for four jeeps, rice and .radios, vaccines for the village children and help in purifying the local water. Richardson also promised a medical review of the rebel camp where Kerubino's daughter and 450 other children had died from disease and unsanitary conditions.

After returning from the Sudan mission, Richardson met with President Clinton, a man who loves hearing about the Indiana Jones-like adventures of his roving ambassador. The President appreciated Richardson's help in New Mexico in the previous fall's reelection campaign and, as reward, appointed him to the top American job at the UN. The new ambassador says that one of his highest priorities is to get the United States to pay its delinquent UN dues, which amount to about $1 billion, while urging the UN to undertake some much-needed reforms. Richardson stresses that in the age of huge global problems and interconnections, American membership in the UN is important and that the United States should not be its "biggest deadbeat." Richardson wants to "symbolize" a "new era in the relationship between the United States and the United Nations."

Though he voted against the Gulf War in Congress in 1991, Richardson is now trying to preserve the coalition that fought to prevent Saddam Hussein from dominating the Middle East. As of early 1998, he was in the thick of the crisis brewing as Hussein seeks to repudiate the Gulf War agreement he signed to allow free access to UN inspectors to investigate Iraqi biological, chemical, and nuclear weapons sites. Security Council members China, France and Russia, believe that Iraq has been punished enough and the UN should relax the trade sanctions it imposed at the end of the Gulf War. They profess to believe that Saddam can be deterred from obstructing the UN inspectors by diplomatic means. Americans and their leaders, on the other hand, are sure that the Iraqi strong man is attempting to deceive the world and perceive Saddam as a continuing threat to world peace. It is Richardson's job to keep the appeasers and the faint of heart from weakening America's resolve to punish Saddam if he does not comply with the agreements he made in 1991.

32

★★★★★★★★★★

★★★★★★★★ A HISTORICAL DOCUMENT ★★★★★★★★

The Ecological Credo

No issue promises to be as urgent in the years ahead as the fate of the natural environment, for it is the very foundation of human society and its preservation is essential to us all. While no one denies this proposition, many disagree about how it is to be applied. At one extreme are those who feel that we are already doing enough to protect the air, the water, the forests, the oceans, the animal world, that to attempt more would be at the expense of human living standards and comfort. At the other extreme are those inclined to place the natural world ahead of human concerns and surrender much of the modern age to a higher ecological ethic. Most Americans fall in the reasonable middle, not denying the necessity for prudent care of the world's physical foundations but believing that these must be balanced against the realities of modern life.

No public figure has been as closely identified with the ecological vision as Vice President Al Gore. In the selection below Gore presents his view of human kind's need not to forget that planet earth is not infinite and that we must treat it with great respect.

"The edifice of civilization has become astonishingly complex, but as it grows ever more elaborate, we feel increasingly distant from our roots in the earth. In one sense, civilization itself has been on a journey from its foundations in the world of nature to an ever more contrived, controlled, and manufactured world of our own imitative and sometimes arrogant design. And in my view, the price has been high. At some point during this journey we lost our feeling of connectedness to the rest of nature. We now dare to wonder: Are we so unique and powerful as to be essentially separate from the earth?

"Many of us act—and think—as if the answer is yes. It is now all too easy to regard the earth as a collection of "resources" having an intrinsic value no larger than their usefulness at the moment. Thanks in part to the scientific revolution, we organize our knowledge of the natural world into smaller and smaller segments and assume that the connections between these separate compartments aren't really important. In our fascination with the parts of nature, we forget to see the whole.

"The ecological perspective begins with a view of the whole, an understanding of how the various parts of nature interact in patterns that tend toward balance and persist over time. But this perspective cannot treat the earth as something separate from human civilization; we are part of the whole too, and looking at it ultimately means also looking at ourselves. And if we do not see that the human part of nature has an increasingly powerful influence over the whole of nature—that we are, in effect, a natural force just like the winds and the tides—then we will not be able to see how dangerously we are threatening to push the earth out of balance."*

*From Al Gore, *Earth in the Balance: Ecology and the Human Spirit* (Boston: Houghton Mifflin Company, 1992, pp. 1–2).

Marian Wright Edelman

Ten days before the United States Supreme Court issued *Brown v. Board of Education of Topeka*, the landmark decision outlawing school segregation, Marian Wright's father, the Reverend Arthur Wright, died. He had followed the case avidly and had spoken often about what it would mean for the future of black children in America. His last words to his daughter, whom he called "Booster" for her vivacious personality, were spoken as she rode to the hospital with him in an ambulance. "Booster," he said, "don't let anything get in the way of your education." His words gave the fourteen-year-old black girl the courage to feel that she "could be and do anything." And to this day she still strongly believes that she can change the world for the better.

Marian was born on June 6, 1939, in Bennettsville, South Carolina, where Jim Crow laws prevented black people from drinking Coke at drugstore soda fountains or playing in local parks. Arthur Wright, minister of Shiloh Baptist Church, was determined to remedy the situation. Bringing together members of the black community he built a playground, complete with a small merry-go-round and a canteen, behind his church. Blacks were forced to swim in a small creek contaminated by hospital sewage, and he hoped to install a swimming pool as well. Unfortunately, he could not raise the money to finish the project. Reverend Wright also became involved in other humane projects. Realizing that older blacks often had no place to live in South Carolina, Reverend White established a home for the aged, the first of its kind in the state, across the road from his house. His wife, Maggie Leola Bowen Wright, ran it with the help of her children who did their share of the home's cooking and cleaning. Helping others was as important a part of Marian's upbringing as her schooling. "Service," she was taught, "is the rent we pay for living."

Named for singer Marian Anderson, Marian was the youngest of Maggie and Arthur Wright's five children. First born was sister Olive, who until recently has taught math and science in the Washington, D.C., public school system. Then came her three brothers, Arthur Jr., Harry, and Julian, who are involved in educational counseling and church activities. Gender, however, played no part in how the children were raised. Both the boys and the girls were expected to go to college and have careers; both were taught how to clean house.

Marian did exceptionally well in school. She was a drum majorette in the school band and studied piano and voice, though her first love was literature and her favorite author was Tolstoy. The only time her father did not give her chores at home was when she was reading, so she says she "read a lot." Although she wanted to go to the more cosmopolitan Fisk University in Nashville where her sister had gone, Marian's now-widowed mother convinced her to attend Spelman College, which was closer to home. Spelman, in Atlanta, founded in 1881, is the largest and most prestigious private liberal arts college for black women. In the late 1950s and early 1960s, its students, advised to wear hats and gloves when they were off campus, were required to attend chapel six days a week and were expected to obey strict laws regarding dormitory curfews. The latter, presumably, were to discourage too much involvement with the black male students at nearby Morehouse College.

Intending to enter the foreign service when she graduated from college, Marian

148

applied for and was awarded a Merrill scholarship for a junior year abroad. She spent the first summer in Paris at the Sorbonne and the academic year at the University of Geneva. The following summer she went to the Soviet Union on a Lisle Fellowship. She had heard that W.E.B. DuBois was living there and she hoped to meet him. He had already left for other parts by the time she arrived in Moscow, but she witnessed the celebrated "kitchen debate" between Nikita Khrushchev and Richard Nixon. The year away from home gave her an enormous amount of confidence and the feeling that she could get along anywhere in the world.

She returned to Spelman for her senior year and found the civil rights movement gathering steam. She soon got into the thick of it. She had been aware of the particular unfairness of segregation from her early childhood when a car and a truck collided near her home and the ambulance driver picked up the slightly hurt white truck driver but refused to take the severely injured black victims to the hospital. In addition, with Spelman located in Atlanta, civil rights leaders including Martin Luther King, Whitney Young, and Carl Holman were a constant presence on the campus. Marian participated in the sit-ins at the Atlanta City Hall cafeteria in 1960 along with a large group of black college students and rallied volunteers at Spelman by putting up a notice on campus reading "Young ladies who can picket, please sign below." She was one of those arrested and spent the night in jail reading C.S. Lewis's *The Screwtape Letters*, which she had brought along to the sit-in just in case.

Her night in jail, and her work cataloguing discrimination complaints at the NAACP office, changed her career plans. After graduating from Spelman, Marian had planned to go to graduate school at Georgetown University to major in Russian studies. Now she decided to go to law school. Although she was not sure she had an aptitude for the law, she believed that as an attorney she would be able to do the greatest good for the civil rights movement. She applied to Yale Law School and was accepted and awarded a John Hay Whitney Fellowship to enable her to attend. It was there that she got to know Robert Moses, a Harvard M.A. who helped found the Student Nonviolent Coordinating Committee, and who came to Yale periodically to meet with members of the Northern Student Movement. At this point he was engaged in the dangerous task of encouraging blacks in Mississippi to register to vote.

Marian went to Mississippi in 1963 during the spring break of her third year in law school to help Moses. There she discovered that there were only three black lawyers in the whole state and they were all in Jackson. When some black would-be voters were arrested in Greenwood, ninety-six miles away, there were no lawyers around to plead their case and the defendants had to spend three weeks in jail until bail money could be raised. The experience in Greenwood, Marian has said in a recent interview, convinced her to finish law school. "I hated every minute of it . . . [but I knew] I was needed in Mississippi."

When she got back to New Haven, she found that the NAACP Legal Defense and Educational Fund had established an internship program to train young lawyers to work in the South. After her graduation from Yale Law School, Marian took a year of training with the NAACP in New York, learning the subtleties of civil rights law, and then in the spring of 1964 returned to Jackson, where she opened a legal office to deal with civil rights cases. Unable to be admitted to the Mississippi bar until she fulfilled the nonresident's yearlong residence requirement, Marian arranged with the three black Jackson lawyers to sign the papers she prepared. When she was finally eligible to take the exam, she passed on her first attempt and became the first black woman admitted to the Mississippi bar.

Marian and the three lawyers were kept very busy from the time she arrived in the state. Nineteen sixty-four was the first year of the Mississippi "summer project" in which hundreds of students, both white and black from all over the country, came to help register black voters. The white authorities were bitterly hostile and clamped down hard on the volunteers. There were many arrests, and some of the students were beaten badly by the police. There was plenty of work for civil rights lawyers. This was also the summer that civil rights workers Andrew Goodman, Michael Schwerner, and James Chaney were killed by members of the Ku Klux Klan. Marian said she had to learn basic survival techniques "like starting up your car in the morning with the door open in case there's a bomb."

She stayed in Mississippi for four years and during that time became active in the community action programs under the federal War on Poverty. Some black activists rejected cooperation with the government. She, however, believed, and still believes to this day, it is always best to work within the system. Her particular interest was in Head Start, a program administered by the Office of Economic Opportunity established under the War on Poverty Act passed by Congress in 1964. Head Start was designed to improve the life chances of poor young children by early educational enrichment as well as health services and nutrition programs. Marian worked as general counsel for the Child Development Group of Mississippi (CDGM), a volunteer organization of private civil rights activists, educators, and ministers formed after Mississippi as a state refused to apply for Head Start money. Bypassing the state authorities CDGM received $1.5 million to launch a Head Start project directly from the federal government. The organization offended powerful people in Mississippi and Washington by its insistence on desegregation and involvement in civil rights activities. But Marian and other friends were able to save the program. Since then, and in spite of almost yearly worries about refunding, Head Start has helped many preschool children in Mississippi.

It was in Mississippi that Marian met Peter Edelman, a Jewish lawyer from Minneapolis and the man she would marry. In 1967, Harvard Law School graduate Edelman was a legislative assistant to Senator Robert F. Kennedy, who came to the state when his Senate Subcommittee on Employment, Manpower, and Poverty held hearings in Jackson. Edelman was advised to look up Marian Wright before the subcommittee convened. They met for dinner and talked for hours into the night. Marian testified before the subcommittee and took the committee on a tour through the Delta where people were living in shacks without heat, electricity, or running water and where unbathed babies had swollen bellies from lack of food. Wright sometimes says that it was hungry children who brought her and her husband together.

In March 1968, Marian Wright moved to Washington, partly to be with Peter and partly because she felt that it would be more effective to deal with the problem of poverty on a federal level. Soon after she arrived, she became counsel to the Poor People's Campaign, which had decided to carry out its campaign to compel the nation to confront economic inequality despite the assassination in April of its leader Martin Luther King, Jr. In addition, she established the Washington Research Project, to explore issues in the public interest and to lobby congress for funds to expand services to children. In July 1968 Peter and Marian were married in the Virginia backyard of Adam Walinsky, Robert Kennedy's other leading legislative assistant. This was the first interracial marriage in the state of Virginia since its "miscegenation" laws were declared unconstitutional.

The wedding took place after Robert Kennedy was assassinated. Edelman, as well as other senior aides to Kennedy, had received a Ford Foundation grant after the senator's death to help them with their passage to other occupations. Peter and

Marian used the money to travel around the world, spending time in Africa, Vietnam, India, and Prague. When they returned to Washington Peter became the associate director of the Robert F. Kennedy Memorial. Marian went back to helping poor children through the Washington Research Project, now focusing on education.

Three years later, Marian again shifted her locale, this time to Boston, when Peter accepted a job as vice president of the University of Massachusetts. Marian was named director of the Center of Law and Education at Harvard University but commuted to Washington on a weekly basis to administer the Washington Research Project. By now the Edelmans had two sons, Joshua and Jonah; another son, Ezra, was born in 1974. With the understanding that raising a biracial, interfaith family would present unusual adjustments, the boys were brought up with strong values and a deep belief in God and instructed to honor and respect the religious traditions of their father and mother. Each one was given what the family likes to refer to as a "Baptist Bar Mitzvah," with both a Baptist minister and a rabbi presiding.

The plight of needy children continued to concern Marian Edelman. Since her Mississippi Head Start days she had been formulating various plans to deal with children's problems. One factor in her choice was the recognition that people were "tired of the concerns of the sixties" but that children always aroused public attention. In 1973 she founded the nonprofit, nonpartisan Children's Defense Fund (CDF) as a spin-off from the Washington Research Project. Obtaining financing only from private individuals and foundations, she staffed the CDF and began to issue flawlessly researched reports on children's issues such as day care, health, and nutrition. Some of the early topics the CDF looked into included a survey of the treatment of institutionalized children, an inquiry on the use of children in medical experiments, and an investigation into why so many of the nation's school-aged youngsters were not actually going to school. Other issues it tackled were the foster care system, child abuse, infant mortality, children's nutrition, drug use, and homelessness.

In 1979 the Edelmans moved back to Washington D.C., where Marian became more and more engrossed in the CDF and Peter became a professor at the Georgetown University School of Law. By 1993 the CDF had a staff of over a hundred and a budget exceeding $10.5 million. In 1983 the CDF became involved in what Marian Edelman saw as an ever-growing priority: babies born out of wedlock. Besides publishing reports and press releases on this problem, the CDF began an advertising campaign aimed directly at adolescents, warning them about the consequences of having sex too early as well as sex without birth control. The CDF aimed at a pragmatic rather than a moralistic strategy. Between 1984 and 1988 it lobbied Congress to expand Medicaid services to poor children, using as a major argument that increasing children's health services actually decreased government future costs in doctor and hospital bills. The CDF had major successes in inducing Congress to expand Head Start and nutrition programs for children and also became involved in working for the passage of a child-care bill that, when enacted in 1990, was the first such measure since 1971. The Act for Better Child Care provides billions of dollars for child-care assistance for low-income working families.

The CDF's basic goals for children include: "a healthy start," through basic health care; a "head start" through quality preschool education; and a "fair start" through economic security for families. Marian Wright Edelman makes sure that she constantly keeps the CDF in the public's mind. She lectures widely, gives frequent interviews, and writes articles and books. She has won a prestigious MacArthur Fellowship and a Rockefeller Foundation award. Her most recent book, published in 1992, is *The Measure of Our Success: A Letter to My Children and Yours*. This ninety-seven-page work, which became a best-seller in hardcover, is mostly a message about parenting, but Chapter 5 "If the Child Is Safe: A Struggle for America's Conscience and Future," implores the government, the community, and families to take concerted action on behalf of American children. Her critics have said that Edelman focuses too much on government's responsibility for children and not enough on the family's role.

One member of CDF's board of directors is Edelman's friend, Hillary Rodham Clinton, whom she has known since 1969. Marian herself is known in Washington as one of the "First Friends" of the Clintons. So far, unlike many other professional friends of the president and First Lady, she has declined to take a job with the Clinton administration and claims she is not interested in competing for the next opening on the Supreme Court or in running for elected office. She wants to stay "focused just on children" and she thinks she can be more effective working outside of government than inside. Marian Edelman, a workaholic who is just now beginning to show gray in her short curly hair, hopes that her personal future will bring a little more time for going to the movies and taking weekend trips to New York City with her husband. But it is difficult to picture her slowing down. She told an interviewer she follows the advice of Martin Luther King, Jr., who instructed his supporters to keep active. "If you can't fly, run," he said. "If you can't run walk. If you can't walk, crawl, but by all means keep moving."